THE BOOK OF
MARGERY KEMPE

THE BOOK OF MARGERY KEMPE

The
Autobiography
of the
Madwoman of God

A NEW TRANSLATION BY

TONY D. TRIGGS

TRIUMPH™ BOOKS
Liguori, Missouri

Published by Triumph™ Books 1995
Liguori, Missouri 63057-9999
An Imprint of Liguori Publications

First published in Great Britain 1995
by Burns & Oates,
Wellwood, North Farm Road,
Tunbridge Wells, Kent TN2 3DR

Library of Congress Cataloging-in-Publication Data

Kempe, Margery, b. ca. 1373
    [Book of Margery Kempe. English]
    The book of Margery Kempe : the autobiography of the madwoman of God / a
new translation by Tony D. Triggs. — 1st ed.
        p. cm. — (A Triumph classic)
    Includes bibliographical references.
    ISBN 0-89243-828-2
    1. Kempe, Margery, b. ca. 1373—Biography. 2. Women authors, English—
Middle English, 1100-1500—Biography. 3. Christian pilgrims and pilgrimages—
Early works to 1800. 4. Mysticism—England. I. Triggs, Tony D. II. Series.
PR2007.K413 1995
248'.2'092—dc20
[B]   95-18591

9 8 7 6 5 4 3 2
First printing
Printed and bound in Finland by Werner Söderström Oy

CONTENTS

Introduction   7

THE BOOK OF MARGERY KEMPE
    First Book   17
    Second Book   187
    Margery Kempe's Prayers   211

Maps of Margery Kempe's Travels   216

Further Reading   219

To Donna and Nigel, in gratitude for all that they are.

INTRODUCTION

Dating from 1436, *The Book of Margery Kempe* is the first autobiography to be written in English. In it, a woman from King's Lynn (then Lynn Bishop) in Norfolk gives a moving account of torments and joys that were so intense as to 'ravish' her soul. She firmly believed that this tumult of inner experience came directly from God. Sometimes it came in the form of visions and sensory hallucinations and sometimes as intimations directly received in her soul.

Margery's *Book* sets all of this in the context of a remarkable life. Unlike her saintly contemporary, Julian of Norwich, who wrote the *Revelations of Divine Love*, she lived in the world and not in a cell, and experienced all its pleasures and pains. A comfortable Norfolk childhood made her snobbish and proud; post-natal depression and business failure chastened her and fired her with religious zeal. A pilgrimage to Jerusalem increased her faith, for it took her, almost literally, to the foot of the Cross.

From this time onwards the person and passion of Christ were almost constantly present to Margery's mind. They counterpointed her workaday experience and suffused it with meaning. Even the sight of a baby boy was enough to set Margery crying and wailing with deep emotion, for in the baby she also saw the infant Christ. In Rome, she went up to handsome adults, mistaking them for Christ the man. (She seems to have had the fortune to be immune to embarrassment.)

Margery freely admitted, at many points in the *Book*, that her weeping and wailing were 'boisterous' (noisy and violent). Her frequent outbursts, coupled with much extempore preaching, tended to alienate those around her. Sometimes she managed to hold the noise in until she was literally blue in the face, but then it broke forth with all its pent-up 'boisterousness', even in church at the solemnest moments of the mass.

Her language, even her very name, have a homely and familiar ring, conjuring up the image of someone down-to-earth, unpretentious, bucolic. The sense of red-cheeked, buxom heartiness has its appeal, but we have to confess that we know almost nothing about her appearance. We do know it took two men to keep her perched on her donkey when intense devotion overcame her sense of balance as she followed the Way of the Cross in Jerusalem. There are other signs, too, that she had a fair deal of brawn and strength. But however we picture her face and bearing we have to remember the tears and the tear-stains.

Medieval hagiographers saw ecstasies and tears as a mark of holiness. However, pilgrim parties and travellers (especially those in holiday spirit) found Margery's company hard to endure. Her declamations and tears disrupted many a meal, and she frequently found herself left behind at inns or even on lonely roads by people eager to make their escape. Strangers sometimes let her join them, only to turn her away again within the day. Margery's account of these rejections is often touchingly naive. An example occurs when she tells us about her return from France at the end of her third and final overseas pilgrimage: 'She had put her things on board the ship when [her companions] ... changed to another ship. She never knew the reason for this.'

Dressed in virginal white (despite having mothered fourteen children), Margery was a conspicuous figure, especially when she was wailing and ranting. With a popular reputation for holiness, and perhaps for clairvoyance, she must have attracted sizable crowds when she came back from distant shrines complete with relics and blistered feet.

Margery's public lamentations and ranting disturbed both church and civil authorities. She lived at the time of the Lollards, a school of preachers and thinkers whose ideas, based on those of John Wycliffe, anticipated Protestantism. There was an anti-clerical strand to the movement, which attracted the church's enmity. Nor did the church approve of Lollard theology, which valued preaching more highly than the sacraments. Margery deplored profane swearing, and this connected with Lollard objections to the swearing of oaths, even solemn oaths of attestation. Perhaps as a woman she excited medieval misogyny; as a woman suspected of preaching she was especially prone to disapproval: she was arrogating a priestly function, and hostile minds saw this as a challenge to ordination and all the other sacraments. No wonder she was arrested about a dozen times! She proved to be irrepressible, though; while under arrest she would shout to passers-by from her cell.

Margery Kempe was used to being spurned and reviled 'for the love of Christ', and she suffered arrest and violence in the same devout spirit. To her, these pains and privations were simply her humble part in bearing the Holy Cross of Christ. Once, when she was under arrest, well-meaning people told her that she should 'spin and card wool like other women do, and not have all this disgrace and bother.' Margery's reply was uncompromising: 'I suffer less than I'd like to do for love for our Lord. All I suffer is cutting words; but our merciful Lord Jesus Christ

... suffered vicious blows, cruel scourging and finally a shameful death.'

When tried before bishops and other churchmen Margery proved to be orthodox in all her beliefs. She was never convicted of any offence and was quickly released from imprisonment, often with letters of recommendation and a suitable escort. The letters and escort ensured her speedy passage into another diocese; with her strident and prophetic voice, she remained a thorn in the church's flesh, and each jurisdiction wanted her out of the way as quickly as possible. In a similar spirit, Margery was sometimes arrested on her return from an overseas pilgrimage but never during the outward journey.

On her final pilgrimage, made when she was sixty years old, she was forced to beg for her sustenance as she stumbled her footsore way across northern and western Europe. Something of her moneyed past seemed to mark her off from common beggars, and well-to-do people offered her companionship, or even shelter in their homes. As usual, her other-worldly zeal turned most of her would-be friends against her, and in the end she was forced to travel with a flea-ridden party who shocked her by stripping naked in order to 'pick themselves'. Margery preferred the discomfort of flea-bites. Severed from her once-proud past, she still remembered its superficial but tempting advantages.

The externals of her medieval world, its religious rites and practices, come through in the book and give it enormous fascination. Not only as autobiography but as travelogue, too, it set a standard that was not surpassed for centuries. However, it is Margery's sheer, intense humanity which engages our feelings so entirely. Like most human beings, she had her pride and she knew what it was to suffer a fall; she went through mental and physical illness and learned to care for the sorrows of others, drawing on her own experience as she helped a woman to cope with severe post-natal depression. As a mother she went through the pain of bereavement; as a wife she knew both the pleasures and burdens of being married. In her younger days her 'mind had been filled with voluptuous thoughts, sexual lust and overwhelming desire for [her husband's] body'. Later, when he was senile and incontinent, she remembered all they had shared together and nursed him with her characteristic compassion and care. It is true that in their middle years the couple took the exceptional step of renouncing sex for the sake of Margery's holiness, but unlike many 'plaster saints', Margery was positive about its appeal. She was a wholehearted, flesh-and-blood person, who in everything from flea-bites to sexual abstinence knew what she was suffering and what she was missing for the sake of her Lord.

Since inner events were prompted by external ones, Margery's *Book* is never dull. The interior and external worlds form the warp and the weft of a tapestry in which holiness interlaces the mundane elements. Margery's habit of mistaking the people around for Christ exemplifies this interplay. So does the spontaneity of her many conversations with God.

Margery often turns to God when faced with detractors, and he usually speaks to her soul in words of support and approval. One has to confess that some of these passages read as if she has told a tale to an over-indulgent parent and received the pampering reassurance she wanted. In cynical moments, one feels she is giving God his lines and unconsciously making them gratifying to herself. True to her abundant humanity, she clearly had her defects and flaws, and was over-ready to credit God with the workings of her own very fallible psyche (which is not to say that God did not work through them).

The Church reflected its final judgment on Margery in the fact that she was never canonized, though Margery says that God went so far as to deify and marry her. In the relevant episode, God invites her to kiss him, embrace him and take him to bed. These crude descriptions could cause offence, but we have to remember that Margery, who was illiterate, was grappling to express in words an experience so sublime (whatever its origin) as to go beyond any human language. The fact remains that most of Margery's visions turn on the person of Margery herself, as she interacts with God and the saints, while other parts of the *Book* turn on Margery's interactions with the people around her. Her work is thus what its title implies: a book of Margery Kempe herself. By contrast, Julian of Norwich was a self-effacing, reflective channel of divine intimation. Her *Revelations of Divine Love* could never be called the *Revelations of Mother Julian*.

At her best, though, Margery Kempe speaks with an amazing power that equals Mother Julian's. Her visions of Christ's passion, crucifixion and first resurrection appearances are clothed in words so intense and fine as to represent language almost transfigured. Though set out in prose, they rank with the greatest religious poetry in the English language.

From first to last, the *Book* is full of beautiful and telling images. For example, Margery likens a sound in her ear to the blowing of bellows and then to a dove, which she thinks is the voice of the Holy Spirit. 'Afterwards, [God] turned it into the voice of a little bird called a redbreast, which often sang very joyfully in my right ear.' She enjoyed this kind of sensory input for twenty-five years or even longer. Some may perhaps attribute it to tinnitus or temporal lobe epilepsy—reminding us that Margery's flawed but saintly spirit saw the glory of God in everything and turned it to holy tears, deep joy or telling poetry.

There is poetry of a different sort in some of Margery's sharp replies when under attack. She never answered insult with insult, but was always ready to rebuke hypocrisy or spiritual blindness. At times she spoke with a quiet, collected dignity which surprised all those who despised her tears. Once, when she was weeping at the thought of Christ's dead body, a priest brusquely told her: 'Woman, he's been dead long enough now.' To which she replied, 'Sir, his death is as fresh to me as if he had died this very day, and so I think it should be to you and to all Christian people.'

The challenge and joy of reading Margery Kempe's strange *Book* is to decide for oneself the wellspring of all her visions and claims. Along the way we will feel the intense devoutness of her medieval world while recoiling from some of the characters who sullied it; and if we sometimes smile at Margery Kempe herself there are moments when we can hardly fail to share in her tears.

Text and translation

As an illiterate, Margery had to dictate her *Book*. Her first scribe proved unworthy of his task, for his writing was almost illegible and his grammar a blend of his native English and the German he had adopted after going abroad. (There are clues in the *Book* which suggest that he was Margery's son, but she forbears to name names!) A priest, working under Margery's direction, later deciphered and re-wrote this text, creating by far the longer of the work's two 'Books'. Margery and this second scribe then prefaced the existing brief introduction with a longer one explaining his role as redactor, and they later wrote Book Two, which is mainly concerned with Margery's final, tormented pilgrimage. They concluded the *Book* by adding some of Margery's very moving prayers.

There has long been debate as to how much influence the scribes exerted over what was set down. The *Book* calls Margery a 'creatur', meaning 'creature' or 'created thing'. Though subtly nuanced, this word is very impersonal and its use may reflect the scribal stance, as may the almost exclusive employment of the third person 'she' when referring to her. However, there are moments when the mask of impersonality slips and the first person 'I' breaks through to the surface, allowing Margery's voice to speak directly down the vista of time.

This translation from the Middle English makes a confident choice in favour of allowing Margery to speak for herself throughout; we hear her account in the first person, just as her scribes must have heard it themselves. The extempore tone which enlivens much of Book One is preserved, though redundancies and verbal tangles have sometimes been eliminated and a few odd words of clarification have been inserted in square brackets.

In working on the new introduction and on Book Two and the Prayers, Margery's priest was untrammelled by the work of a previous, semi-literate scribe. The present translation preserves the relatively lofty tone which sometimes emerges in his work. It serves to highlight the homely, colloquial flavour of the *Book* as a whole, a flavour which underlies even some of the most sublime passages (as, for example, when Margery, in a vision, makes 'a nice hot drink' for Christ's sorrowing mother). One almost regrets that Margery and her initial scribe could not have managed without the help of the bookish priest.

There are certain points, including one or two in Book One, where a lofty tone may perhaps be a mark of passages which the priest went as far as to put into Margery's mouth or at least adapt substantially. Be that as it may, the locutions which Margery attributes to God show little sign of priestly editing. Some are sublime but most are banal—so much so that Louise Collis, in her book about Margery Kempe entitled *The Apprentice Saint* (Michael Joseph, 1964), mocks their banality by rounding off brief quotations with words like 'God remarked'. This translation attempts to preserve the original in all its range and variety, including its revealing flaws.

Lost for several centuries, the *Book* was rediscovered in 1934 in an early manuscript copy. Rodents had feasted on a few of Margery's precious words but otherwise the text shows every sign of integrity, save for one major error, presumably made when a copyist muddled the leaves of his source: he misplaced at the end of chapter 18 material concerning Margery's somewhat acrimonious clashes with widows, and this translation restores it to its obvious context a chapter later. (It begins with the words 'On a previous occasion, I had gone to pray.')

It is sad to feature the one bad mistake of a man to whom we owe so much. Unlike Margery's scribes he left us a note of his name, for he added at the end of the manuscript the touching words:

Ihesu mercy quod Salthows
[Jesus have mercy, said Salthows].

If Margery's multifaceted *Book* has a single message it is a plea for God's mercy on herself, and on 'all who have lived, live now or shall live in the future'. In a few short words the fallible Salthows had echoed the keynote of Margery's work.

Nondum amabam et amare amabam;
Quaerebam quid amarem, amans amare.

(St Augustine)

... hir mende and hir thowt was so ioynyd to God þat sche neuyr
forȝate hym but contynualy had mende of hym & behelde hym in
alle creaturys.

(Margery Kempe)

THE BOOK OF
MARGERY KEMPE

First Book

Margery Kempe's Introductions

Here begins a short study which offers sinful wretches great reassurance, consolation and comfort, and an understanding of the sublime and inexpressible mercy of our sovereign saviour Christ Jesus. May his name be worshipped and praised for ever, for in our own lifetimes he has deigned to show us his majesty and goodness in spite of our unworthiness. All our saviour's works are for our instruction and guidance, and the favour he shows to any of his created souls brings benefit to all who have the grace to respond. To the glory of his holy name our merciful Lord Jesus Christ has therefore allowed this little treatise to be set down. It will touch on some of his wonderful works—on how mercifully, kindly and lovingly he stirred and incited a wicked wretch like me to love ✓ him; and how, at the prompting of the Holy Spirit, I then spent many years doing my best to follow our saviour, with vows of fasting and many other penances.

In times of temptation I was constantly suffering setbacks; I was like a reed that bends with every breath of wind and only stays upright when all is calm. This was the case until our merciful Lord Christ Jesus took pity on me. Out of compassion for his handiwork and his creation, he turned my health into sickness, my success into failure, the good opinion of others to blame and their love into hatred. For many years I had gone my own uncertain way but all these reverses inescapably drew and incited me to follow the way of his perfection—the way which Christ our Saviour had exemplified in his own person, having duly followed the path before us and trodden it with dignity.

By the mercy of Jesus this study will show you something of my way of life. It will show how the hand of our Lord touched my body with serious illness, causing me to go out of my mind and suffer a lengthy spell of insanity. It lasted until our Lord, by his grace, made me well again, as I shall reveal more fully below. At that time I was richly endowed with worldly goods, but before very long I was totally devoid of means, and I had to abandon my pomp and pride. Those who had previously looked up to me started condemning me in no uncertain terms; my family and former friends were now my biggest enemies.

In the light of this amazing change I sought refuge under the wings of my spiritual mother, Holy Church, and I went and submitted myself to my confessor. I confessed my misdeeds and imposed severe penances on my body. Soon afterwards, our merciful Lord began to visit me day

17

by day with freely-flowing tears of contrition. I shed so many tears that some people slandered the work of God by claiming that I was putting them on.

So much did people slander me and condemn me, criticize and rebuke me for the grace and virtue which suffused me by the strength of the Holy Spirit that I found some measure of consolation and comfort in suffering any trial out of love for God and in witnessing to the acts of grace he performed within me. The more slander and criticism I suffered the more I grew in grace and the more would I devote myself to holy meditation, the contemplation of things divine and the wonderful speech and conversation of our Lord in my soul, which warned me about the contempt I would suffer for loving him and advised me to show forbearance, placing all my trust and love and affection in him alone.

By the inspiration of the Holy Spirit I knew and understood many secret and hidden things that were going to happen. I often wept and sobbed when I was preoccupied with God's holy speech and conversation—so much so that many people were amazed; they had no idea that God was so intimate with my soul. Even I could never describe the grace I felt within me, it was so heavenly, so far beyond my understanding and natural powers of comprehension, and the power of my feeble frame to endure its visitations. Words could never give fit expression to what I felt within my soul.

At such times I was afraid of being deluded and deceived by my unseen enemy, but the Holy Spirit told me to go to many illustrious clerics, including archbishops, bishops, and doctors and bachelors of divinity. I also consulted many anchorites, describing to the best of my abilities my way of life and the works of grace which the Holy Spirit of his goodness performed in my mind and soul. Everyone to whom I revealed my secrets said that I owed our Lord great love for the grace he had shown me; they advised me to follow my inclinations and inner stirrings and trust in the fact that they came from the Holy Spirit and not from a devil. Some of these good and noteworthy clerics took it on pain of their souls, as they would answer to God, that I was filled with the Holy Spirit, and they told me that I should have my feelings and revelations described in a book. Some of them offered to record them themselves but I firmly refused, having received an inner command not to commit them to writing so soon. From the time when I first had my inner feelings and revelations it was at least twenty years before I had any written down. That was when our Lord saw fit to command and require me to have them recorded, along with details of how I lived my life, so that all the world would know of his goodness.

I had no scribe to help me or take my experiences seriously—not until an Englishman living in Germany (he had married there and lived there with his wife and child) was apparently moved by the Holy Spirit to come to England with his wife and his property. He knew about me and what I wanted, and he lived with me until he had written down as much as I chose to tell him during our time together, after which he died.

There was a priest I liked a lot, and I told him all about it and gave him the book to read. However, it was so badly written that it was almost beyond him to do so; it wasn't in proper English or proper German, and the letters weren't formed in the normal way. The priest was convinced that no one would ever be able to read it without special help. Even so, he promised me that if he did succeed in reading it he would gladly copy it out and make a better job of it.

Soon afterwards, there was so much evil talk about me and my weeping that the priest was nervous of speaking with me except on odd occasions, and he wouldn't do the writing out he had previously promised to do. As a result, he avoided and put off writing this book for as much as four years or more, despite the fact that I frequently pressed him to get it done. In the end, he refused to make the attempt; he wasn't prepared to run personal risks over something he couldn't even read. He advised me to go to a good man who had been closely acquainted with the book's first scribe, thinking that he would be better able to read the writing than anyone else; he had sometimes read letters in the same hand, sent while their writer was living abroad in Germany.

I went to the man, asking him to write out this book and keep its existence secret for as long as I lived, and I offered to pay him a generous sum in return for his effort. He filled about one sheet of paper, but to little purpose: he wasn't able to make much progress because the original was so badly written and so confused. At this point, the priest's conscience began to trouble him because, having promised to write out this book if he could decipher the original, he had failed to make his best effort. He therefore asked me to get the book back if I possibly could. I did so, and I was more than happy to bring it to the priest. I asked him to try and carry out his good intentions, and I said I would pray to God to obtain the grace he needed for the reading and writing. The priest put his faith in my prayers and began to read the book, and it seemed to him much easier than it had been before. He read it out to me word for word, though I sometimes had to prompt him where he found it difficult.

The arrangement is not chronological, with things described in the order they happened; they were set down just as they came to me during the process of writing. This was done such a long time after the events had occurred that I couldn't remember when or in what order they had taken place, which made me all the more careful only to put things down if I knew for a fact that they were true.

When the priest first started to write this book he had trouble with his eyes, and he couldn't see to form the letters or mend his pen, though everything else was perfectly clear. He tried to write with a pair of spectacles perched on his nose but they made things much worse. When he told me about the trouble he was having I said that his unseen enemy resented the good act which he was performing and would do his best to hinder him. I told him to do the best he could by the grace of God and not give up. When he resumed his work on the book it seemed to him that he could see as well as he'd ever done, both by daylight and by candlelight. Having filled a quire of paper he therefore added a leaf at the start and wrote this new introduction. Written in 1436, it gives more detail than the following one, which was written earlier.

This is a short account of someone who had high status and worldly reputation but was later drawn to our Lord by severe poverty, sickness, humiliation and other salutary experiences in many different countries and places.

Some of the tribulations in the following account will be recorded not in the order in which they occurred but as I could call them to mind when the time came for setting them down; for it was not until I had forsaken the world and fervently embraced our Lord for over twenty years that this book was written.

From the start, people pressed me to make a record of what I went through and what I felt, and a Carmelite friar freely offered to act as scribe if I wished him to do so. But I had an inner sense that I should not set everything down at once; and many years passed before I felt prompted to have it done.

In the event, my first scribe was a man who had little idea of how to write either English or German. As a result, only those who were full of God's grace could follow my meaning, for I was so condemned and slandered that very few people would believe what I said.

In the end, a priest felt a strong desire to record this account, and he struggled to read the first account for a full four years on end. Later, prompted by me and spurred on by his conscience, he made another attempt to read it and he found it much easier than he had done before.

And so he began to write in the year of our Lord 1436, on the day following the feast of Mary Magdalene, using the information which I myself gave him.

Chapter 1

When I was twenty, or a little older, I was married to a well-respected burgess, and, things being what they are, I quickly found myself pregnant. During the pregnancy and up to the time the child was born I suffered from severe attacks of illness; and then, what with the labour of giving birth on top of my previous illness, I despaired of my life and thought that I would not survive.

At that point I sent for my priest, because I had something on my conscience which I had never before divulged in my life. For I was constantly hindered by my enemy, the devil, who was always telling me that so long as I was in good health I had no need to make confession; I should just do penance by myself, in private, and God, in his all-sufficient mercy, would forgive me for everything.

And therefore I often did harsh penances, restricting myself to bread and water; I also did other godly deeds, praying devoutly but never revealing my guilty secret in the course of confession.

But when I was ever sick or out of spirits, the devil whispered to me that I would be damned because I had not been absolved of that special sin. Therefore, not expecting to survive the birth of my child, I sent for my priest, as I've already told you, fully intending to be absolved for everything I had done in my life.

But when I was on the point of revealing my long-concealed secret, my confessor was a little too hasty with me; he began to tell me off in no uncertain terms, before I had even covered all I meant to say; and after that, try as he might, he couldn't get me to say a word.

Eventually, what with my fear of damnation on one hand and the priest's sharp tongue on the other, I became insane, and for half a year, eight weeks and a few days I was prodigiously plagued and tormented by spirits.

During that time I saw (or I believed I saw) devils opening their mouths as if to swallow me, and revealing waves of fire that were burning inside their bodies. Sometimes they grabbed at me, sometimes they threatened me; they tugged and pulled me, night and day for a whole eight months. They also bayed at me fearsomely, and told me to forsake the church and its faith and deny my God, his mother and all the saints in heaven.

They told me to deny my good works and all my good qualities, and turn my back on my father, my mother and all my friends. And that's what I did: I slandered my husband, my friends and my own self. I said many wicked and cruel things; I was empty of any virtue or goodness;

I was bent on every wickedness; I said and did whatever the spirits tempted me to say and do. At their instigation I would have destroyed myself many times over and been damned to hell; and as if to show determination I bit my own hand so savagely that the mark has been visible ever since.

What's more, I used my nails (for I had no other instrument) to scratch myself viciously, ripping the skin on my chest near my heart. And if I'd had my own way I would have done even more to myself, but I was bound and restrained by force day and night. I suffered from these and other temptations for such a long while that people thought I'd never recover or even survive, but then something happened: as I lay by myself, without my attendants, our merciful Lord Jesus Christ—ever to be trusted! his name be praised!—never forsaking his servant in a time of need, appeared to me—his creature who had forsaken him—in human form, the most pleasing, most beautiful, loveliest sight that human eyes could ever behold. Dressed in a mantle of purple silk, he sat by the bed, looking at me with so much holiness in his face that I felt myself inwardly fortified. And he spoke to me in the following way:

'Daughter, why have you abandoned me, when I never thought to abandon you?'

And instantly, as he spoke these words, I swear that I saw the air open up as brightly as any shaft of lightning. And he rose up into the air, not very fast or quickly but with grace and ease, so that I could clearly see him in the air until it closed again.

And at once my composure and mental faculties came back to me, just as they had been before, and I begged my husband, as soon as he came, for the keys of the cellar so that I could get myself food and drink as I had done in the past. My maids and attendants advised him not to hand over any keys; they said I would only give away any such stores as we had, for they thought that I was beside myself.

Nevertheless, my husband, who was always kind and sympathetic to me, ordered them to give me the keys; and I got myself food and drink, insofar as my physical health would allow me to do so. And I recognized my friends, the members of my household and all the others who came to see the act of mercy which our Lord Jesus Christ had performed on me. Blessed may he be, who is always close to us in our troubles. When people think he is far away he is right beside them, full of grace.

Afterwards, I returned to all my other household duties, doing everything in a quite level-headed and sober way but not really knowing the call of our Lord.

Chapter 2

When, mercifully, I had thus returned to my right mind, I fancied that I was bound to God and would be his servant. However, neither my husband nor anyone else could persuade me to give up being vain or enjoying the trappings of wealth I was used to. Yet I knew very well that people said some very unpleasant things about me, for I wore gold braid in my hair, and my hoods and tippets were slashed [to show the silken linings]. As for my cloaks, the fabric was cut so that pieces of various colours could be sewn in place, thus attracting men's eyes and gaining ever more adulation for myself.

And when my husband told me to stop being proud he got a short, sharp answer. I said I had come from a good family—too good for him to have married into—for my father had been Mayor of Lynn and afterwards the alderman of the town's Holy Guild of the Trinity; so I meant to keep my family's respect whatever people might say about me.

My neighbours were very jealous of me, and wished that they were as well-dressed as I was. My only wish was to be admired. I would not take correction, and unlike my husband I wasn't content with the things God gave me; I always wanted more than I had.

Then out of sheer greed I began to brew ale, and for three or four years I was one of the leading brewers in Lynn. In the end, though, I lost a great deal of money, for I lacked experience in the trade. I had excellent servants who knew a lot about brewing ale, yet they never seemed to get it quite right. The ale foamed up as well as anyone could wish—but then the foam disappeared and the ale went to waste. This affected batch after batch, and my servants felt so bad that they left.

Then I remembered how God had punished me before—not that I had heeded it. Now he was punishing me again, this time with financial loss. As a result, I gave up brewing altogether.

Then I asked my husband to forgive me because I had not followed his advice sooner. I said that my pride and sinfulness were the reason for the punishments, and resolved to lead a better life, though I'd acted with the best of intentions.

Yet I did not entirely renounce worldly things, for I turned my mind to a new line of business. I had a mill that was powered by horses, so I got two good horses and a servant, and reckoned on earning my living by grinding people's corn. This enterprise did not last long, for shortly afterwards, on the eve of the feast of Corpus Christi, a miracle happened.

The servant was in good physical health and both the horses were sturdy and reliable, having always worked the machinery well. Now on this occasion the man took one of the horses and put it in the mill as usual, but the horse refused to pull no matter what the man did. The man was upset and racked his brains as to how he could get the horse to pull. Sometimes he led him by the head, sometimes he beat him, sometimes he coaxed him. Nothing worked, for the horse would rather go backwards than forwards. Then the man put a sharp pair of spurs on his heels and got on the horse's back to make him pull, but to no avail.

When the man realized how hopeless it was he put the horse back in the stable and gave him corn, and he ate well, with a good appetite. And later he took the other horse and put him in the mill, and this horse behaved like its partner had done before, for nothing the man did would make him pull. Then the man gave up his job and would not remain with me any longer. It was soon being said round the town of Lynn that neither man nor beast would give me service.

Then some people said that I was cursed or that God was taking vengeance on me for all to see. Some said one thing and some said another. Some wise men, whose thinking reflected their love of our Lord, said that our Lord Jesus Christ was showing his ineffable mercy by calling me from the pride and vanity of the wretched world.

Then I decided that all these troubles besetting me on every side were the scourges by which our Lord would punish my sinfulness. Asking God's mercy, I renounced my pride, my greed and my love of worldly renown. I mortified my body and set out on the path to everlasting life, as I mean to explain in the pages that follow.

Chapter 3

One night, as I lay in bed with my husband, I heard a melodious sound that was so sweet and lovely I thought that I must be in paradise. So straightaway I jumped out of bed saying, 'What a shame that I ever sinned! It's so joyful in heaven!' This melody was so sweet that it surpassed all the melody that anyone could hear in this world; there was no comparison. And so, after that, whenever I heard any music or revelry I wept profusely, shedding copious tears of deep devotion, sobbing and sighing for the bliss of heaven without a thought for the shame and contempt of this wretched world.

And always, after this holy call, I kept the joy and the melody of heaven in my mind—so much so that I could hardly stop myself speaking about it. For when I was in company I would often say, 'It's so joyful in heaven!' And those who knew how I'd lived beforehand and now heard me saying so much about the joys of heaven said to me, 'Why are you always talking about the joy of heaven? You don't know what it's like; you haven't been there any more than us!' And they were angry with me because I wouldn't (like them) either hear or speak about worldly things, though I had done before.

And from this time onwards I never wanted sexual intercourse with my husband, for this matrimonial duty was so loathsome to me that I felt that I would rather eat or drink the oozing slime in the gutter than consent to any physical relationship (except on my obedience). So I said to my husband, 'It isn't for me to deny you my body, but my heart and my feelings are drawn away from all earthly things and devoted to God.' He insisted on having his own way and I let him do so, but I was full of tears and sorrow because I couldn't live my life chastely. And I frequently asked my husband to live a life of sexual abstinence, and I said that I was very conscious of how we had often displeased God by our passionate love and the high degree of sensual pleasure we had had from each other, so by common desire and common consent we should now deliberately punish ourselves and mend our ways by refusing to serve our bodily lust. My husband said it was right to do so, but not just yet— he would do so when it was God's will. And so he availed himself of me as he had done before; he wouldn't desist. And all the time I prayed to God to let me live chastely, and three or four years later, when it pleased our Lord, he made a vow of chastity, as I shall later recount if Jesus gives me leave to do so.

And also, after hearing this celestial melody, I subjected my body to severe penance. Sometimes I confessed my sins two or three times a day—and especially the sin I'd concealed and covered up for so long, as I've mentioned at the start of the book. I subjected myself to severe fasting and lengthy vigils. I got up at two or three in the morning and went to church and stayed there at prayer until midday and all the afternoon as well. Then many people criticized me behind my back and to my face for living so strictly.

Next, I got a hair cloth from a kiln—the sort of cloth that malt is dried on—and wore it inside my gown as discreetly and secretly as I could so that my husband wouldn't notice it. And he didn't notice it, despite the fact that I lay with him in his bed each night, and wore the hair shirt every day, and had children during this part of my life.

Then for three years I had a great struggle against temptation, and I bore it as meekly as I could, thanking our Lord for all his gifts. And I stayed in good spirits when I was rebuked, scorned or mocked because of my love for our Lord; I was much more cheerful than I had been before, while enjoying public adulation. For I was well aware that I had committed a serious sin against God and deserved more shame and remorse than anyone could heap on me; and I knew that being despised by the world was the way to heaven, since Christ himself had chosen it. All his apostles, martyrs, confessors and virgins and all who ever entered heaven took the way of suffering; and as for me, there was nothing I wanted as much as heaven.

I was glad at heart to think I was setting forth on the path that would lead me to the place I most desired. I also felt great sorrow and compunction for wronging my Maker, shedding copious tears and sobbing loudly. And many a time our Lord put it into my mind to think of my wayward behaviour ever since childhood. And then, face to face with my own wickedness, all I could do was sorrow and weep, and constantly pray for mercy and forgiveness.

My tears were so profuse and continuous that many folk thought I could turn them on and off at will, and they said that I was a false hypocrite who wept just to get worldly comfort and gain. And a great many folk who had loved me when I belonged to the world now abandoned me and didn't want to know me. And all the while I thanked God for everything, for all I desired was mercy and forgiveness of sin.

Chapter 4

For the first two years after being called to our Lord in this way I wasn't troubled by any temptation. I could easily stand fasting—it didn't bother me—and I despised the pleasures of the world. My body didn't seem to rebel at all. I thought myself strong enough to face up to any devil in hell, for I had mortified my flesh so much. I thought I loved God more than he loved me. I was smitten with the deadly wound of vainglory but I didn't feel it, for I often wanted the crucified one to free his hands from the cross and embrace me as a sign of his love. Our merciful Lord Jesus Christ, seeing my presumption, sent me, as I have already said, three years of temptations.

I mean to give an account of one of the worst temptations, to show those who come after me that they should not have faith or delight in themselves, as I did; for without doubt our unseen enemy never sleeps, but busies himself examining our constitutions and personalities. By our Lord's consent he lays his snare where he finds us weakest, and no one can escape it by their own power.

And so he lay before me the snare of lechery, just when I thought that all my fleshly lust had been entirely quenched. The temptation lasted for quite some time, and there was nothing I could do about it. I made frequent confessions, I wore the hair shirt and severely mortified my body. I wept many bitter tears and frequently implored our Lord to preserve me and keep me from falling into sin, for I would rather have died than given way. And throughout this time I had no desire for sex with my husband; it was very painful and unpleasant for me.

In the second year of my temptation it came about that a man I thought a lot of told me on St Margaret's Eve before evensong that he'd give anything to lie with me and satisfy his bodily urges; and he told me I shouldn't resist him, because if he didn't have his own way this time he'd have it some other—I had no option. He did this to test how I would react, but I thought he really meant what he said and I did not say very much in reply. So for the time being we separated, and both went to hear evensong, for the church was dedicated to St Margaret.

I was so exercised by the man's words that I couldn't keep my mind on the service, nor say the Lord's prayer or think any other worthwhile thought, but was more troubled than ever before. The Devil put it into my mind that God had forsaken me, otherwise I would not be tempted in such a way. I believed the Devil's persuasive talk and began to give in to it because I couldn't think any wholesome thoughts. And so I accepted that God had abandoned me.

And when evensong was over I went to the man I have told you about to let him have his way with me, as I thought he wanted. But he was so evasive that I couldn't tell what he did want, so we parted for the night. And all night long I was so bothered and agitated that I hadn't the slightest idea what to do. I lay by my husband, but I couldn't bear to have intercourse with him—it seemed so repulsive to me, though it would have been quite in order if I'd wanted to, and this was a suitable time to do it. But all the while I was troubled about the other man and about sinning with him in the way he'd proposed.

In the end, temptation and lack of discretion overcame me. I consented inwardly and went to the man to see if he was ready for me. And he said that he wouldn't have me for all the wealth in the world; he would rather be cut up as small as meat for the cooking pot.

I went away feeling thoroughly humiliated and confused, seeing his own fidelity and my own lack of it. Then I reflected on the grace that God had given me earlier, and how my soul had been deeply at peace for two years. I'd repented of my sin with many bitter tears of compunction and a total desire never to sin again; I'd rather have died, or so I thought. And now, seeing how I'd wilfully consented to commit a sin, I was half way to total despair. Such was my sorrow that I thought that I was in hell. I thought I deserved no mercy, for I'd given my consent so willingly; I thought myself unfit to serve God, having been so false to him. Even so, I was confessed time and time again, and did whatever penances my confessor laid down, and conducted myself according to the rules of the Church. May God be blessed for the grace he gave me; but far from removing my temptation he increased it, or so it seemed to me. And so I felt he'd forsaken me, and I did not dare to trust in his mercy.

I was beset with dreadful temptations for almost all the next year—temptations to lechery and despair. But our merciful Lord, as I myself acknowledged, made me grieve and shed many bitter tears each day for my sins—usually lasting for two hours. But afterwards I could hardly help despairing again, and I was as far from any sense of grace as those who have never felt grace in their lives. I couldn't bear this and I despaired all the more. Except for the time when I did feel God's grace my torments were so extreme that I could hardly cope with them, but constantly mourned and sorrowed, just as if God had forsaken me.

Chapter 5

Then, on the day before Christmas Day, as I was kneeling in St Margaret's church, Lynn, in the chapel of St John, weeping my heart out and asking for mercy and forgiveness for my sins and wrongdoing, our merciful Lord Jesus Christ—blessed be his name—ravished my spirit and said to me, 'Daughter, why are you weeping so bitterly? I am by your side—Jesus Christ who died on the cross suffering cruel pains and torments for you. I, the same God, absolutely forgive you for all your sins. And you shall never go to hell or purgatory; but when you pass from this world you will enter the bliss of heaven in the twinkling of an eye.

'I am the God who has brought your sins before your mind and made you confess them. So do as I say and boldly call me Jesus, your love, for your love I am, and your love I shall be for ever more. And, Daughter, I want you to do away with the hair shirt on your back, for I will give you a scourge in your heart that will please me much better than all the hair shirts in the world. Also, my beloved Daughter, you must give up what you like best in this world, which is eating meat. And instead of that flesh you shall eat the flesh and blood of Christ—my body truly present in the sacrament of the altar. And, Daughter, I want you to receive my body every Sunday, and I shall infuse you with so much grace that all the world will marvel at it. And everyone will bite and gnaw at

you like rats gnawing at dried cod. Daughter, don't be afraid, for you
will triumph over all your enemies. I will give you sufficient grace to
answer every cleric on matters concerning the love of God. And I swear
to you by my majesty that I shall never forsake you, come what may. I
shall aid and preserve you so that no devil in hell shall ever part you from
me, nor shall any angel in heaven or man on earth—for devils in hell
may not, angels in heaven will not and men on earth shall not. And,
Daughter, I want you to give up your praying of many prayers and
ponder the things I shall put in your mind. I shall give you the freedom
to pray until six o'clock to say what you want to say. Then you must be
silent and speak to me through your innermost thoughts, and I shall give
you deep meditation and genuine insight. And I want you to go to the
anchorite at the house of the Preaching Friars and let him know of the
secrets and advice I've given you. Do as he advises you, for my spirit will
speak to you through him.'

I went to the anchorite, as I had been ordered, and told him everything
that had been revealed to me. Then, with great reverence and weeping,
the anchorite thanked God and said, 'Daughter, you are sucking from
the very breast of Christ, and have received a token of heaven to come.
I charge you to receive such thoughts as God may give you as meekly
and as devoutly as you can, then come and tell me what they are; and,
if our Lord Jesus Christ so desires, I shall tell you whether they have
come from the Holy Spirit or else from your enemy the Devil.'

Chapter 6

On another day I composed myself to meditate, as I had already been
told to do, and I lay motionless, not knowing what direction my
thinking should take. Then I said to our Lord Jesus Christ, 'Jesus, what
shall I think?'

Our Lord Jesus spoke to me inwardly: 'Daughter, think about my
mother, for she is the source of all the grace which you enjoy.'

And at that instant I saw St Anne, almost at the end of her pregnancy,
and I begged St Anne to let me be her maid and her servant. And straight
away our Lady was born, and I eagerly took her into my care, and kept
her until she was twelve years old. She had good food and drink, lovely
white clothes and white headcloths. And then I said to the blessed child,
'Lady, you shall be the mother of God.'

The blessed child answered, 'I only wish I were fit to be the servant
of the woman who'll conceive God's son.'

And I said, 'Lady, if that grace falls on you I beg you to let me stay in your service.'

As my vision continued, the blessed child passed out of my sight for a certain time and then returned. 'Daughter,' she said, 'I have now become the mother of God.'

Then I fell on my knees in great devotion, weeping profusely, and said, 'Lady, I am unworthy to serve you.'

'Daughter,' she said. 'Follow me. I'm happy to have you serve me.'

Then I set out with our Lady and Joseph, and I carried with me a jar of ointment and also some spices. And we went to see Elizabeth, John the Baptist's mother, and when we met we paid our respects to one another, and our twelve weeks together were full of happiness. At the end of that time St John was born, and our Lady picked him up from the ground with every mark of reverence. Giving him to his mother, she blessed him and said he would live a holy life. Then we said goodbye to one another with tears of affection. And I fell on my knees in front of St Elizabeth and begged her to ask our Lady to let me serve her and bring her happiness.

'Daughter,' replied Elizabeth, 'It seems to me that you do your duties really well.'

And then I set out with our Lady on the way to Bethlehem, and every night I got lodgings for her with great reverence, and our Lady received a warm welcome. And I made people give our Lady fine white clothes and cloths to wrap her son in when he was born; and when the time came, I ordered bedding for our Lady and her son to lie in. And then I begged for food for our Lady and her blessed child. And I bathed him in bitter tears of compassion, calling to mind the cruel death he would suffer for love of sinful mankind. And I said to him, 'Lord, I will treat you kindly; I will not bind you painfully. I beg you not to be displeased with me.'

Chapter 7

And afterwards, on the Twelfth Day, three kings came with their gifts and worshipped our Lord Jesus Christ as he lay in his mother's lap. As our Lady's servant I was inwardly watching it all take place, and I wept intensely. And when I saw that they were ready to take their leave and return to their own country I could not bear them to depart from the presence of our Lord, and I was so dismayed that they wanted to leave that I cried my heart out.

Soon afterwards an angel came and told our Lady and Joseph to leave the Bethlehem area and go to Egypt. Then I set out with our Lady, and every day I devotedly obtained her lodging with many sweet thoughts and meditations, and also with many sublime inner visions.

And often I cried for two hours or more as I fixed my mind on our Lord's passion. Sometimes I wept for my own sins and sometimes for the sins of others, sometimes for the souls in purgatory and sometimes for those in poverty or any hardship, for I dearly wanted to comfort them all.

Sometimes I wept uncontrollably and very noisily, for I yearned for the bliss of heaven and had to wait so long before I could go there. Then I pined for deliverance from this wretched world.

Our Lord Jesus Christ spoke inwardly to me and said that I must wait and endure the pangs of love: 'For I have chosen you to kneel before the Trinity to intercede for the whole world, for many hundreds of thousands of souls will be saved by your prayers. So ask for what you want, Daughter, and what you ask for I shall grant.'

I replied, 'Lord, I ask you mercifully to preserve me and everyone else from everlasting damnation. Punish us in this life as you wish, and in purgatory too, but by your great mercy keep us from hellfire.'

Chapter 8

Another time, as I lay in prayer, the Mother of Mercy appeared to me and said, 'May blessings fall upon you, Daughter. A place has been prepared for you in heaven before my son's throne—for you and for whoever you want to have with you.'

Then her blessed son asked me, 'Daughter, who will you have as your companion?'

'My beloved Lord, I would like to have my spiritual father, Master R[obert Spryngolde].'

'Why do you ask for him rather than your natural father or your husband?'

'Because I can never reward him for his goodness towards me and the gracious pains he has taken in hearing my confession.'

'I grant you what you wish for him; but your father, your husband and your children will be saved as well.'

Then I said, 'Lord, you have forgiven me my sins, and I now put all the good works that you are doing in me at your disposal. Whether I pray, think, weep, go on pilgrimage, fast or speak to any good purpose, my will is that you should definitely give half the merit to Master R[obert] as if he had done these things himself. And, Lord, share the other half among your friends and your enemies, and among my friends and enemies, for I will have only yourself for my reward.'

'Daughter, I will be a faithful executor and carry out all your wishes. Because of your great concern for the welfare of your fellow Christians, your reward in heaven will be redoubled.'

Chapter 9

On another occasion, I was praying to God to let me live chastely with my husband's permission, and I heard Christ say to me inwardly, 'On Fridays you must go without both food and drink, and your wish will be granted before Whit Sunday, for I will suddenly strike your husband dead.' Then, on the Wednesday in Easter Week, when my husband wanted to have intercourse with me as usual, and was making the first moves, I said, 'Jesus, help me,' and there and then he just couldn't touch me in that way, and he couldn't manage physical relations with me ever again.

On the Friday before Whitsun Eve, when I was in St Margaret's church at Lynn hearing mass, I happened to hear a loud, frightening noise. I was very scared, for I'd been unnerved by people saying that God would take his revenge upon me. I knelt on my knees, bowing my head and holding my prayer book in my hand, and begging our Lord Jesus Christ for his grace and mercy. Suddenly a stone weighing three pounds and a stump of beam weighing six pounds fell from the highest point of an archway, where they had been supporting the central beam, and landed on my head and my back. I thought my back was broken, and I was afraid I hadn't long to live. Promptly I cried out, 'Jesus, have mercy,' and my pain disappeared.

A good man called John Wyreham, seeing this strange event and thinking that I was badly hurt, came and tugged my sleeve and said, 'How are you, madam?' I was completely well and unharmed, and I thanked him for his kindness and concern. I just marvelled and wondered at the fact that I wasn't in any pain after having been in so much pain only just before. Nor did I feel any pain in the twelve weeks afterwards. Then the Holy Spirit spoke within my soul and said, 'Take this as a great miracle, and if the people won't believe in it I shall work many others.'

A well respected doctor of divinity called Master Aleyn, who was a

Carmelite friar, heard about this strange act of God and asked me all the details of what happened. Wishing God's works to be glorified, he got the stone that fell on my back and weighed it, and afterwards he got the end of the beam that fell on my head, which one of the church wardens had put on the fire, ready to burn. And this worshipful doctor said it was a great miracle, and that God should be highly praised for preserving me from the malice of my enemy. He told a great many people about it, and a lot of them greatly glorified God for his presence within me. But there were also others who would not take it seriously. Rather than believe that it signalled any mercy or favour, they took it as a sign of anger and vengeance.

Chapter 10

Soon afterwards, I was inwardly moved to visit certain places for the good of my soul because God had saved me from being injured; but I was not free to do it unless I had my husband's consent. I asked my husband to give me permission, and fully trusting that it was the will of God he readily agreed, and we went together to the places I was moved to visit. And then our Lord Jesus Christ said to me, 'My servants are very keen to see you.' And I was welcomed and fêted in all sorts of places. Because of this I was frightened of giving way to vainglory; it scared me a lot.

Our merciful Lord Jesus Christ—may his name be worshipped—said to me, 'Daughter, don't be afraid. I shall free you from vainglory. For those who worship you worship me; and those who despise you despise me, and I shall punish them for it. I am in you and you are in me, and those who hear you hear the voice of God. Daughter, if any living person forsakes his sin and acts according to your advice, then no matter how sinful he may have been, I will show my love for you by agreeing to whatever grace you promise him.' Then my husband and I went on our way to York and various other places.

Chapter 11

One Friday—it was Midsummer Eve and the weather was hot—I was coming away from York with a bottle of beer in my hand and my husband carrying a cake in his clothes, against his chest, when he happened to ask me the following question: 'Margery, if a man appeared with a sword and threatened to chop off my head unless I had intimate relations with you, as I used to do, tell me honestly what your conscience would say—for you assure me you won't lie. Would you let my head be cut off or would you let me make love to you again, as I've done in the past?'

'Oh sir,' I said. 'Why bring this up? Haven't we been chaste for the last eight weeks?'

'Because I want to know what you feel deep down.'

And then I said with great regret, 'The truth is that I'd rather see you killed than have us go back to our unclean ways.'

And he rejoined, 'There's no way you're a proper wife.'

And then I asked my husband why he hadn't made love to me for the last eight weeks, since I'd slept with him every night in his bed. And he said it made him so scared to touch me that he didn't dare do it any more.

'Well then, sir, turn to God and ask him for mercy. It's nearly three years since I told you that you'd suddenly be killed. It's now the third year, and I'm still hoping to have what I wish [a life of perpetual chastity]. Good sir, I beg you to give me what I'm going to ask, and I shall pray for you to be spared through the mercy of our Lord Jesus Christ; and you'll have more reward in heaven than if you wore a hair shirt or a coat of mail. I beg you to let me make a vow of chastity before whatever bishop God may choose.'

'No,' he said, 'I won't agree to it, because at the moment I can have sex with you without committing a mortal sin, and if you do it I won't be able to.'

Then I replied, 'If the Holy Spirit wants to bring about what I've proposed, then I pray God that you will give your consent; and if it isn't the will of the Holy Spirit, I pray God that you will never allow it.'

Then we went on our way to Bridlington in really hot weather, and I was very upset and afraid about my chastity. And we came to a cross and my husband sat himself down beneath it. He asked me to join him and said these words: 'Margery, let me have what I want and you can have what you want. My first wish is that we shall still sleep in the same bed as we have done up to now; the second is that you shall pay my debts before you go to Jerusalem; and the third is that you shall eat and drink with me on Fridays as you used to.'

'No, sir,' I said, 'I shall never agree to break the Friday fast for as long as I live.'

'Well,' he said, 'in that case we'll make love again.'

I begged him to let me say my prayers, and he readily agreed. Then

I knelt down beside a cross in the field and in floods of tears I prayed as follows: 'Lord God, you know all things. You know the pains I have taken to keep my body chaste for you for these three whole years, and now I could have what I want and my love for you holds me back. For I could have it if I broke the fast which you commanded me to keep on Fridays, and started having food and drink. But, blessed Lord, you know I will not disobey your will, and even now my sorrow is far less than the comfort I find in you. Now, blessed Jesus, show me your will, unworthy as I am, so that henceforth I can follow and fulfil it with all my strength.'

And then our Lord Jesus Christ spoke to me with great tenderness, commanding me to return to my husband and beg him to let me have what I wanted. 'And he shall have what he wants. For, beloved Daughter, I told you to fast so that you'd more quickly and easily get your wish, which has now been granted. I don't require you to fast any longer, and in Jesus' name I am asking you to eat and drink as your husband does.'

Then I thanked our Lord Jesus Christ for his grace and his goodness, and afterwards I got up and went to my husband and said to him, 'Sir, if it pleases you, you can grant my wish and I'll grant you yours. Promise that you won't come into my bed, and I promise to clear your debts before I go to Jerusalem. And let my body be totally at God's disposal, which means that from now to your dying day you must never make any claim on me by asking for your matrimonial rights; and I shall eat and drink on Fridays, just as you ask.'

Then my husband replied, 'May your body be as freely devoted to God as it has been to me.'

I thanked God wholeheartedly, very pleased that I had my wish, and I pressed my husband to say the Lord's Prayer three times over in honour of the Trinity and the grace that God had granted us. And we did this kneeling under a cross, and then we ate and drank together in very high spirits. This was on Midsummer Eve, on a Friday. Then we carried on towards Bridlington and we also visited many other districts. Wherever we went we spoke with God's servants—anchorites, hermits, and many others who love our Lord, including many fine scholars, doctors of divinity and students too. And in accordance with God's commands I told many of them about my feelings and visions, to see if they were of any value.

Chapter 12

Our Lord sent me to various religious houses, including a monastery where, for love of our Lord, I was very welcome, except that a monk who held high office there treated me with disdain and contempt. In spite of this, they sat me down for a meal with the abbot, and frequently during the meal I said all sorts of good things which God put into my mind.

The monk who had so despised me was there to hear what I said, and so were many others. And the things I said began to win him round towards me, and he started to have a great liking for what I had to say. So afterwards, when he and I were both in church, this monk came to me and said, 'Woman, I understand God speaks to you. Please tell me whether I shall be saved or not and by what sins I have most displeased God, for I will not believe in you unless you tell me what sins they are.'

I said to the monk, 'Go to mass, and I'll see if I can weep for you and win you grace.' He did as I said and went to mass, and I wept profusely for his sins.

When mass was over, I said to our Lord Jesus Christ, 'Blessed Lord, what answer shall I give to this man?'

'My beloved Daughter, say in the name of Jesus that he has committed the sins of lechery, despair and covetousness.'

'Oh gracious Lord, this is a hard thing for me to say. He will put me to shame if I make a mistake.'

'Don't be afraid; speak forthrightly in my name and in the name of Jesus, for all the things I'm saying are true.'

And then I said again to our Lord Jesus Christ, 'Good Lord, will he be saved?'

'Yes,' said our Lord Jesus, 'if he gives up his sins and follows your advice. So charge him to forsake his sins, make his confession, and give up the post that he holds outside the religious house.'

Then the monk returned and said, 'Margery, tell me my sins.'

I said, 'Sir, I beg you not to ask about them. I assure you that if you take my advice your soul will be saved.'

'But I won't take you seriously unless you tell me my sins.'

'Sir, I understand that you have committed the sins of lechery, despair and covetousness.'

At this the monk was taken aback and he stood transfixed. And then he said, 'So have I sinned with married women or single women?'

'Sir, with wives.'

And then he asked, 'Shall I be saved?'

'Yes, sir, if you do as I say. With my help, you must repent of your sins.

You must make confession and give them up. Abandon the outside post that you have, and God will give you grace because of his love for me.'

The monk took me by the hand and led me into a lovely kitchen, made me a great dinner and then gave me gold to pray for him. And thereupon I took my leave.

On another occasion I visited that place again, and the monk of whom I have spoken had given up his outside job, just as I had advised, and had turned from his sins. He had been made the sub-prior of the place, and thanks be to God all was well with him both outwardly and inwardly. He made me very welcome and praised God with all his heart for the fact that he'd met me in the first place.

Chapter 13

Once I was with the monks at the church in Canterbury, and they bitterly despised and condemned me because I was weeping so much. I wept for nearly the whole day, morning and afternoon alike, both for the monks and priests and for those in the secular life. I wept so much that my husband went away, as if he didn't know me, and like it or not I was left by myself among them, and I didn't have his company again for the rest of that day.

So an elderly monk, a rich and highly respected man who had been treasurer to the queen before taking the habit, grasped my hand and said to me, 'What can you say about God?'

'Sir,' I said, 'I like to hear about him as well as speak about him,' and I told the monk a story from scripture.

The monk said, 'I wish you were shut up in a house of stone so that no one could speak to you.'

'Ah, sir,' I said, 'you should uphold God's servants, but you are the first to hinder them. May our Lord set you right.'

Then a young monk said to me, 'Either you have the Holy Ghost in you or else a devil, for what you're saying to us comes from scripture, and it isn't something you've made up yourself.'

Then I replied, 'Sir, would you allow me to tell you a story?'

And the people said to the monk, 'Let her say what she wants.'

And so I began, 'There was once a man who had committed a serious sin against God. When he made his confession his confessor told him as part of his penance to hire some men for a year to rebuke and reprove him for his sins, and he was to give them silver for their work. And one day he found himself surrounded by lofty men like yourselves—God save you all—and he stood among them as I am standing among you now, and they reviled him just like you revile me, and the man was laughing or smirking and finding their words really funny. The greatest scholar among them said to the man, "Why are you laughing, you wretch, when we despise you so much?"

"Ah, sir, I've every cause to laugh. For days I've been paying silver from my purse and hiring men to rebuke me so as to gain remission of my sins, and thanks to you all I can keep my silver in my purse today."

'In just the same way I tell you, dear sirs, that while I was in my home district I grieved each day, weeping and mourning because I didn't suffer the shame, scorn and despite I deserved. I thank you all, sirs, very much for the profitable morning and afternoon I've had today. May God be blessed for it.'

Then I left the monastery, and they followed and cried at me, 'You'll be burned, you false Lollard. Here's a cartload of briars and a barrel ready to burn you with.' And I stood outside the gates of Canterbury—it was evening and there were a lot of people who didn't know what to make of me.

Then the people said, 'Take her and burn her.' And I stood there, with my body trembling and shuddering very violently and with nothing whatsoever to comfort me, and with no idea where my husband had gone.

Then inwardly I prayed to our Lord along these lines: 'I came here, Lord, out of love for you. Blessed Lord, help me and have mercy on me.' And as soon as I had offered up these silent prayers to our Lord two handsome young men appeared and said to me, 'Woman, do you deny being a heretic or a Lollard?'

And I replied, 'Sirs, I am neither a heretic nor a Lollard.'

Then they asked me where my inn was. I said I didn't know what street it was in, but it would be the German's house. Then these two young men took me home to my inn, where I found my husband, and they made a great fuss of me and begged me to pray for them.

And many people in Lynn had maligned me while I was away, telling untrue stories about all sorts of things I was supposed to have done while roaming the country.

Then after this I had great peace of spirit for a long time, and sublime visions day by day, and much holy talk and conversation from our Lord Jesus Christ at all hours. And I shed many sweet tears of high devotion so plenteously and so continually that it was a wonder that my eyes survived or that my heart could endure the fire of love which was kindled by the holy talk of our Lord when he said to me (as he often did),

'Beloved Daughter, love me with all your heart, for I love you with all my heart and with all the strength of my Godhead, for from everlasting you were a chosen soul in my sight, and a pillar of my Holy Church. My merciful eyes are always upon you. It would be impossible for you to endure the scorn and despite that lie ahead of you except that you have my grace to be your only support.'

Chapter 14

Then I thought it was a real joy to be criticized because of my love for God. It was a great pleasure and comfort to me when I was chided and scolded for loving Jesus, for condemning sin, for upholding virtue, for talking about the scriptural texts I'd learned in sermons and for conversing with scholars.

I pictured to myself what death I might die for Christ's sake. For the love of God I could almost have suffered execution, but the process of dying terrified me. I feared my own lack of fortitude and imagined for myself what I thought would be the easiest death, which was to be bound head and foot to a piece of timber and have my head struck off with a sharp axe, for the love of God.

Then our Lord spoke to my mind: 'I thank you, Daughter, that you are willing to die out of love for me, for whenever you think these thoughts you earn the same reward in heaven as if you had actually suffered death. But no one will kill you, and no fire will burn you, nor water drown you nor wind buffet you, for I cannot forget that you are written in my hands and my feet; and I am glad to have suffered pains for your sake. I shall never turn against you in anger, but I shall love you forever.

'Don't be afraid, even if all the world is against you, because no one can harm you. I swear to your mind that if I could go through my torments again, then just for your soul I would do so rather than have you depart from my presence forever. And so, Daughter, just as you see the priest take the child at the font and dip it in the water and wash away its original sin, so in just the same way shall I wash away all your sin in my precious blood.

'And don't be afraid if I sometimes take away from you the grace of holy speech or tears, for I am working secretly in you to stop you having any vainglory, and to show you clearly that you can only have such tears and talk when God sends them to you; God gives them freely—they're not to be earned—and he can give them to whoever he likes without in any way wronging you. And therefore receive them meekly and thankfully when I send them to you. If I withdraw them accept it with a good grace but seek them conscientiously until you get them back again, for tears of compunction, devotion and compassion are the greatest and surest gifts that I can give on earth.

'What more could I do for you, short of taking your soul from your body and putting it in heaven—which I won't do yet. But heaven and God are found together and God is in your soul, along with many an angel to preserve it from harm both night and day. For when you go to church I go with you; and when you sit down to eat I sit with you; when you go to bed I go with you; and when you leave the town I leave too. Daughter, no father ever cared for his child as much as I'll care for you, and help you and keep you.

'I sometimes treat the grace I give you in just the same way as I treat the sun. You know that the sun sometimes shines far and wide, so that many can see it. At other times I hide it from people's eyes with a cloud, yet its true heat and brightness are never diminished. And that is just how I treat the souls whom I have chosen. Although you cannot always weep when you wish to do so my grace is in you just the same. I declare you to be my true daughter, and a mother, a sister, a wife and a spouse, for in the Gospel our Lord says to his disciples, "He who does the will of my Father in heaven is mother, brother and sister to me." When you seek to please me you are a true daughter; when you weep and sorrow for my pain and my passion you are a true mother, taking pity upon your child; when you weep for the sins and troubles of others you are a true sister; and when it grieves you to wait so long for the joys of heaven you are a true spouse and wife, for it's right for a wife to be with her husband, and to lack true joy until she is in his company.'

Chapter 15

When our Lord had forgiven me my sins, as I have explained, I had a desire to see the places where he was born, suffered his passion and died, along with other holy places which he visited in his lifetime and also after his resurrection. And while I was feeling these desires, our Lord spoke in my mind and told me to go to Rome, Jerusalem and the shrine of St James. This was two years before I went, because I wanted to go but could not afford it.

And then I said to our Lord, 'Where shall I get the money to visit these holy places?'

Our Lord replied, 'I will give you friends all over England to help you. And Daughter, I will go to every country with you and provide for your needs. I will take you there and bring you back safely, and no Englishman will die in any ship you are in. I shall save you from the clutches of all who are wicked. And Daughter, I command you to wear white clothes, and no other colour; you must dress as I say.'

'Ah, dear Lord, I'm afraid that people will slander me if I go around dressed differently from other chaste women. They'll they stare at me and call me a show-off.'

'But Daughter, the more ridicule you suffer out of love for me the more you please me.'

Then I didn't dare do otherwise than follow the command I'd received in my soul, and I set out into the countryside. My husband went with me, for he always treated me kindly and well. Although out of baseless fear he sometimes left me for a while he always came back, and he felt sorry for me and spoke up for me as well as his fear of the people allowed. But everyone else who went with me forsook me, and the Devil tempted them into falsely accusing me of things I was never guilty of. This was the case with a man I trusted very much. He offered to accompany me on my travels, and I was glad of his offer, believing that I could rely on his support and help when I needed it, for he had spent a long while living with an anchorite who was a doctor of divinity, a holy man and my confessor.

And so this man—the anchorite's servant—followed his inclinations and set off with me on my travels. As for my maid, she accompanied me for as long as things went smoothly and no one spoke against us. But our Lord allowed our unseen foe to whisper into the people's ears, and as soon as this happened they criticized me for weeping so bitterly and said that I was a hypocrite and a false deceiver, and they threatened to burn me. Then the man I've mentioned, who was reckoned to be such a holy man, and in whom I'd placed such a lot of trust, condemned me utterly, treated me with foul contempt and wouldn't go any further with me.

My maid, seeing trouble on every side, decided to pit herself against me. She wouldn't obey me or take my advice. She let me go by myself into many prosperous towns and wouldn't go with me. But my husband was always ready when everyone else let me down, and he went with me where our Lord sent me; and all the while he trusted that everything was for the best and would turn out well in God's good time.

During these travels he took me to speak with the Bishop of Lincoln, whose name was Philip; and we had to wait three weeks before we could see him because he was not in residence at his palace. When the bishop came home he was told how a certain woman had waited all that time to speak with him and he sent for me at once, impatient to find out what I wanted. And then I went up to him and greeted him, and he welcomed me warmly and said that he had been wanting to speak with me for a long time and was very glad I had come. And so I asked for the chance to speak with him privately and tell him all my spiritual secrets, and he set a convenient time for this.

When the time came, I told him about my meditations and holy visions, and the other secret things about life and death that our Lord had revealed to my soul. He was very glad to hear all this, and he encouraged me to tell him whatever I wanted. He commended my insights and visions highly, saying that they concerned lofty and deeply religious matters. He urged me to set them down in writing, and said that the Holy Spirit had inspired them. And I said it was not God's will to have them written down so soon (and in fact they weren't set down for over twenty years). And then I added, 'I have received a command in my soul: if you are willing to do so, you are to give me the mantle and the ring and clothe me entirely in white, for I know by revelation that as you clothe me on earth our Lord Jesus Christ will clothe you in heaven.'

Then the bishop said to me, 'I will grant your wish if your husband agrees to it.'

Then I said to the bishop, 'Please let my husband come and see you, and you can hear what he says.'

And so my husband came before the bishop, and the bishop asked him, 'John, do you want your wife to take the mantle and the ring so that the two of you live celibate lives?'

'Yes, my Lord,' he said, 'and as a sign that we both undertake to live chastely I here and now place my hands in yours,' and he put them between the bishop's hands. And that was the end of our dealings with the bishop that day, except that he had us well entertained and said that we were thoroughly welcome.

On another day, the bishop invited me to come and eat with him. And before he started eating I saw him hand out thirteen pence, and thirteen loaves and other food to thirteen poor men, and he did the same thing every day. The sight of it stirred me to deep devotion, and I praised and worshipped God for the fact that he had given the bishop the grace to do these good deeds, and I wept so profusely that the bishop's whole household wondered what was wrong with me.

And after this I was sat down to eat with many of the bishop's best clerks, priests and squires, and the bishop courteously sent me food from his own dish. The clerks asked me many searching questions, and by the grace of Jesus I answered them, and the bishop was very pleased with my answers. As for the clerks, they could only marvel at the fact that I answered so readily and with such deep significance.

When the bishop had eaten he had me go to his room and said to me, 'You and your husband asked me to give you the mantle and the ring. I've put this matter to my advisors and they won't let me sanction the wearing of such distinctive clothing without more thought. You say that by the grace of God you are going to Jerusalem, so pray to God that the matter may wait until you return, by which time you will be better tested and proved.'

On the following day I went to church and prayed to God with all my heart that I might know how to act in this matter and the answer I should give to the bishop. Our Lord Jesus Christ answered to my mind in the following way: 'Daughter, tell the bishop that he is more concerned about worldly disgrace than about the perfect love of God. Tell him that I would have excused him for meeting your wishes just as I excused the children of Israel when I told them to borrow and remove the Egyptians' property. Tell him, Daughter, that though he will not do it now, it will be done at another time when God wishes.'

I gave my message to the Bishop of Lincoln as I had been commanded, and he asked me to go to the Archbishop of Canterbury, [Thomas] Arundel. I was to ask on the Bishop of Lincoln's behalf for permission for him to give me the mantle and ring, though I did not belong to his diocese. This was a way of stalling which his clerks put him up to because they disliked me.

I said to him, 'Sir, I'm more than willing to go to my Lord of Canterbury because there are other issues and matters which I have to broach with his Reverence. But I won't be going on this account, for God does not want me to ask about it.' Then I took my leave of the Bishop of Lincoln, and he gave me twenty-six shillings and eight pence to buy myself clothes and to pray for him.

Chapter 16

Then my husband and I set out for Lambeth in London, where the Archbishop was staying at the time. It was afternoon when we entered his hall, and it was thronged with the Archbishop's clerks and other irresponsible men—both squires and yeomen—who were coming out with all sorts of horrid oaths and ill-considered remarks, and I rebuked them in no uncertain terms and said that they would be damned unless they gave up their swearing and other sinful habits.

And straight away an ill-dressed woman from the same town stepped forward and scolded and damned me for all she was worth, and she said in a really malicious way: 'I'd like to see you in Smithfield, and I'd light a faggot to burn you with; I wish you were dead.'

I stood there and didn't answer, and my husband was very hurt and upset to hear his wife scolded in such a way. Then the archbishop sent for me to go into his garden. I went up to him and greeted him in the best way I could, and begged him to use his gracious authority to empower me, with his letter and seal, which were valid throughout the whole of his province, to choose my own confessor and to receive communion every Sunday, if God so moved me. In a thoroughly pleasant way he granted all I wanted without taking any silver or gold, nor would he let his clerks take anything for writing the letter or adding the seal.

When I found that I was in such good standing with him I felt great inner comfort and strength, so I told this worshipful lord about my way of life and the graces God imparted to my mind and soul. I wanted to know what he'd say about it and whether he found any fault in either my visions or weeping. And I also told him the cause of my weeping, and the way our Lord conversed with my soul. And he found nothing wrong but approved the way in which I lived; he was thoroughly pleased that our merciful Lord Jesus Christ was showing such grace in our day and age. May his name be blessed!

Then I spoke forthrightly to him about the need to discipline his staff, saying respectfully, 'My Lord, Almighty God the Lord of all has not given you your benefice and all your worldly goods so that you can maintain traitors to him who slay him every day by swearing horrid oaths. You will answer for their behaviour unless you correct them or dismiss them from your service.'

He listened gently and humbly as I told him what was on my mind and he gave me a gracious answer, from which I gathered that the matter would be put to rights, and so we continued talking until the stars began to shine in the sky. Then my husband and I took our leave.

On a later occasion my husband and I returned to London, and many worthy men were keen to hear me speak, for I had so much to say about the love of God that my hearers often wept with great emotion. And so I was thoroughly well received there, and so was my husband on my account, and this was the case for as long as we chose to stay in the city.

Afterwards we returned to Lynn, and I went to the anchorite at the house of the Preaching Friars in Lynn and told him about the welcome I had had, and how I'd got on while away from home. And he was very glad to see me back, and he reckoned that it was a great miracle that I'd travelled so far and wide. And he said to me, 'I have heard a lot of unpleasant talk about you while you've been away; I have been advised to abandon you and not to mix with you any more, and important people have promised me their friendship if I give you up. And I spoke up for you saying that if you were still the same as you were when I last saw you, then I could safely say that you were a good woman, a lover of God, and highly inspired by the Holy Spirit. And I said to these people, 'I will not forsake her for any lady in this realm. How could I talk to the lady if it meant abandoning her? If I couldn't be friendly with both of them I'd abandon the lady. I'd rather speak just to Margery if I had to choose.'

First read chapter 21 and then, after that, read the following chapter.

Chapter 17

One day long before this time, when I was still bearing children and had just given birth, our Lord Jesus Christ informed me that my childbearing days had come to an end and he said I should therefore go to Norwich.

And I replied, 'Ah, dear Lord, how shall I get there? I am faint and weak.'

'Don't worry. I'll make you strong enough. I want you to go to the vicar of St Stephen's and tell him that I greet him warmly and that he is a specially chosen soul of mine. Tell him that his preaching pleases me greatly. Share your secrets with him and tell him the things which I reveal to you.'

Then I made my way to Norwich and entered his church on Thursday shortly before midday. And the vicar was walking up and down with another priest. (This priest was the vicar's confessor, and was still alive when the things in this book were first written down.) Wearing black at the time, I greeted the vicar and asked for an hour or two of his time in the afternoon, once he had eaten, to speak with him about God's love.

Raising his hands and crossing himself he said, 'God preserve us! How could a woman take up an hour or two hours talking about God? I won't eat a thing till I know how you can fill an hour with talk of our Lord.' And he sat himself down inside the church.

Sitting near him, I told him all the words which God had spoken within my soul. Afterwards, I told him all about my way of life right from childhood, as well as I could remember things: how rebellious I had been to our Lord Jesus Christ, how proudly and vainly I had carried myself, how hostile to the laws of God and how jealous towards my fellow Christians; and I told him how it had afterwards pleased our Lord Jesus Christ to chasten me with many troubles and vile temptations, and how I had then been fed and consoled with my holy meditations, and especially with thoughts of our Lord's passion.

And while I was talking about the passion of our Lord Jesus Christ I heard such a terrible melody that I couldn't bear it. Then I fell down as if I was paralysed and lay motionless for a long while. I wanted to get the melody out of my mind but couldn't.

And then I had an inward assurance that there was great joy in heaven, and that each smallest part of heavenly bliss surpasses without comparison all the joy that could ever be imagined or felt in our present life. I felt greatly confirmed in my faith and all the more ready to tell the vicar the things which had been revealed to me about the living, the dead and his own self.

I told him how the Father of Heaven sometimes spoke to my soul as plainly and unmistakably as a friend speaking to another friend by word of mouth. Sometimes it was the Second Person of the Trinity and sometimes all three Persons of the Trinity, united in Godhead, who spoke to my soul and informed me, by my faith and through his love, of how I should love him, worship him and fear him. This was so exquisite that I had never come across any book—neither Hilton's book, Bridget's book, the *Stimulus Amoris*, the *Incendium Amoris*, nor any other book I had ever heard read—that spoke so sublimely of the love of God as to match what I felt in my soul, so powerfully working if only I could have explained what I felt.

Sometimes our Lady spoke to my mind, sometimes St Peter, sometimes St Paul, sometimes St Catherine or whatever saint I was praying to. They appeared in my soul and taught me how I should love our Lord and how I should please him. Their talk was so sweet, so holy and so devout that I frequently found it unbearable but fell down and writhed, wearing strange expressions on my face and sobbing loudly. I shed many tears, and sometimes I said, 'Jesus, have mercy' and sometimes, 'I'm dying.' Because of this many people slandered me. Denying that it was the work of God, they preferred to believe that an evil spirit was afflicting my body or else that I had some physical illness.

Despite the way people gossiped and complained about me, this holy man, the vicar of St Stephen's church in Norwich, remained on my side, and God has since exalted him and showed and proved his holiness by his marvellous works. From the time God prompted me to tell him how I governed myself and lived my life he did all he could to support me against my enemies, for he confidently believed that I genuinely knew the truth about God and was filled with grace by the Holy Spirit, who has the right to breathe and inspire wherever he wishes. And though we may hear his voice, no one in the world can tell where it comes from or where it is going.

From this time onward this holy vicar was always my confessor when I went to Norwich and he gave me communion with his own hands. On one occasion, I was ordered to appear before some of the bishop's officers to answer some charges. These were being levelled against me at the instigation of envious people, and the good vicar, more concerned with the love of God than the shame of the world, went with me to my examination and saved me from the malice of my enemies. And then it was revealed to me that the good vicar would live for seven more years before departing from this world in a state of grace, and he died as I had predicted.

Chapter 18

In my soul I was charged and commanded to go to a white friar in the same city of Norwich. He was called William Southfield, and he was a good man living a holy life. I was to show him the grace that God had given me, just as I'd done with the good vicar I've already mentioned.

I did as I was commanded and met with the friar one morning. I spent a long while with him in a chapel and told him about my meditations and the other things which God had been doing in my soul, for I wanted to know if I was being deceived by anything false.

All the while I was telling him about my inner feelings, the white friar, with his hands raised up, said, 'Jesus, have mercy! Thanks be to Jesus!' And then he said to me, 'Sister, don't worry about your way of life, for the Holy Spirit is working his grace abundantly within your soul. Thank him freely for his goodness, for we all owe him thanks on your account. In our day and age he is breathing his grace into you and others like you, to the help and comfort of all of us who are sustained by your prayers. We deserve to suffer many evils and troubles on account of our sins, but having such worthy people among us saves us from them. May Almighty God be blessed for his goodness.

'And therefore, Sister, my advice is that you dispose yourself to receive the gifts of God as humbly and meekly as you can. Do not raise any obstacle or objection against the goodness of the Holy Spirit: he may give his gifts wherever he wishes; he makes the unrighteous worthy of them, and he makes wrong-doers virtuous. His mercy is always available to us unless the fault is in ourselves, for he will not dwell in a body which is subject to sin. He shuns all hypocrisy and falsehood; he asks us to have a humble, meek and contrite heart of our own free will. Our Lord himself says, "My spirit will dwell in a meek and contrite man, and one who fears my words." Sister, I trust to our Lord that you have these qualities, either by the exercise of will or by natural inclination— perhaps by both. And I cannot believe that our Lord allows people to be permanently deceived if they trust him completely and hunger and thirst for nothing but him alone, as I hope you do yourself. And therefore be sure that our Lord loves you and is doing works of grace within you; and may he increase and continue it to his everlasting glory, for his mercy's sake.' This good man's words did a lot to ease my body and soul, and they also greatly strengthened my faith.

And then our good Lord commanded me to go to an anchoress called Dame Julian, who was in the same city. I made my visit and told her about the graces of compunction, contrition, sweetness and devotion which God had imparted to my soul, along with compassion, holy meditation and the contemplation of things divine. I also told her about the many holy sayings and intimations which our Lord had spoken direct to my soul, and all the wonderful revelations. My reason for telling the anchoress was to find out whether I was deceived, for the good anchoress was an expert in such things and could give sound advice.

The anchoress, on hearing about the marvellous goodness of our Lord, thanked God with all her heart for visiting me in such a way. She advised me to obey the will of our Lord God and do my best to fulfil the promptings in my soul as long as they didn't conflict with the worship of God or the well-being of my fellow Christians; for if they did then they sprang from the workings of an evil spirit and not a good one. The Holy Spirit never prompts us to act unkindly; if he did he would be acting contrary to his own nature, for he is pure love. What is more, he stirs each soul to perfect chastity, for those who live chastely are known as temples of the Holy Spirit, and the Holy Spirit makes every soul unswerving and steadfast in the true faith and teaching.

'A man who tries to face two ways always wavers and varies in all he does. And anyone who constantly doubts is the like the ebb and flow of the sea, which is moved and carried about by the wind. Such people have little chance of receiving the gifts of God.

'Any creature who does have these marks of holiness must faithfully believe that the Holy Spirit is dwelling in his soul. And he can and should believe all the more that the Holy Spirit is in his soul when God visits him with tears of contrition, devotion or compassion.

'Saint Paul says that the Holy Spirit pleads for us with sighs and tears beyond all number; that is to say, he causes us to plead and pray with so much sighing and weeping that the tears are too many to count. No evil spirit can give these signs, for Jerome says that tears cause the Devil more torment than he suffers from the fires of hell.

'God and the Devil are eternally opposite and can never dwell together in a single place. The Devil has no power in a person's soul, for scripture says that the soul of a righteous person is the seat of God, which is what I think that you are, Sister. I pray that God will give you the strength to persevere. Put all your trust in God and don't be afraid of wagging tongues, for the more contempt, disgrace and criticism you meet in the world the more worthy you are in the sight of God. You need to show forbearance, for that is how you will preserve your soul.'

The anchoress and I had a great deal of holy conversation as we talked about the love of our Lord Jesus Christ during the many days we were together. I also revealed my way of life to many good clerks and famous doctors of divinity, both religious and secular, and they said that God was doing great works of grace within me and told me not to be afraid— I was not deceived in living in the way I did.

They advised me to pursue my course, for their greatest fear was that I would turn back and not continue in the way of perfection. I had so many enemies and suffered such slander that it seemed to them that I would not be able to bear it without a great deal of grace and a very strong faith; for those who had no idea of how I conducted myself, except from what they saw on the surface or heard from gossips, twisted the truth and said really evil things about me. Because of this I met with a lot of opposition and trouble—far more than I would have suffered had there not been all this evil talk.

In spite of all this, the anchorite who belonged to the Preaching Friars in Lynn and was my principal confessor, as I have already said, staked his soul on the fact that my apprehensions were good and genuine and not in any way ill-founded. And through the gift of prophecy he told me that when I went to Jerusalem I would have a lot of trouble with my maid, and that our Lord would try me out and test me severely.

So then I replied, 'Ah, good sir, what shall I do when I am far from home in foreign countries and my maid has turned against me? I will have lost my bodily comfort, and I won't know where to get spiritual comfort from any confessor such as you.'

'Daughter, don't be afraid, for our Lord will comfort you himself, and his comfort surpasses all other forms of consolation. And when all your friends have forsaken you our Lord will cause a broken-backed man to lead you where you want to go.' And in every detail things turned out as the anchorite had prophesied—as I hope to explain more fully below.

Then in a sort of complaining way I said to the anchorite, 'Good sir, what shall I do? The man who confesses me in your absence is very sharp with me. He won't take my feelings seriously; he doesn't value them and thinks they're no better than trifles and jokes. It hurts me a lot because I think well of him and I'm keen to follow his advice.'

By way of reply, the anchorite said, 'Daughter, it is not surprising if he cannot trust your feelings so soon. He knows that you've been a sinful woman in the past, and he thinks that God would not come so close to you in such a short time. After all our conversations I wouldn't for all the world be as sharp with you as he is. Because of your virtues, God has chosen him as your scourge and he is treating you like a smith with a file who makes the iron bright and shiny where before it looked rusty, dark and unpleasant. The sharper he is with you the more your soul shines out in God's sight, and God has chosen me to nurture your spirit and bring you comfort. Be humble and meek and thank God for him and for me as well.'

Chapter 19

Before I went to Jerusalem, our Lord sent me to a respectable lady to speak to her confidentially and pass on something he wanted me to tell her. The lady would not speak to me without her confessor being present, and I said that I was happy with this. Then when the lady's confessor had come, all three of us went into a chapel together, and I said with great respect and many tears, 'Madam, our Lord Jesus Christ asked me to tell you that your husband is in purgatory, and that though he'll be saved it will be a long while before he enters heaven.'

The lady was displeased with this and said her husband had been a good man—she could not believe that he was in purgatory. However, her confessor supported me and said it could easily be as I said, and he backed up my words with holy tales. Thereupon this woman sent her daughter, along with other members of her household, to tell the anchorite who was my main confessor that he must either forsake me or lose her friendship. The anchorite told the messengers that he would not forsake me for anyone in the world. If people asked him about my conduct and his opinion of me he told them I was God's personal servant, and he said that I was God's tabernacle. And to fortify me in my faith, the anchorite told me to my face, 'Though God may deprive you completely of tears and the sound of his voice, you must still accept that God loves you and that the gifts which you have already had assure you of a place in heaven, for tears of love are the greatest gift God can give on earth, and all God-loving people should thank him for having created you.'

Another widow begged me to pray for her husband and find out if he needed help. And as I prayed for him I was assured that his soul would be in purgatory for thirty years unless he had better friends on earth. I told the widow and said to her, 'If you give three or four pounds in alms to buy masses for him and help the poor you will please God greatly and do a lot to ease his soul.' The widow paid little attention and let the matter pass.

Then I went to the anchorite and told him the feeling I had, and he said that the feeling had come from God. The almsgiving would be good in itself, even if the soul had no need of it, and he recommended that it should be done. Then I told this confessor what the problem was in the hope that he would speak to the widow, and for a long time I heard no more about it.

Afterwards, our Lord Jesus Christ said to me, 'The thing I wanted done for that soul has not been done. Ask your confessor about it now.' I did so and he confirmed that it had not been done; to which I replied, 'My Lord Jesus Christ has just told me as much.'

On a previous occasion, I had gone to pray to find out what answer I should give the widow, and I felt God commanding me inwardly to tell her that if she wished to please God she should leave the man who was then her confessor and go to the anchorite at the house of the Preaching Friars in Lynn and tell him all about her life. When I gave her this message neither the widow nor her confessor would believe it unless God gave her the same marks of grace he had given me, and she told me to keep away from her. And when I told her that she was duty bound to feel love and affection for her confessor the widow said I'd have done well to place my love and affection where she placed hers.

Then our Lord commanded me to have someone write a letter and send it to her. A master of divinity wrote the letter at my request and it went to the widow. It included these remarks: in one place it said that the widow would never have the same signs of grace as me; in another it said that God would be well pleased if I never entered her house.

Soon afterwards our Lord said to me, 'It would be worth more to her than the whole of this world if her love were set on the same things as yours. I want you to go to her confessor and tell him that because he won't believe what you say they will be parted sooner than he thinks, and whether he likes it or not strangers will know about it before he does. Daughter, you will see from this how hard it is to get someone to go against their own wishes.'

Within twelve years this whole affair occurred exactly as I had said. But at the time I suffered great torment and sorrow at having to say these things at our Lord's command. And all the while my love of God grew, and I became more confident than I had been before.

Chapter 20

One day, as I was hearing mass and the priest, who was a young and upright man, was holding the sacrament above his head, it shook and fluttered to and fro in his hands like a dove fluttering its wings. And when he held up the chalice containing the precious sacrament the chalice moved to and fro as if it was going to fall from his hands. After the consecration, I marvelled at the way the blessed sacrament had stirred and moved, and I wanted to see more consecrations to find out if it would happen again.

Then our Lord Jesus Christ said to me, 'You won't see this sort of thing any more; thank God that you have seen it once. My daughter St Bridget never saw me acting in this way.'

Then I answered inwardly, 'Lord, what does this mean?'

'It means vengeance to come.'

'What vengeance, dear Lord?'

And our Lord replied to me, 'There shall be an earthquake. Tell whoever you like in the name of Jesus. For I promise you that I speak to you, Daughter, as surely as I spoke to St Bridget, and I promise you that every word written in St Bridget's book is true, and its perfect truth will be known through you. And things will go well for you, Daughter, in spite of all your enemies. The more they envy you for my grace within you the more I shall love you. I would not be truly God unless I loved you, for I know you better than you know yourself, whatever people may say about you. You say I am very patient with people about their sins, and you are right to say so, but if you saw their sins as I do you would marvel at my patience and grieve for their sins far more than you do.'

Then I said, 'Oh beloved Lord, what can I do for all these people?'

Our Lord answered, 'It is enough for you to do as you are doing.'

Then I prayed, 'Merciful Lord Jesus Christ, all mercy, grace and goodness are yours. Have mercy, pity and compassion on them. Let them see your mercy and goodness; help them and send them true contrition and never let them die in their sins.'

Our merciful Lord said, 'Being righteous, Daughter, I can do no more for them than I do. I send them preachers and teachers, plagues and wars, hunger and famine, deprivation and grievous illness and many other tribulations, yet they will not heed my words, and they will not take any notice of my visitations. And so I shall tell them, "I caused my servants to pray for you and you despised their deeds and their good lives."'

Chapter 21

In the time when I used to have revelations, our Lord said to me, 'Daughter, you are to have a child.'

I replied, 'Lord, what shall I do about looking after my child?'

Our Lord said, 'Daughter, don't worry—I shall arrange for someone to look after it.'

'Lord, I am not worthy to hear your voice while I'm communing in this way with my husband—though it causes me great pain and distress.'

'But that means that far from being sinful, Daughter, it's a source of reward and merit for you. Your grace will not be any less, for I want you to bear me more fruits of the spirit.'

Then I replied, 'Lord Jesus, such a way of life is for holy virgins.'

'Yes, Daughter, but rest assured that I also think highly of married women, and especially those wives who wish to live chastely, if only they could have their way, and make it their business to please me as you do; for though the state of maidenhood is more perfect than the state of wedlock, yet, my Daughter, I love you as much as any maiden in the world. No one can stop me loving whoever I wish to love and as much as I wish, for love, my Daughter, quenches all sin. So ask me to give you the gifts of love. No gift is as holy as the gift of love, and nothing is so desirable, for love can obtain whatever it wants. And therefore, Daughter, you cannot please God better than to think about his love all the while.'

Then I asked our Lord how best to love him. And our Lord replied, 'Keep your wickedness in mind and think of my goodness.'

I replied, 'I am the most unworthy creature you have ever shown your grace to on earth.'

'Don't worry, Daughter,' said our Lord. 'I am not concerned with anyone's past but only with what they will be in future. Daughter, you have despised yourself and therefore you will never be despised by God. Remember, Daughter, what Mary Magdelene used to be, and Mary of Egypt, Saint Paul and many other saints who are now in heaven, for I make the unworthy worthy and I make the sinful virtuous. And so I have made you worthy of me, loved once and for all. There is no saint in heaven who will not come to you if you want to speak with them, for as God loves so they love. When you please God you please his mother and all the saints in heaven. Daughter, I ask my mother, all the angels in heaven and all the saints in heaven to witness to the fact that I love you with all my heart and cannot forgo your love for me.'

Then our Lord said to his blessed mother, 'Blessed Mother, tell my Daughter how greatly I love her.'

Then I lay unmoving, consumed with weeping and sobbing as if my heart would burst, and all because of the sweetness with which our Lord had spoken to my soul.

Soon afterwards the Queen of Mercy, the Mother of God, spoke to my soul saying, 'My darling Daughter, I have come to bear sure and certain witness to my sweet son Jesus, along with all the angels and saints in heaven who love you dearly. Daughter, I am your mother, your lady and your mistress, and I am to teach you how to please God best in every way.' She taught me and instructed me so wonderfully and the matters were so sublime and holy that I was nervous of repeating it or telling it to anyone other than the anchorite who was my principal confessor, for he had the greatest skill in such matters. And he charged me on my obedience to tell him whatever came into my heart, and I did as he asked.

Chapter 22

As I lay meditating and inwardly weeping bitterly, I said to our Lord Jesus Christ, 'Lord, there are maidens dancing with joy in heaven. Shall I not be able to do so too? For I am no virgin, and nowadays I very much regret having lost my maidenhead. If only I had been murdered when I was taken from the font so that I would never have displeased you— then, blessed Lord, my maidenhead would have been yours forever. Ah, dear Lord, I have not loved you all the days of my life, and that upsets me very much. I have run away from you and you have run after me;

I have fallen into despair and you have lifted me up.'

'Daughter, how often have I told you that your sins are forgiven and that we are united to one other for ever more? I love you, Daughter, in a special way, and because of this I promise that you will enjoy special grace in heaven, Daughter, and I promise to be with you at the end of your life, when you are dying; and with me will be my blessed mother, my holy angels and twelve apostles, St Catherine, St Margaret, St Mary Magdelene and many other servants in heaven who worship me highly because of the grace that I—your God, your Lord Jesus—bestow on you. Don't be afraid of suffering severe pain when you die, for you'll have what you wish, which is to be more concerned with my passion than with your own pain. You must not be afraid of the Devil of hell, for he does not have any power over you. He fears you more than you fear him. He is angry with you because your weeping torments him more than all the fire in hell; you deprive him of many souls with your weeping. And I have promised that you will not suffer any purgatory other than the slander and evil talk of this world, for I have chastised you to my own satisfaction with the many terrors and torments that you've suffered for years from evil spirits, both while asleep and awake; so when you die I shall have mercy on you and preserve you from them, so that they do not have any power over either your body or soul. It is a wonder that you still have your natural wits, considering how they have vexed you in the past.

'I have also, Daughter, chastised you with the fear of my Godhead, for I have often beset you with great stormy winds, making you think that vengeance was falling on you for your sins. I have tested you with many troubles and grievous sorrows, and with many illnesses so severe that you have been anointed in the expectation of death, and yet because of my grace you escaped it. So don't be afraid, Daughter, for with my own hands, which were nailed to the cross, I shall take your soul from your body with great joy and melody, with sweet scents and pleasant odours, and offer it to my Father in heaven, for there you will see him face to face and dwell with him eternally.

'Daughter, you will be thoroughly welcome to my Father, my mother and all my saints in heaven, for you have often given them the tears of your eyes to be their drink. All my hallowed saints will rejoice at your homecoming. You will be filled with every kind of love you desire. Then you will bless the time when you were made and the body that redeemed you, for he will rejoice in you and you in him for ever more. Daughter, I promise you the same grace I promised St Catherine, St Margaret, St Barbara and St Paul, for until the Day of Judgement whatever created being on earth seeks favour from you, believing that you are beloved of God, shall have what he wants or else something better. And so it is that those who believe God loves you will be forever blessed.

'The souls in purgatory will rejoice at your homecoming, for they know of God's special love for you. And men on earth will rejoice in God on your account, for the many acts of grace performed on your behalf will make his love for you known to all throughout the world. For love of me you have been despised, and so for my love you will be adored. Daughter, when you are in heaven you will be able to ask for what you want and I will give you all you wish. I have already told you that your love is special, and therefore you will receive a special love in heaven, a special reward and a special honour.

'And because, in spirit, you are a virgin, I shall take you by one hand in heaven and my mother by the other hand, and you will dance in heaven with other holy maidens and virgins, for I shall say to you, my own blessed wife, 'I welcome you with every sort of joy and gladness. You are here to live and remain with me for ever more; you will dwell with me always in joy and bliss, which no eye may see, nor ear hear, nor tongue tell, nor heart conceive, for I have ordained it for you and for all your servants who wish to love me and please me as you do.''

Chapter 23

A vicar once came to me, asking me to pray for him and find out whether he would please God better by giving up his ministry and his benefice or by staying on, for he felt he was getting nowhere with his parishioners. And while I was praying with this in mind, Christ said to my spirit, 'Tell the vicar to continue with his ministry and keep his benefice. He should do the best he can in the way of preaching and teaching, but sometimes he should get someone else to teach them my laws and commandments so that he cannot be at fault at all; and if they still don't do any better his reward will not be in any way less.' And so I passed the message on as I was commanded, and the vicar carried on with his ministry.

Once, I was in the choir of St Margaret's church and there was a woman's corpse there. The widower, who was in sound health, had come to offer a mass penny for her, in accordance with the local custom; and our Lord said to me, 'Listen, Daughter: the soul of this corpse is in purgatory, and although the widower is in good health at the moment he will die before long.' And this occurred as God had revealed to my inner sense.

On another occasion, as I lay in the choir praying, a priest came up to me and asked me to pray for a woman who was on her death bed. And as I began to pray for her our Lord said to me, 'Daughter, it is very important to pray for her, for she has been a wicked woman and she will definitely die.'

And I answered, 'Lord, save her soul from damnation because of her love for me,' and then I wept for her soul, and I shed a great many tears. And our Lord granted my wish for the soul to be treated with mercy, and he told me to carry on praying for her.

And my confessor came to me, urging me to pray for a woman who was lying on the point of death, or so people thought. And straight away our Lord said that she would live and be well, and so it turned out.

Also, there was a good man who was a close friend of mine and a great help to those in need. He was seriously ill for weeks on end, and people were very despondent about him, for they did not think he could possibly live, so severe was the pain in all his joints and throughout his body. Our Lord Jesus Christ said to my spirit, 'Daughter, do not be afraid for this man. He will survive and be thoroughly well.' And sure enough, he lived on for many years, enjoying good health and fortune.

And then a good man, a dyer, was ill in bed too, and when I prayed for him I was told in my heart that he would linger for a while and then die from his illness, and he did so shortly afterwards. But a well respected woman—a special friend of mine who was thought to be holy—was so sick that she was expected to die, yet when I was praying for her our Lord replied, 'She won't be dead for ten years or more, and soon you'll be making merry together and talking happily as you have in the past.' And that's how it actually was, because this holy woman lived for many more years.

Many other, similar things were inwardly revealed to me. To write them all down might get in the way of more valuable things. I have had these examples set down to show the warmth and goodness of our merciful Lord Jesus Christ and not to make any claim for myself. These intuitions and similar ones (more by far than are set down in writing), concerned as they were with life and death, with those to be saved and those to be damned, were a source of pain and punishment to me. I would rather have suffered any physical penance than have these feelings, and I could easily have dismissed them because of the fear I had of being deluded and deceived by my unseen enemy. When they didn't fit in with the way I saw things, these feelings sometimes troubled me so much that my confessor was afraid they would drive me to despair. Then after having suffered such turmoil and deep anxiety I was shown how my feelings should be interpreted.

Chapter 24

The priest who wrote this book down tested my intuitions on many and varied occasions by asking me questions and demanding information about things that lay in the future - things whose outcome was obscure and uncertain for everyone. He begged me to pray to God and learn what the future held, although I was unwilling and reluctant to do such a thing. He said that I should do it when our Lord incited devotion within me, and afterwards I should tell him honestly and without pretence, for otherwise he would not be prepared to write this book. And so, driven by the fear that he would give up his plan of writing this book, I did as he asked me and told him what I sensed would happen in the matters where he put my feelings to the test.

He proved that my feelings were reliable, yet he would not always trust what I said, and this caused him trouble in the following way. A young man whom this priest had never seen before once came to him and told a sorry tale about the poverty and hardship into which he had had the misfortune to fall. He said he had been ordained to the priesthood, and he also explained the cause of his troubles. He had been pursued by enemies, and had had no choice but to die or else defend himself. He had been slightly hasty and struck a man—possibly two—and he said his victims were dead or else in danger of dying. Because of this he had lost his standing with the Church and he could not serve as a priest without a dispensation from the Court of Rome; he had fled from his neighbourhood and couldn't return for fear of being arrested for murder.

My priest believed the young man's story because he was a likeable, good-looking man with an engaging manner and facial expression; he talked and conversed in a serious way and was priestly in his bearing and clothes.

Taking pity on his troubles, and hoping to find him friends who would give him help and support, my priest approached a highly respected burgess in Lynn. This burgess was a compassionate man who was fit to be mayor, but had been laid up for a long time with a serious illness. Speaking to both the man and his wife—a really good woman— the priest bemoaned the young man's troubles, hoping to receive a generous gift of alms, as he often did when he asked on behalf of others in need.

But I (of whom this book is written) happened to be there at the time, and I heard how the priest pressed the young man's case and how he praised him. But my spirit was strongly moved against him; I said they had many other neighbours who, as they were well aware, were in serious need of help and relief, and it was better to give alms to help those who they know for sure were of good character, and neighbours of theirs, than to strangers whom they did not know, for many people give a good impression with their speech and outward appearance, but God knows what their souls are like.

The good man and his wife agreed with what I said, so they decided not to give any alms. The priest felt annoyed with me at the time, and when he met me by myself he went on about how I'd stopped him getting the young man alms. He considered the man to be well-intentioned and praised the way he conducted himself.

I replied, 'Sir, God knows how he lives his life, for as far as I know I've never seen him. But I do know how he might behave, so if you'll follow my advice and inclinations you'll let him make his own decisions and fend for himself as best he can. Don't have anything to do with him, because in the end he's going to cheat you.'

The young man kept coming to the priest, getting round him and saying that he had good friends in the country who would come to his aid if they knew where he was—and quickly at that—and would not forget those who had helped him in his time of need.

The priest, trusting that things would turn out as the young man had said, willingly gave him silver in order to help him out. The young man asked the priest to forgive him if he didn't see him for two or three days, for he had to pay a visit to somewhere nearby; he would soon come back and return his money safe and sound. The priest was perfectly happy with this, for he trusted the young man to keep his word; he wished him well and let him go away until the time when he had promised to return.

Once he had gone, I understood, from the feelings I had within my soul, that our Lord would reveal his dishonesty, and that he wouldn't ever come back again. To test whether my feelings were true or false, I asked the priest where the young man he had praised so much was. The priest was sure he'd soon be back, having gone a short way off on foot. I told him I didn't think he would ever see him again—and that's how it was. So then he wished he had taken my advice.

Soon after this happened another dishonest rogue—an old man— came to the same priest and offered to sell him a nice little prayer book. The priest came to me, asking me to pray for him and find out whether God wanted him to buy the book. While I was praying he did his best to make conversation with the man, and then he came back to me and asked me what my feelings were.

'Sir,' I said, 'don't buy any books from him—he can't be trusted, and you'll find that out if you try to have any dealings with him.'

Then the priest asked the man to show him this book. The man said he didn't have it on him. The priest asked him how he came to have it, and he said that he was acting for a priest who was a relative of his and had given him the task of selling it for him.

'Father,' said the priest respectfully, 'why are you offering the book to me rather than to other laymen or priests? The church has many priests who are better off and richer than I am, and I'm sure you've never heard of me before today.'

'It's true that I hadn't heard of you, sir,' he answered, 'but I feel well disposed to you, even so. And anyway, the priest who owned it said that if I knew any young priest who I considered sober and well governed he should have this book before anyone else—and for less price too, in the hope that he would pray for him. These are the reasons I've come to you rather than anyone else.'

The priest asked him where he lived.

'Sir,' he said, 'just five miles away in Pentney Abbey.'

'I've been there,' said the priest, 'and I haven't seen you.'

'No, sir,' he answered, 'I've only been there a little while, but—God be praised—they now provide for my daily needs.'

The priest asked to have a look at the book in the hope that they could agree a price.

He answered, 'Sir, I hope to be here again next week, so I'll bring it with me. And I promise you, sir, that if you like it you'll have it in preference to anyone else.'

The priest thanked him for his kindness and they went their separate ways, but the priest never saw the man again, which showed him that my suspicion was justified.

Chapter 25

What follows is a very notable example of my intuition. It is set down here for convenience, because it seems similar to the examples that have been given before, even though it happened long after the things which follow it. It took place in an important town where there was one parish church with two dependent chapels.

With the parson's permission the chapels contained and administered all the sacraments except for christening and purification. The parson was a Benedictine monk who had been sent from the order's house in Norwich and was residing with three of his brother monks in the important town I have already mentioned.

Some of the parishioners wanted the chapels to be on equal terms with the parish church, and they sought a bull from the Court of Rome. This caused a great deal of litigation and ill feeling between the prior (who was the parson and curate) and the parishioners, who wanted to have baptisms and purifications in the chapels as well as the parish church. They particularly wanted a font in the bigger, more outlying chapel, and they obtained a bull which granted them a font in the chapel provided that this in no way downgraded the parish church. The bull was appealed, and days were spent in legal proceedings to establish whether installing the font would lower the status of the parish church. The parishioners who were pressing their case were influential, and they had the help of people in positions of power. Also, and most important of all, they were wealthy men, leading merchants with more than enough money—something that gets results whatever the circumstances, sad though it is that inducements should carry more weight than justice. Even so, the prior who was their parish priest, though poor, stood up to them manfully with the help of some parishioners who were friends of his and loved to worship in the parish church.

The matter was under appeal for so long that both sides began to feel frustrated, and no conclusion seemed in sight. The issue was therefore referred to William of Alnwick, who was the Bishop of Norwich, to see if he could bring it to an end by negotiation. He did his best to bring things to a peaceful conclusion, offering the first group of parishioners much of what they wanted, though on certain conditions. Those who were on the parson's side and favoured the parish church were upset. They were terrified that in getting what they wanted those who had pressed to have a font would make the chapel equal to the parish church.

Then the priest who later wrote out this book came to me as he had done earlier, when the matter was before the courts. He asked me about my innermost feelings on this issue of whether or not they should have a font in the chapel.

'Sir,' I replied, 'don't worry, for I know in my soul that even if they paid a bushel of nobles they wouldn't get it.'

'Oh, Mother,' said the priest, 'the Bishop of Norwich has granted it to them on certain conditions. They have a period in which to consider it and give their answer, and I'm afraid that far from turning it down they'll accept it readily.'

I prayed to God that things would turn out as the parson wanted, and because it had been revealed to me that they would not get a font I was all the more ready to pray to our Lord to resist their desires and prick their vanity. And so, in accordance with our Lord's wishes, they did not approve or accept the settlement which had been offered to them. Instead, they relied on getting what they wanted through influence and legal action. And as God would have it their hopes were thwarted, and because they wanted everything they gained nothing. So—God be praised!—the worship and status of the parish church continued unchanged as they had been for two hundred years and more, and the outcome proved that God truly spoke within my heart.

Chapter 26

When the time came for me to visit the holy places where our Lord lived and died, in accordance with the inner voice I had heard years before, I asked the parish priest of the town where I lived to make an announcement from the pulpit for me: any man or woman with a claim for debt against myself or my husband was to come and have a word with me before I left and I would settle things to their satisfaction—which is what I did. Then I said goodbye to my husband and the holy anchorite, who had previously told me the details of my departure from Lynn, the many troubles I would have on the journey, and how, when my party abandoned me, a hunch-backed man would guide me safely onwards by the help of our Lord (which, as I shall explain in due course, is exactly what happened).

I said goodbye to Master Robert and begged for his blessing, and I did the same with other friends. Then I went on my way to Norwich and made an offering at the shrine of the Trinity. I continued to Yarmouth and made an offering at a statue of our Lady before I boarded my ship.

On the following day we reached a sizeable town called Zierikzee, where by virtue of his abundant goodness our Lord gave me copious tears of contrition for my own sins and sometimes for the sins of others too. And in particular I shed tears of pity when I thought about our Lord's passion. On Sundays I received the sacrament wherever time and place allowed, and I wept and sobbed so violently that many people were struck with amazement that God had given me so much grace.

Before leaving England I had eaten no meat and drunk no wine for four years. However, my present confessor commanded me on my obedience to have them both, and I did so for a little while. I then asked my confessor to excuse me from eating meat; he could grant me this favour just so long as he wished. But nearly everyone in the party soon became annoyed with me for not eating meat, and some made sure that my confessor was also annoyed about it. But what annoyed them most was that the fact that I wept so much and was always talking about our Lord's love and goodness, both at meal times and at other times too.

They had no compunction about criticizing me and condemning me to my face and said they would not put up with me like my husband did when I was at home in England. And I replied meekly, 'Our Lord God Almighty is as great a Lord here as he is in England, and I've as much cause to love him here as there. May his name be blessed!'

These words made my party angrier than they had been before and their hostility and unkindness to me made me very unhappy; they were very respectable people and I wanted their high opinion if I could have it with God's approval. And I said to one of them in particular, 'You cause me a lot of shame and hurt.'

He answered back, 'I pray to God that you'll die the same death as the Devil did—and quickly too.' And he said more cruel words to me than I can repeat.

And soon afterwards some of the party who I trusted most—and my own maid too—said I could no longer travel with them, and they said they would take my maid away from me so that she wouldn't have to prostitute herself by keeping my company. And the one who was looking after my money gave me a noble in a really angry, spiteful way. He told me to clear off and fend for myself as best I could. They said I wasn't to stay with them a moment longer, and they abandoned me that very night.

Then the next morning one of the party—a man I liked a lot—came and asked me to go to the others and make my peace with them, and ask them if I could stay with them as far as Constance. So I did as he said, but as I travelled to Constance with them I suffered a lot of trouble and bother, for in various places along the way they humiliated me and condemned me. They cut my gown so short that it hardly came below my knees, and they made me wear a piece of white canvas—it looked like an apron made of sacking—so that people would think I was a fool, or slight me and treat me disrespectfully. They made me sit at the end of the table, so that I was the lowest of the low and scarcely dared to speak a word.

But despite all their malice I enjoyed more respect than the others did, and this was true wherever we went. The owner of the house where we stayed for the night constantly did his best to give me better service than he gave the others, despite the fact that I sat in the lowliest place at the table; he sent me food from his own dish, which annoyed my companions very much.

And as they proceeded towards Constance they were told that unless they enjoyed God's favour they would suffer harm and serious hardship. As soon as we arrived at a church I went in to pray, and I prayed wholeheartedly, weeping and shedding many tears, for help and support against our enemies. And at once our Lord, speaking inwardly to me, said, 'Don't be afraid, Daughter. Your party won't suffer any harm while you are with them.' And so we proceeded safely to Constance.

Chapter 27

When my party and I had arrived in Constance I heard people mentioning an English friar who was in the city. He was a master of divinity and the representative of the Pope. So I went to see this important man and told him all about my life from my earliest days right up until then, and knowing that he was the Pope's legate and a leading scholar I was as frank as I would have been in confession. I told him about the trouble I was having with my companions, and also about God's gifts to me—gifts of contrition and compunction, sweetness and devotion—and the many and varied revelations which our Lord had made to me. I told him that I was afraid of being deluded and deceived by my unseen enemies; I lived in dread of them, wishing I could stand up to them and drive them away and not feel them near me.

When I had finished speaking, the worthy clerk spoke to me very comfortingly. He said that the Holy Spirit was working within me, and he strongly urged me to receive and accept things as and when God chose to give them; he'd doubtless given me gifts in the past, for the Devil cannot impart such grace to anyone's soul. He also said that he would help me to deal with the evil people in my party.

Later, my party decided to invite this fine scholar to dinner. He told me about it, advising me to sit at the table when he was there in just the same way as I did when he wasn't and to conduct myself as I did in his absence.

When it was time for us all to sit down and eat our meal each person chose the place he preferred. The first to sit down was the legate—the doctor of divinity; then the others took their places, leaving me till last. I sat at the end of the table, not saying a word, just as I did when the legate wasn't there. Then the legate said to me, 'Why aren't you more cheerful?'

I sat there and didn't answer him, just as the legate had told me to do.

When they had eaten, everyone complained bitterly about me to the legate. They insisted that I could no longer stay in their company unless he ordered me to eat meat as they did, give up my weeping and not say so much about holy things.

Then the illustrious doctor replied, 'No, sirs, I cannot insist on her eating meat when by doing without she is better able to love our Lord. Those of you who vowed to go to Rome barefooted I would hold to your vows for as long as you were able to keep them. In the same way, while our Lord gives her the strength to abstain from eating meat I cannot tell her to eat it again. As for her weeping, it is not for me to prohibit it when it comes as a gift from the Holy Spirit. And as for the things she says, I will ask her to stop till she finds herself with people who are more prepared to listen to her.'

The party was annoyed and very angry. They gave me over to the legate and insisted that they would have nothing else to do with me. He received me calmly and graciously as if I was his mother and he also took charge of my gold—about twenty pounds, since one of them wrongfully kept back sixteen pounds or so. They also kept my maid, refusing to let her go with her mistress, despite the promise and assurance she had given me that she would never forsake me, come what may.

And the legate looked after me, and changed my gold into local currency, just as a son would look after his mother.

Then I went into church and prayed to our Lord to provide me with a guide. Our Lord immediately spoke to me and said, 'You will have excellent help and a good leader.'

Straightaway an old man with a white beard approached me. He was a Devonshire man and he said to me, 'Madam, since your companions from England have abandoned you, will you invite me, for love of God and for love of our Lady, to accompany you and be your guide?'

I asked him his name and he replied, 'It's William Weaver.'

So in the holy name of God and our Lady, I asked him to help me out of my predicament, and I told him that I would pay him well for his trouble. Then I went to the legate and told him how well our Lord had provided for me, and I took my leave of him, of my companions who had so unkindly turned me away, and of my maid, who had been duty bound to go with me.

I left feeling thoroughly sad and miserable. I was in a foreign country, and neither I nor my guide knew a word of the language. And so we went on our way together in considerable fear and unhappiness. And on the road, the man said to me, 'I am scared that you'll be abducted, and that because of you I'll be beaten up and robbed of my coat.'

I replied, 'William, don't be afraid. God will look after us really well.' And every day I remembered the gospel story about the woman who was taken in adultery and brought before our Lord. And as I called it to mind I prayed, 'Lord, as you drove away her enemies so drive away mine, and preserve my chastity which I have dedicated to you; may I never be defiled, for if I am, Lord, I vow that I shall never return to England for as long as I live.'

And so we went on our way each day and met all sorts of friendly people, and they didn't say anything offensive to me but gave me and my companion food and drink; and in many places where we called the good wives at inns let me share their beds out of love for God.

And as I travelled, our Lord gave me the great blessing of an untroubled spirit. And so God brought me all the way to Bologna.

And after my arrival, who should turn up but the companions who had previously left me behind. They were amazed when they heard that I had got to Bologna before them, and one of their number came and begged me to go and see if they would let me rejoin their fellowship, and that's what I did.

'If you want to travel with us,' they answered, 'you must make a new agreement with us: that you won't keep on about the Gospel in all our stopping places, but will sit in there and enjoy yourself at mealtimes like the rest of us.' I agreed to this and they let me join their company again.

Afterwards they moved on to Venice, and they stayed there for thirteen weeks. And every Sunday I took communion in a large house of nuns, who treated me very hospitably. And when I was there our merciful Lord Jesus Christ used to overcome me with deep devotion and copious tears, to the great amazement of the ladies who lived there. And some time later, as I sat eating with my travelling companions, I quoted gospel texts that I had learned in the past along with other useful words. And straight away my companions said I had broken my promise. And I replied 'Yes, sirs, the fact is that I can no longer keep my agreement with you. I cannot help speaking of my Lord Jesus Christ, even if the whole world forbids me to do so.'

Then I took to my room and ate alone for six weeks, until our Lord made me so ill that I thought myself as good as dead, only for the Lord to suddenly make me well again. And my maid left me by myself the whole time, preferring to prepare the company's food and wash their clothes than to lift a finger for me—the mistress she had promised to serve.

Chapter 28

This company which had excluded me from their table so that I could no longer eat with them engaged a ship to carry them [to the Holy Land]. They bought containers for their wine and organized bedding for themselves but nothing for me. Seeing their unkindness, I went to the same supplier as them, and provided myself with bedding just as they had done. And I went where they were and showed them what I had done, intending to sail with them in the ship they had hired.

Afterwards, when I was thinking things over, our Lord spoke to me inwardly and warned me not to sail in that ship, and he chose a different ship for my voyage—a galley, in fact. I told some of the company about it and they passed it on to all the rest, and as a result they didn't dare to put to sea in the ship which they had arranged for themselves. They sold the containers they had got for their wine and fell over themselves to get on board the galley where I was. And so, much against my wishes, they became my fellow passengers, for they didn't dare do otherwise.

When it was time to make their beds they locked up my bedclothes, and a priest who was in the party took one of my sheets and said it was his. I took God as my witness that it was mine. Then the priest swore a great oath: by the Bible in his hand I was an out-and-out liar; he despised and condemned me. And so I suffered endless torment until I reached Jerusalem.

Before I arrived there I spoke to those who I thought had some sort of grievance against me. 'I beg you, sirs,' I said to them, 'be on good terms with me just as I am with you, and forgive me for having upset you on the journey. And if any of you have wronged me at all, I forgive you for it—and may God forgive you too.'

And so we proceeded into the Holy Land until we could see Jerusalem. And when I saw it—riding, as I was, on the back of an ass—I thanked God with all my heart; and I prayed that just as he had brought me to see this earthly city of Jerusalem so, of his mercy, he would give me the grace to see the city of Jerusalem on high—the city of heaven. Our Lord Jesus Christ, responding to the thought that had passed through my mind, said that I would have my desire. Communing with the Lord brought me such a feeling of joy and sweetness that I was on the point of falling from my ass, for the God-given sweetness and grace in my soul were too much to bear. Then two German pilgrims came to me and saved me from falling. One was a priest, and he put spices in my mouth to make me better, for he thought I was ill. And so they helped me into Jerusalem.

And when I arrived I said, 'Sirs, I beg you not to be annoyed if I weep bitter tears in this holy place where Jesus Christ our Lord lived and died.' Then we went to the temple in Jerusalem, and we were let in that day at the time for saying evensong, and we stayed there until the time for saying evensong on the following day. Then the friars lifted up a cross and led the pilgrims from place to place to see where Christ had suffered the torments of his passion, and every man and woman had a wax candle. All the while as we went about, the friars explained what our Lord had endured at every point. And I wept and sobbed as profusely as if I could see our Lord before my very eyes, suffering his passion there and then.

And by using my imagination I could see him clearly in my mind's eye, standing before me, and so I shared in his suffering. And when we ascended onto Mount Calvary I couldn't stand or kneel but fell down. My body writhed and tossed about, I flung my arms wide and cried out as though my heart would burst, for in the city of my soul I saw the stark truth of our Lord's crucifixion. Right in front of my face I heard and saw with my inner perception the grief of our Lady, St John, Mary Magdalene, and many others who loved our Lord. And I had such great compassion and pain at seeing our Lord's suffering that I couldn't have helped crying and shouting out, even if it had cost me my life. And this was the first outcry I ever made during a vision.

And this sort of crying out persisted for many years afterwards. No one could stop it, and I was severely condemned and criticized for it. So loud and so remarkable was it that people were astounded unless they had heard it before or knew the cause of the yelling. And I had these attacks so often that they sapped my bodily strength, especially if I heard about our Lord's passion. And sometimes when I saw the crucifix, or if I saw a man or any animal with an open wound, or if a man beat a child in front of me, or if I saw or heard someone striking a horse or another beast with a whip, I imagined that I was witnessing our Lord being beaten or wounded just like the man or the beast; and this was so as much in the country as in the town, and when I was by myself as well as with other people.

When my cryings began I had them frequently. This was the case in Jerusalem and also in Rome. But when I first came home to England they occurred only seldom—say once a month—but then once a week, and afterwards daily. Once I had fourteen in a day, on another day seven—all according to God's visitations. Sometimes when I was in the church God sent them: at other times I was in the street, or indoors, or in the countryside, for I never knew the time or hour when they would come. And they never came without overwhelmingly sweet devotion and intense inner vision.

As soon as I realized that I was going to cry out I contained it for as long as I could, so that people would not be disturbed by the noise. For some said I was troubled by an evil spirit; some said it was an illness and some said I had drunk too much wine; some cursed me and wanted me in an asylum; some wished that I was out at sea in a bottomless boat: everyone had his own idea. Other, spiritually-minded, people loved me and favoured me all the more. Some great scholars said that neither our Lady nor any of the saints in heaven had ever cried so much, but they had very little idea what I felt; nor would they accept that I couldn't stop myself crying out, even if I had wanted to. So, when I knew that I was about to cry out, I kept it in for as long as I could and did my best to hold it back. I suppressed it until I had turned a greyish blue like lead, but it kept growing bigger and bigger inside me, ready for the time when it would escape. And when my body could no longer stand the inner ferment, when it was overcome with the inexpressible love that worked so fervently in my soul, then I fell down and cried out wondrously loud. And the more I tried to keep it in or hold it at bay the longer and louder I cried in the end. That is what I did at Mount Calvary, as I have already said.

I witnessed things so vividly with my inner vision that it seemed as if Christ was hanging before my eyes in his manhood. And when, by the outpouring of the high mercy of our sovereign saviour Jesus Christ, I was allowed to see so palpably his precious tender body, ripped and torn by scourges, with more gashes than the holes in a dovecote, hanging on the cross and bearing the crown of thorns on his head, his blessed hands and his tender feet nailed to the hard wood, the rivers of blood profusely flowing from every part, the grave and dreadful wound in his precious side shedding blood and water out of love for me and for my salvation, then I fell to the ground and cried out aloud, twisting and turning amazingly in every direction, flinging out my arms as if I was in my death throes. And nothing could keep me from crying out or from making these bodily movements, such was the fire of love that burned so ardently in my soul with pure pity and compassion.

It is no wonder if I cried out and showed my joy in my face and countenance. After all, we only have to use our eyes and every day we can see men and women crying, roaring and wringing their hands as if they had gone clean out of their minds, though they know well enough that it displeases God. Some do it because they have lost their worldly goods, some for love of their relatives or because of giving too much thought and earthbound care to worldly friendships; and most of all through inordinate lust and desire of the flesh when their special friends leave them. And if anyone tells them to stop or cease their weeping or crying they'll say they can't: they loved the friend so much and he was so gentle and kind to them that they cannot forget him.

They would weep, cry out and scream all the more if their closest friend was snatched away before their eyes, put in front of a judge and wrongly condemned to death—a death as cruel as our merciful Lord underwent for us. How could they bear it? Without doubt they would cry and scream and seek revenge, or people would say they had failed in friendship. Oh how shameful it is to feel such excessive grief and sorrow for the death of a creature who has often sinned and wronged her maker. It offends God and hinders the soul of the living and of the dead. And the merciful death of our saviour, by which we are all restored to life, we forget—we are such unnatural wretches. And as for those who know the Lord's secrets and are full of his love, we fail to support them but scorn and oppose them as much as we can.

Chapter 29

My companions and I came to the grave where our Lord was buried and as I entered it, candle in hand, I suddenly fell down as if I had died of sorrow. And as I got up I was weeping and sobbing as if I had seen our Lord being buried right in front of my eyes. And then I thought that inwardly I could see our Lady, and how she mourned and wept because of her son's death, and our Lady's sorrow became my own sorrow.

And so it was that everywhere the friars led us in that holy place I was all the while weeping and sobbing my heart out, especially when I came to the spot where our Lord was nailed to the cross, for then I cried and wept so uncontrollably that I couldn't stop myself. We also saw the marble slab where they laid our Lord when he was taken down from the cross, and there I wept with intense pity as I thought about our Lord's passion. Afterwards I was given communion on Mount Calvary, and it made me weep and sob and cry so loudly that it was amazing to hear it.

I was full of holy thoughts and meditations, full of devout contemplation of our Lord Jesus Christ's passion, full of the holy intimations that our Lord Jesus Christ made to my soul—so much so that I could never put these things into words once they were over, for they were so high and holy. Great was the grace which our Lord showed towards me during my three weeks in Jerusalem.

On another day, in the early morning, we went up into the hills and our guides told us where our Lord had carried the cross on his back, where his mother had met him and how she fainted, how she fell to the ground and how he fell too. And so we continued all morning until we came to Mount Zion, and all along the way I wept profusely for pity of our Lord's passion.

The place where our Lord washed his disciples' feet is on Mount Zion, and a little way off is the site where he had his last supper with them. I very much wanted to receive communion in that holy place where our merciful Lord Jesus Christ first consecrated his precious body in the form of bread and gave it to his disciples. And I did so with great devotion, shedding copious tears and sobbing noisily, for to take communion on this spot earns full remission. The same applies in four places in the church of the Holy Sepulchre: one is Mount Calvary, another is the place where our Lord was buried, the third is the marble stone where they laid his precious body after taking it down from the cross; and the fourth is the place where the holy cross was buried—but there are many other such places in Jerusalem.

When I came to the place where the apostles received the Holy Spirit our Lord filled me with great devotion. And then I went to the place where our Lady was buried, and I knelt on my knees while I heard two masses, and our Lord Jesus Christ said to me, 'You have come here, Daughter, not because you need to but to increase your merit and reward, for your sins were forgiven before you came. I am pleased with you, Daughter, because you place yourself under obedience to Holy Church, obeying and heeding the things which your confessor says. By authority of Holy Church he has absolved you of your sins and given you a dispensation so that you do not have to go to Rome or the shrine of St James unless you wish to do so. Nonetheless, in the name of Jesus, I command you, Daughter, to go and visit these holy places, for I am above all Holy Church and I shall go with you and take good care of you.'

Then our Lady spoke to my soul in the following manner: 'Daughter, you are greatly blessed, for my son Jesus will suffuse you with so much grace that everyone will be amazed. Don't be ashamed, dear Daughter, to receive the gifts which my son will give you. I promise that they will be great gifts indeed; and so, dear Daughter, you should not be ashamed to own him as your God, your Lord and your love, for I was not ashamed, when I saw my sweet son Jesus hanging on the cross, to cry and weep for the pain of my sweet son Jesus Christ; and Mary Magdelene was not ashamed to cry and weep for love of my son. Daughter, if you wish to share in our joy you must share in our sorrow.' I had these lovely words and conversations at our Lady's grave—far more of them than I could ever repeat.

Afterwards I rode to Bethlehem on an ass, and when I came to the church of the Nativity I went inside to see the crib where our Lord was born. I was overcome with deep devotion and I received many words and intimations in my soul and a great sense of inner consolation, but I also wept and sobbed so much that my companions would not let me share their table and I had to eat completely alone. And then the grey friars who had led me from place to place let me join them, and to save me having to eat by myself they sat me down to eat with them.

One of the friars asked one of my companions if I was the English woman who they'd heard spoke with God. When this came to my notice I realized the truth of what God had told me before I left England: 'Daughter, I shall make all the world wonder at you. Many men and women will worship me through their love for you, and will worship me in you.'

Chapter 30

On another occasion, my companions wanted to visit the River Jordan and they would not let me go with them. I prayed to our Lord Jesus that I should go with them, and he told me to go with them whether they liked it or not. So, by the grace of God I joined them without asking their permission. When I came to the River Jordan the weather was so hot that the heat seemed enough to burn my feet.

Next, my companions and I set out for Mount Quarantine, where our Lord fasted for forty days. I asked my companions to help me to get up onto the hill-top and they refused, for they were having trouble getting up themselves. I was very upset that I couldn't get up onto the hill.

Just then, a strong-looking Saracen happened to come upon me, and I put a groat in his hand, signalling to him to help me up to the top of the hill. And straight away he took my arm and helped me right up onto the hill where our Lord had fasted for forty days.

Once I was there I felt very thirsty but my companions wouldn't do anything for me. Then, out of his great goodness, God stirred the grey friars' hearts with compassion and they comforted me when my countrymen wouldn't have anything to do with me. As a result, my love of our Lord became all the stronger, and wherever I went I was all the more ready to suffer, for his sake, humiliations and rebukes because of the gift of weeping, sobbing and crying out which he had given me— a gift which I could not refuse when God chose to send it to me. And I always found that my feelings about things were correct, and the promises God had made to me in England and in other places came true in just the way I'd expected. Because of this I was more confident in receiving God's speech and inner communing, and I sought it with greater assurance.

Later, when I had come down the Mount, I followed God's prompting and went to the place where St John the Baptist was born. And then I went to Bethany where Mary and Martha used to live, and I visited the grave where Lazarus was buried and came back to life. I also visited the chapel where our blessed Lord appeared to his blessed mother on Easter morning before he appeared to anyone else, and I stood in the very place where Mary Magdalene stood when Christ said to her, 'Mary, why are you weeping?'

I cannot describe all the places I visited, for I was in Jerusalem and the surrounding area for three weeks, and all the while I was there I was full of deep devotion. And the friars of the church of the Holy Sepulcre welcomed me warmly and gave me many important relics. They had so much faith in me that they would have liked me to stay with them longer, if I had wished. The Saracens also fêted me; they escorted me and guided me to all the places I wanted to visit throughout the country, and I found everyone good and kind to me except my own countrymen.

As I travelled from Jerusalem to Ramleh I found myself wanting to turn back to Jerusalem because of all the grace and spiritual comfort I had experienced while I was there, and also because I wanted to obtain more remission of sins. But then our Lord commanded me to go to Rome and then continue home to England. He said to me, 'Daughter, whenever you say or think to yourself "Worshipped be all the holy places in Jerusalem where Christ suffered bitter pain and passion" you will have as much pardon as if you were there in the flesh and so will everyone you give it to.' And when I was on my way to Venice many of my companions were very ill, and our Lord said to me, 'Don't be afraid, Daughter, no one will die in the ship that you're in,' and this proved to be perfectly true.

And when our Lord had brought us safely back to Venice my

countrymen abandoned me and went off leaving me by myself. Some of them said that they wouldn't travel with me for a hundred pounds. And when they had gone, our Lord Jesus Christ, who always helps us in time of need and never forsakes any servant of his who truly trusts in his mercy, said to me, 'Don't be afraid, Daughter, for I will look after you really well. If you wear white clothes, as I told you to do before you left England, I will see that you reach Rome safely and then get back home to England without being attacked.'

Then, because I was feeling very depressed and unsure, I inwardly answered, 'If I can satisfy myself, by taking advice from the Church, that you are truly the Spirit of God that I can hear speaking in my mind, I shall do as you want, and if you get me to Rome in safety I shall wear white clothes out of love of you, even if everyone marvels at me.'

'Daughter, set out in the name of Jesus, for I am the Spirit of God and I will help you in every adversity. I will travel with you and support you wherever you go, so do not distrust me. You have never known me to deceive you, and I never tell you to do anything which, if you obey me, does not bring glory to God and good to your soul, and I shall pour my grace upon you freely.'

Just at that moment I glanced to one side and saw, sitting near me, a poor man with a hump on his back. All his clothes were covered in patches, and he seemed to be about fifty years old. I went over to him and said, 'Sir, what's wrong with your back?'

He replied, 'It's deformed by disease, madam.'

I asked him his name and what country he came from. He said he was called Richard and he was from Ireland. Then I remembered what my confessor, the holy anchorite, had told me while I was still in England. His words, which I have quoted above, were, 'Daughter, when your companions have forsaken you, God will provide a hunch-backed man to take you where you want to go.'

So I said to the man, 'Good Richard, take me to Rome and you'll be well rewarded for your trouble.'

'No, madam,' he replied, 'I know that your countrymen have abandoned you, and escorting you would be difficult for me. Your countrymen have bows and arrows to defend you and themselves. As for me, the only form of defence I've got is a cloak full of patches. I'm afraid my enemies will rob me and perhaps take you away from me and defile your body, so I daren't escort you. Even for a hundred pounds I wouldn't want you to suffer such dishonour while we were travelling together.'

I replied, 'Richard, don't be afraid; God will take good care of us, and

I will give you two nobles for your trouble.' He agreed to my offer and we set out together.

Soon afterwards, we were joined by two grey friars and a woman who had travelled with them from Jerusalem. The woman had an ass, and on its back was a chest with a statue of our Lord inside it. Richard said to me, 'You must go on your way with these men and this woman and I will meet you each morning and night, for I have to follow my occupation and beg for my living.'

I did as he said and went on my way with the friars and the woman. None of them could understand my language, but every day they arranged my food, drink and lodgings as well as they arranged their own—better, in fact—so that I always felt that I owed them my prayers.

Every evening and morning Richard the hunchback came and gave me his company as he had promised. And when we entered fine cities the woman with the image in the chest took it out of the chest and put it in the laps of respectable wives, and they dressed it in shirts and kissed it as though it was God himself. When I saw how they worshipped and honoured the image I was seized with such sweet devotion and such lovely meditations that I was shaken with sobs and loud crying. What made it all the more moving for me was that in England I had meditated profoundly on the birth and childhood of Christ; now I thanked God because I saw that these creatures had as much faith in what I could see with my bodily eye as I had had in what I had seen with my inward eye.

When these good women saw me weeping, sobbing and crying so prodigiously and mightily that I was nearly overcome with it, they made me a good soft bed and laid me on it and comforted me as much as they could out of love of our Lord. May his name be blessed!

Chapter 31

I had a ring that our Lord had commanded me to have made while I was in England, and to have engraved with the words 'Jesus is my love.' As I travelled through various lands I was exercised as to how I should keep this ring from thieves, because I wouldn't have lost it for a thousand pounds or more, having had it made at God's command. It was also at God's bidding that I wore the ring, for before God revealed his wishes I had made up my mind that I would never wear one.

I happened to be lodged in a good man's house, and many neighbours came to greet me because of my gifts and my holiness. I told them the measurements of Christ's grave and they were very grateful and joyful to have them; they couldn't thank me enough for bringing them. I then went to my bedroom, letting my ring hang from the string of my purse, which I had at my chest.

On the morning of the following day I wanted my ring but it had disappeared and I couldn't find it. I was very unhappy and complained to the woman who owned the house in the following way: 'Madam, the special ring that shows I'm a bride of Christ, so to speak—it's gone.'

The good wife, understanding my meaning, begged me to pray for her, and her face and expression changed completely as though she was guilty. Then I took a candle in my hand and searched all round the bed where I had slept that night, and the woman took another candle in her hand and she too set about searching all around the bed. And at last I discovered it, lying on the floorboards under the bed, and I joyfully told the woman I'd found it. Then, at my prompting, the woman did her best to ask for my forgiveness: 'Good Christian, pray for me,' she said.

After this I reached Assisi, where I met an English friar minor with a reputation for serious scholarship. I told him about my way of life, my intuitions and the revelations I received. I also told him about God's gracious workings within me—the holy inspirations, the sublime insights and how our Lord communed with my soul almost as if he was holding a conversation with me.

This noteworthy scholar said that I owed a great debt to God: he had never heard of anyone in the world living as close to God in love and intimate speech as I did, and he said that God should be thanked for his gifts, which arise from his goodness and not because human beings deserve them.

Once, when I was in church at Assisi, the veil which our Lady wore on earth was displayed with many lights and great reverence, and I was overcome with great devotion. I wept, sobbed and cried aloud with copious tears and holy thoughts. I was also there on Lammas Day, when there is pardon and plenary remission of sins, to obtain grace, mercy and forgiveness for myself, for all my friends and enemies and for all the souls in purgatory.

There was a lady there who had come from Rome to obtain her pardon. Her name was Madam Florentine, and she had travelled to Assisi with her many Knights of Rhodes, her gentle-women and a fine set of horses. Then Richard (the hunchback) went to her and asked if he and I could travel to Rome with her when she returned so that we would not be set upon by thieves. And by God's providence, this noble lady allowed us to join her retinue and go to Rome with her.

When I reached Rome, and my former companions—who had

turned me out of the group—got there too, they heard people saying that a woman answering my description had arrived in the city, and they were amazed that I had got there safely. And then I went and obtained my white clothes, and I dressed myself entirely in white, just as I had been ordered to do years earlier, so that what had been revealed to my soul was now fulfilled.

Next, I was given accommodation at the Hostel of St Thomas of Canterbury, Rome, and I received communion there every Sunday, weeping profusely, sobbing loudly and crying out. I was highly regarded by the dean of the hostel and all his brothers but then, through the prompting of my unseen enemy, there came a priest who was considered, at the hostel and elsewhere in Rome, to be full of holiness. This priest was a fellow countryman and was also one of my former companions. In spite of his holiness he spoke such evil of me and so badly slandered my name at the hostel that I was turned out thanks to his evil tongue, and I could no longer make my confession or my communion there.

Chapter 32

When I realized that these worthy men were rejecting me and turning me out I was very miserable, mainly because I had no confessor and could no longer receive communion as I liked to do. Weeping profusely, I begged our Lord for mercy and asked him to meet my needs in whatever way he thought was best.

After that I called Richard (the hunchback) to come to me, and I asked him to go to the church by the hostel and tell the priest at the church how I lived my life, how unhappy I was, and how much I wept because I couldn't be confessed or receive communion, and how ashamed and contrite I was for my sins.

Richard went to the priest and told him about me. He explained that our Lord moved me to contrition and compunction and copious tears, that I wanted to receive communion every Sunday if that was possible, and that I did not have a priest to confess to. The priest was very pleased to hear how contrite and full of compunction I was, and he said I should come to him in the name of Jesus and say my 'confiteor' and he would give me communion with his own hands.

Because the priest could not understand any English our Lord sent John the Evangelist to hear my confession. I said 'benedicite' and he said 'Dominus', and by spiritual insight I saw him and heard him as clearly as I would have seen and heard any other priest with my eyes and ears. Amid sorrowful tears, I told him all my sins and sadness. He listened to me gently and kindly, and then he told me the penance I should do for my wrongdoing, and he absolved me of all my sins with sweet and gentle words. The things he said greatly strengthened my faith in the mercy of our Lord Jesus Christ. Before going away he told me to receive the sacrament of the altar in the name of Jesus.

Once he had gone I prayed with all my heart throughout mass, 'Lord, to show that you are not angry with me grant me a spring of tears so that to glorify you and increase my merit I can receive your precious body with tears that express every kind of devotion, for you are my joy, my Lord, my bliss, my comfort and all the treasure that I have in the world, and I covet no other joy in the world but you alone. So do not forsake me, beloved Lord.'

Then our blessed Lord Jesus Christ answered my soul saying, 'Beloved Daughter, I swear by my lofty majesty that I shall never forsake you. The more shame, despite and condemnation you suffer out of love for me the greater is my love for you. I am like a man who loves his wife; the more jealous of her his enemies are the better he will dress her to spite them, and I will treat you in just the same way.

'Daughter, there is nothing you can do or say that can please God better than to believe he loves you, for if I could weep with you, Daughter, I would do so out of the feeling which I have for you. A time will come when you will think yourself well satisfied, for you will be living proof of the well-known proverb, "He is blessed indeed who can sit in his chair of happiness and tell of his chair of grief." And that is how it will be with you, Daughter: all your weeping and sorrow will turn to joy and bliss, which will never fail you.'

Chapter 33

On another occasion, when I was in the nave of the church of St John Lateran hearing mass, I was struck by the goodness and devoutness of the celebrant. I very much wanted to speak to him so I asked my hunch-backed man to go to the priest and ask him to have a word with me.

The priest didn't know a word of English and I didn't know any other language. Since he couldn't understand me we spoke through an interpreter, a man who explained to each of us what the other was saying. I asked the priest to pray, in the name of Jesus, to the blessed Trinity, to our Lady and to all the blessed saints in heaven for the gift of understanding my language and speech because by the grace of God there were certain things that I wanted to tell him and inform him about. I also asked him to get others who loved our Lord to pray for this gift.

The priest, a German by birth, was a good man, a capable scholar and very learned. He was well liked and highly valued and trusted in the city of Rome, and he was one of its most important priests. Wanting to please God, he followed my advice and did his best to pray devoutly to God every day for the grace to understand what I said, and he also got others who loved our Lord to pray for him too. They said these prayers for thirteen days, and after that time the priest returned to me to test out what effect they had had. He understood when I spoke in English and I understood when he spoke to me. In spite of this he didn't understand the English that other people spoke; even if they spoke the same words as me he could only understand them if I said them myself.

I then confessed all my sins to the priest, so far as I could remember them, right from childhood up to that very moment, and I received my penance joyfully. After that, I told him the secret things that had come to me by revelation and deep meditation, and how I fixed my mind on Christ's passion, and how God sometimes sent me such intense compassion that I fell to the ground, unable to bear it, weeping bitterly, sobbing noisily and wailing so loudly and horribly that people were often amazed and frightened. They thought that I was troubled by an evil spirit or a sudden illness and they couldn't believe God was working within me. They thought if it wasn't an evil spirit or a sudden illness I must be pretending and deceiving people—just putting it on.

The priest was very sure that God was working within me; when he did have doubts our Lord, speaking through me, sent him signs of his own misconduct and wrongful living. Our Lord revealed them to me and told me to tell him, and they were things of which no one knew except God and the priest himself. After this, he was sure that my feelings were reliable, and he treated me very respectfully as if I was both his wife and his sister. He said that he would stand up for me against my enemies and he did so all the while I was in Rome, although he had to put up with a lot of trouble and evil words. He even gave up his high office so that he could stand up for me when I sobbed and cried after all my English companions had abandoned me. They were always my biggest enemies and caused me a lot of unhappiness wherever we went, for they wished I would never sob or cry. They wouldn't believe that I couldn't help it, and they set their hearts against me and the good man who supported me.

This man, seeing me sobbing and crying so prodigiously, especially on Sundays when I received communion in public, made up his mind to check whether it was a gift from God, as I claimed, or just something which I put on out of hypocrisy, as others claimed. One Sunday he therefore took me off by myself to another church where mass had already been said and everyone had gone home. No one knew what was happening except for himself and the priest. And when he gave me communion I wept so profusely and sobbed and cried so loudly that even he was astonished, for on the evidence of his own ears I had never cried so loudly before. This convinced him that it was the working of the Holy Spirit and neither pretence nor hypocrisy on my part.

After that he was not afraid of taking my side and speaking up against the people who chose to defame me and slander me. In the end, the enemies of virtue spoke almost as badly of him as of me, and he was happy to put up with it in the cause of holiness.

But there were a number of right-minded people in Rome who admired him and also me all the more, and they often asked me to meals and entertained me well, begging me to pray for them. But my fellow Englishmen were obstinate. In particular, a priest among their numbers incited people against me. He spoke all sorts of evil about me because I wore white clothes far more than people he considered holier or better than I was. The reason for his malice was that I would not obey him, but it was clear to me that it would have been bad for the health of my soul to obey him and do as he wanted me to.

Chapter 34

Then, at the prompting of the English priest who was hostile to me, the good German priest who was my confessor asked me whether or not I was willing to obey him.

'Yes sir,' I answered.

'Will you do what I tell you?'

'Gladly, sir.'

'Well, I am telling you to give up wearing your white clothes and wear your black clothes again.'

I did as he told me, and I felt my obedience had been pleasing to God. But the women of Rome subjected me to a lot of mockery. They asked if I'd been robbed by bandits and I answered, 'No, madam.'

And afterwards, in the course of visiting the holy places, I met the priest who disliked me and he was over the moon to see that I'd had to give up doing what I wanted to do. He said to me, 'I'm glad to see you wearing black as you always did.'

And I replied, 'Sir, our Lord was not displeased with me for wearing white, for he wants me to do so.'

Then the priest answered back, 'Now I'm sure you've a devil inside you, for I've just heard him speaking through your mouth.'

'Ah, good sir, I beg you to drive him away from me, for God knows how determined I am to act righteously and please him if I possibly can.'

This made the priest really angry and he came out with a lot of cutting remarks.

And I said to him, 'Sir, it's to be hoped that I haven't a devil inside me, because if I did have a devil you can be sure I'd lose my temper with you. But you don't seem to be able to make me lose my temper with you, no matter what you do to me.' And the priest went off in a sullen mood.

And then our Lord spoke in my soul and said, 'Daughter, don't worry about what he says to you, because even though he goes trotting off to Jerusalem every year I don't have any regard for him. When he speaks against you he speaks against me, because you are in me and I am in you and it means that I suffer many sharp words. I have often told you that cutting words would crucify me again in you, for you will not be put to death except by having cutting words inflicted on you. This priest who pits himself against you is just a hypocrite.'

Then the good priest who was my confessor required me on my obedience and also by way of penance to care for a poor old woman who lived in Rome. I did this for six weeks, waiting on her as I would have waited on our Lady. And the woman did not have a bed to lie in or any bed clothes to cover her except for her cloak. To make matters worse, she was alive with vermin, which caused her a great deal of irritation. And I brought the poor woman water and sticks on my shoulders, and I begged for her food and also her wine. And when the poor woman's wine was sour I drank it myself and gave the poor woman good wine which I had bought for myself.

Chapter 35

On St Lateran's Day I was in the church of the Holy Apostles in Rome when the Father of Heaven said to me, 'Daughter, I am well pleased with you because you believe in all the sacraments of Holy Church and you hold to all its teachings. I am especially pleased that you believe in the manhood of my son and have so much pity for his bitter passion.'

The Father also said to me, 'Daughter, I will have you wedded to my Godhead, and I shall reveal my secrets and decisions to you, for you will live with me for ever more.'

Then I kept silence in my soul and did not reply, for I was deeply afraid of the Godhead and was not adept in the Godhead's manner of conversation, for all my love and affection were devoted to the manhood of Christ; I understood it well and would not be parted from it for anything.

I was so much affected by the manhood of Christ that if I saw any women in Rome with children in their arms and learned that the children were little boys I cried out, roared and wept as though I was seeing Christ as a child. And if I could have had my way I would have taken the children from their mothers' arms and kissed them as if they were Christ himself.

And if I saw a handsome man it pained me to look at him for fear of seeing the one who was both God and man. If I did come face to face with any handsome man I was liable to burst into tears. And so I went through the streets of Rome weeping and sobbing my heart out over the manhood of Christ, and those who saw me were very puzzled because they didn't know why I was crying.

Because of all this it was not surprising that I was rooted to the spot and failed to answer the Father of Heaven when he told me that I was to be married to his Godhead. Then the Second Person, Christ Jesus, whose manhood I loved so much, said to me, 'Margery—Daughter— what have you got to say to what my Father is asking you? Do you like what he's saying?'

And then I would not answer the Second Person but wept with amazing intensity, wanting to keep him and not be parted from him at all.

Then the Second Person of the Trinity answered his Father for me and said, 'Father, forgive her, for she is only young and hasn't properly learned how to answer.'

And then, as it seemed to me inwardly, the Father took me by the hand before the Son, the Holy Spirit, the Mother of Jesus, the twelve Apostles, St Catherine, St Margaret and many other saints and holy virgins and a mighty multitude of angels, and he said to my soul, 'I take you, Margery, to be my wedded wife, for better, for worse, for richer, for poorer, and you must be humble and meek in fulfilling my wishes. For Daughter, I give you my solemn word that no child was ever so gracious to its mother as I shall be to you, both in joy and in sorrow, to help you and to comfort you.'

Then the mother of God and all the saints who were present in my soul prayed that we should have great joy together. And with high devotion and copious tears I thanked God for the inner blessings which I enjoyed, reckoning myself to be totally unworthy of any such grace, for my life was filled with all sorts of comforts, both of soul and of body. Sometimes I detected sweet smells with my nose—sweeter, I thought, than any sweet thing on the earth I had ever smelled before. I could never explain how sweet they were; I felt that I could have lived on them if they had lasted. Sometimes I heard with my bodily ears such sounds and melodies that I could hardly hear what anyone was saying to me unless they spoke sufficiently loudly.

By the time this book was written I had heard these sounds and melodies for nearly twenty-five years, especially when I was praying devoutly not only in Rome but in England too.

With my bodily eyes I saw white things flying all about me on every side—as numerous, you could almost say, as specks of dust in a beam of light. They were very delicate and comforting, and the brighter the sun the better I could see them. I saw them at all sorts of times and places: in church, in my bedroom, at mealtimes and prayers; in country, in town, while walking, while sitting. I was often afraid of what they might be, for I saw them as much in the darkness at night as I did in the daylight. When I was afraid of them our Lord said to me, 'Daughter, take them as a sign that God speaks within you. Wherever God is heaven is too, and where there is God there are many angels, and God is in you and you are in him. So don't be afraid, Daughter, for they show that you are surrounded by angels who protect you both by night and by day; no devil will have the power to hurt you and no evil people will cause you harm.'

After that, I used to say when I saw them coming, 'Blessed be he who comes in the name of the Lord.' Our Lord also gave me another sign, which lasted for about sixteen years, growing more and more intense all the time. It was a fiery flame of love, wonderfully hot, exquisite and comforting, never dying down but always increasing. No matter how cold the weather was I felt its heat burning in my breast and in my heart. It was as real to me as a blaze would be to anyone who put his hand or his finger into it. When I first felt the fire of love burning in my heart I was afraid of it, and our Lord answered in my mind and said, 'Daughter, don't be afraid, for the heat is the heat of the Holy Spirit, and it will burn all your sins away, for the fire of love extinguishes every sin.

'The fire is a sign that the Holy Spirit resides within you, and wherever the Holy Spirit is the Father is too, and the Son is where the Father is, so you know that the Persons of the Holy Trinity are in your soul, entire and complete. Because of this you have every reason to love me well, but you shall have greater cause than ever to love me, for you will hear what you have never heard and see what you have never seen and feel what you have never felt. For, Daughter, as surely as God is God you can trust in his love. Your soul rests in the love of God more securely than it rests in your body, for your soul will depart from your body but God will never depart from your soul; they are joined together for ever more. And so, Daughter, if you knew how much you please me when you willingly let me speak within you you would never do other than hear my voice, for to do so is a holy life and time well spent. For, Daughter, you please me by such a way of life more than if you dressed yourself in chain mail or a hair shirt, or fasted on nothing but bread and water. If you said a thousand Pater Nosters you would not please me as much as when you are silent and let me speak in your soul.'

Chapter 36

'Daughter, fasting is a good beginning for the young, and it is good for them as a penance if their confessor recommends it or imposes it on a specific occasion. In a similar way, saying numerous prayers is good for those who can do no better; it is not the ideal, but it is a good step on the way to perfection. I tell you, Daughter, that those who set great store by fasting and penances want their way of life to be thought the best; and so do those who go in for saying many devotions; and those who are free in giving alms want that way of life to be prized most highly. But I have often told you, Daughter, that the best life on earth is to spend your time in contemplation, weeping and deep meditation. In the sight of heaven you gain more merit by a year of inward contemplation than by praying aloud for a hundred years. And yet you refuse to believe me, for you choose to say a great many prayers whether I wish you to do so or not. Even so, I will not disapprove of what you do, Daughter, and whether you ponder inwardly or speak aloud, I always hold you in high regard.

'If I were on earth in as physical a form as I was before I died on the cross I wouldn't shun you as so many other people do; I would publicly take you by the hand and make a great fuss of you so that people would know how much I love you. For it is right for a wife to be on familiar terms with her husband. No matter how great a lord and how poor a woman they are when they marry they must nonetheless lie together in bed and live together in joy and peace. It must be just the same between you and me. What matters is not what you've been in the past—I have often said I completely forgive you for all your sins—but what you wish to be in the future. Well then, I must surely be familiar with you and lie beside you in your bed.

'Daughter, you very much want to see me, and when you are in your bed you can unashamedly take me to yourself as your wedded husband, your beloved darling and your sweet son, for I want to be loved as a son should be loved by his mother; and, Daughter, I want you to love me as a good wife should love her husband. So boldly take me in the arms of your soul and kiss my mouth, my head and my feet as sweetly as you like; and as often as you think of me or wish to do me any good service you shall have the same reward in heaven as if you did it to my own precious body in heaven, for I ask no more of you but that your heart should love me as I love you, for my love is always available to you.'

Then I thanked and praised our Lord Jesus Christ for his grace and mercy towards me, an unworthy wretch.

I received all sorts of signs in my ears. One was a sound like a pair of bellows blowing in my ear. I was nervous of it but I was inwardly told not to be afraid, for it was the sound of the Holy Spirit. And then our Lord turned the sound into the voice of a dove, and afterwards into the voice of a little bird called a redbreast, which often sang very joyfully in my right ear. And after having had such signs I always received great gifts of grace.

Then our Lord Jesus Christ said to me, 'You can tell from these signs that I love you, because the plenteous love that is in you makes you a true mother to me and to the whole world. I myself am the source of your goodness, which will bring you great reward in heaven.'

Chapter 37

'Daughter, you obey my wishes and stick to me as tenaciously as a cod's skin sticks to a man's hand when it is boiled. You do not forsake me, no matter what humiliation anyone imposes on you, and you say to me, Daughter, that you would never in all this life forsake me or love me less or try any less to please me even if I stood in person in front of you and told you that you would never enjoy my love, nor enter heaven, nor see my face, but were destined to languish in hell forever.

'On this earth you cannot do without my love, nor can you have any other comfort apart from me, For I am your God and all your joy and all your bliss. So I say to you, darling Daughter, that it is impossible for any soul which is as meek and well-disposed towards me to be damned or sent away from me. Daughter, you need never fear, for when the time comes I shall honour and fulfil all the momentous promises I have made to you, your family and all your confessors. Do not have any doubt about it.'

On another occasion—I was in Rome and it was just before Christmas—our Lord Jesus Christ told me to go to my confessor, whose name was Wenslawe. I was to ask him to let me wear my white clothes again, for he had made me give them up as a point of obedience, as I have already explained. When I told him that it was God's will he didn't dare to think of refusing, and from that time onwards I always wore white.

Then our Lord told me that at Christmas I should return to the house where I had lodged before, so I went to the poor woman I was caring for at my confessor's command and told her that I was forced to leave her. The poor woman was very disappointed and made a lot of fuss at the idea of losing me, but when I explained that this was God's will she took it less badly.

Afterwards, while I was still in Rome, our Lord told me to give away all I had and make myself destitute out of love for him. I fervently wanted to please God so I lost no time in giving the things I had away, and I also gave away what I had borrowed from the hunch-backed man who travelled with me.

When he found out that I had given away his property he was very angry and annoyed that I had done such a thing and he told me what he thought in no uncertain terms. So I said to him, 'Richard, by the grace of God we shall get back to England without any trouble, and at Whitsun you can meet me at Bristol and by the grace of God I shall pay you back in full, for I am sure that God, having told me to give it away out of love for him, will help me to pay it back again.' And so he did.

Chapter 38

After I had given everything away and hadn't so much as a halfpenny—let alone a silver piece—with which to meet my needs, I spent some time in St Marcellus's church in Rome, racking my brains as to how I would sustain myself. In answer to my thoughts our Lord said, 'Daughter, you are still not as poor as I was when I hung naked on the cross out of love for you, for you have clothes to cover yourself and I had none. And you have told others to be poor for my sake, so you must follow your own advice. But don't be afraid, Daughter, for in the past I promised you that I would never let you down, and money will come to you. You have often begged for me and my mother so I ask my mother to beg for you - you have nothing to fear. I have friends everywhere and I shall see that they help you.'

When our Lord had spoken to my soul in this sweet way I thanked him for giving me so much comfort, firmly trusting that things would turn out as he had said. Then I got up and went out into the street and I happened to meet a very nice man. We fell into conversation as we went along the street together, and I told him all sorts of edifying tales and moral precepts till God blessed him with tears of devotion and sorrow, to his great comfort and consolation. And after this he gave me some money, which relieved my wants and supplied my needs for quite a while.

Soon afterwards I had a night-time vision in which our Lady appeared to be sitting and eating with a large number of respectable people, and she asked them to give me some food. It occurred to me that the vision had fulfilled our Lord's words in a mystical sense, for it wasn't long since he had promised to ask his mother to beg for me.

Shortly after having this vision I met a respectable lady called Dame Margaret Florentine (the same one who had brought me from Assisi to Rome). Neither of us could easily understand the other, except by means of signals and signs and a few common words. And this lady said to me, 'Margery in poverté?'

I understood what the lady meant and I answered, 'Yes, grand poverté, Madam.'

Then the Lady insisted on my eating with her every Sunday. She sat me down above herself at her own table and she served my food with her own hands. I sat there, overcome with tears and thanking our Lord that people who could not understand my language welcomed me and treated me so kindly out of love for him.

After each Sunday meal the good lady used to give me a hamper containing ingredients with which to make myself soup for two days, and she filled my bottle with good wine, and sometimes she gave me eight bolendine coins.

Someone else who lived in Rome, a man called Marcellus, asked me to meals two days a week. His wife was almost due to give birth and she was keen for me to be the child's godmother when it was born, but I did not stay in Rome that long. There was also a pious simple lady who gave me my food each Wednesday. On days when I was not being fed I begged for my food from door to door.

Chapter 39

On another occasion I was passing a house where a poor woman lived and she called me in and made me sit by her little fire while she gave me a stone cup full of wine. She had a little boy and for part of the time he was sucking from his mother's breast, then he ran over to be with me for a while and his mother sat there dejected and sad. At this I burst into tears as though I had seen our Lady and her son at the time of his passion, and I had so many holy thoughts that I could never recount even half of them. I sat there weeping copious tears for such a long time that the poor woman, who didn't know why I was weeping, sympathetically tried to get me to stop.

Then our Lord Jesus Christ said to me, 'This place is holy,' and I got up and went out into Rome and saw a great deal of poverty among the people. I thanked God highly for the fact that I was also in poverty, trusting that through my poverty I would share the merit of the city's poor.

There was a woman in Rome who was one of the city's leading citizens, and when she asked me to be godmother to her child, I agreed. She named it after St Bridget, who they had known when she was alive.

By the grace of God I was well liked in Rome from about this time, for the people, both the men and the women, held me in high esteem. The master and brothers of the Hostel of St Thomas, where, as I have already explained, I had been refused accommodation, heard tell of the love and favour I enjoyed in the city, and they asked me to return to them. They said I would be more welcome than ever I was before, for they were very sorry that they had turned me out.

I thanked them for their kindness and did as they asked, and once I'd returned they made me very welcome and were thoroughly glad to see me. At the hostel I found the girl who had previously been my maid (and by rights should still have been my maid). She was staying at the hostel in considerable wealth and prosperity, for she was in charge of the wine. And occasionally, as an act of humility, I went to her and begged her to give me some food and drink and she did so cheerfully—and sometimes she gave me a groat as well.

I broached with my maid the shameful way in which she had left me, and I told her people were saying evil things about her behind her back because we were living separately, but she still didn't wish to attend me again.

Afterwards, I spoke with St Bridget's former maid in Rome but she could not understand what I said. Then I got a man who could understand my language, and he told St Bridget's maid what I said and the things I wanted to know about her former mistress. The girl replied that St Bridget had always been kind and gentle to every living thing, and that her face had always been full of laughter. In addition, the landlord where I had lodged told me that he had known her personally. He had never realized how holy she was, but she had always been kind and good to everyone who wanted to speak with her.

In the room where St Bridget died I heard a German priest preaching about her and I heard about the revelations she received and the way in which she lived her life. And on one of St Bridget's holy days I knelt on the stone where our Lord appeared to her and told her the day on which she would die. This room, her former bedroom, was now a chapel to St Bridget.

Our Lord sent such tempests—such winds and rains and turbulent weather—that people in the fields or working outside were forced to shelter in houses to save themselves from injuries and various dangers. I assumed that these were signs sent by God to show that St Bridget's Day should be kept holy and that St Bridget should be venerated more than she was.

And once, when I was planning to go in solemn procession from church to church, our Lord came to me in the night, in bed, and warned me not to venture far from the hostel because during the day he was going to send a violent storm, with thunder and lightning—and so he did.

The storms that year were so severe, with thunder and lightning, torrential rain and freak conditions of every sort, that very old people who lived in Rome said they had never seen anything like it before. There was so much lightning, and it flashed so brightly inside their houses, that they half expected it to burn their homes and everything in them. They begged me to pray for them, for they had no doubt that I was Almighty God's servant and that my prayers would help them and keep them safe. And when I prayed to God to show mercy, as they had asked, he answered me in my soul and said, 'Daughter, don't be afraid, for no sort of weather or storm will harm you; don't doubt me because I shall never deceive you.' And our merciful Lord Jesus Christ decided to put an end to the storms and save the people from any harm.

Chapter 40

By the providence of our merciful Lord Jesus Christ there came from England to Rome a company of people which included a priest, a good man I had never seen before. He had not seen me either, but he was diligently asking and enquiring about me because while in England he had heard people talking about me and saying that I was in Rome, and he longed to speak to me if God would grant him this favour. While he was still in his own country, and meaning to see me when God allowed him to make the journey, he provided himself with money to bring me to help me out if I needed it.

His enquiries led him to the place where I was, and he meekly and humbly called me 'Mother' and asked me to be so kind as to treat him as my son. I said that God accepted him as a mother would, and so did I.

From talking and conversing about holy things I felt sure that this priest was a good man, so I opened my heart up to him and told him the gifts which God had imparted to my soul through his holy inspiration, and I also told him something about my way of life.

On hearing this he would no longer let me beg for my food from door to door; he asked me to eat with him and his companions instead, or else with men and women who invited me to meals out of kindness and for the comfort I would bring to their souls. He persuaded me to accept their offers in the name of our Lord; but otherwise I ate with him and his companions each day, and he gave me enough money for my journey home to England. This bore out the words 'God favours you,' which God had spoken to me shortly before. Thanks be to God that it proved to be true.

Then some of the companions I had been with in Jerusalem approached this good priest, who had only just arrived in Rome, and complained about me. They said I had received absolution from a priest who could not understand my language or my confession. But the priest, who trusted me like a child and was only concerned for my soul's well-being, asked me whether my confessor had understood me when I spoke to him. 'Good Son,' I said, 'I beg you to ask him to dine with you and your companions when I am there, and you'll find out the truth.'

My confessor was invited to a meal and in due course came and sat down to eat with this good priest and his companions. I was there too, and the good priest from England talked and conversed with me in my own language, English. As I have already said, the German priest who was my confessor was a worthy man of the Church. He sat there looking miserable because he couldn't understand them when they spoke in English, only when they spoke in Latin. They were doing it on purpose without his knowing to find out whether he understood English.

In the end, seeing that my confessor clearly did not understand English and was bored, I told him a story from scripture which I had learned from scholars while at home in England, for I was not prepared to say anything trivial or concocted. I did this partly to cheer him up and partly or mainly to show God at work, for I was using my native language, English. The others asked my confessor if he understood what I had said, and he straight away repeated in Latin, word for word, what I had just been saying in English, for he couldn't speak English and he couldn't understand it except when it came from my lips.

This surprised them a lot, for they realized that we understood each other although he couldn't understand any other Englishman. Praise be to God, who enabled a foreigner to understand me when my own compatriots had forsaken me and wouldn't hear my confession unless I gave up weeping and holy talk.

I could only weep when God brought it upon me, but often he gave me so many tears that I couldn't hold them back. The more I wanted to hold them back or keep them at bay the more strongly they welled up inside my soul, and I had such holy thoughts that I couldn't stop myself. Quite against my will I sobbed and cried aloud and there were many men, and women too, who marvelled at me because of it.

Chapter 41

Sometimes, when I attended sermons where Germans and others preached and taught the laws of God, my heart was filled with sudden sorrow and heaviness, and my face showed how unhappy I was as I mourned my lack of understanding. To restore me I wanted the bread of spiritual insight into my most trusted and supremely beloved saviour, Christ Jesus, whose melodious voice, the sweetest of all aromas, sounded softly in my soul and said, 'I shall preach to you and teach you myself, for I am happy with what you want and desire.'

Then with my soul so delectably fed with the sweet communion of our Lord and so filled with his love, I writhed like a drunkard first to one side and then to the other, full of tears and sobs and quite unable to keep myself still, such was the unquenchable fire of love which flamed exquisitely in my soul. Then many people stared at me, asking what was wrong with me, and I cried aloud to them like a creature which had been pierced with love and whose reason had failed, 'Christ's passion is killing me.'

The good women, pitying my sorrow and amazed at my weeping and crying, loved me all the more. They wanted to comfort and console me after my inner labour, so because I couldn't understand their speech they made signs and signals half inviting and half compelling me to go to their homes, for they did not want to lose my company. So by our Lord's grace I enjoyed great love and favour among many people in Rome, both religious and lay. Some religious people went to those of my countrymen who had a high opinion of me and said, 'This woman has sown a lot of good seed in Rome since she came here.' In other words, I had set the people a good example so that they loved God more than they had before.

Once, I was in the church in Rome where St Jerome's body is buried. (It was miraculously moved there from Bethlehem and is now venerated just by the place where St Lawrence is buried.) St Jerome appeared to me in a vision and said to my soul, 'Daughter, the tears you weep for people's sins are a great blessing, for they will save many souls. And, Daughter, you must not be afraid, for your weeping is a unique and special gift from God—a spring of tears which no one can ever take away from you.' With talk of that kind he did a lot to comfort my spirits. And he gave God a great deal of praise and thanks for all his acts of grace in my soul. Without such inner comforts it would have been impossible for me to show patience and meekness when I suffered scorn and unwanted attention because of the grace which God displayed within me.

Chapter 42

When Easter (or Pasques) had come and gone, my pilgrim party and I made up our minds to go home to our native land, but we were told that there were a lot of thieves on the way who would rob us of our goods and possibly kill us. Then, with many sad tears in my eyes I prayed to our Lord Jesus Christ and said, 'Christ Jesus, in whom I place all my trust, you have often assured me that none of my companions would come to harm. I have trusted you completely and your promises have never failed me or let me down. So hear your unworthy servant's prayers, for I trust your mercy absolutely. Lovingly grant that just as we came here safely my companions and I may return to our homeland without any harm to our persons or our property—for no one has power to harm our souls.

Lord, please do not let us fall prey to our enemies, but in all things may your will be done.'

Then our Lord Jesus Christ said to me inwardly, 'Don't be afraid, Daughter, for you and all your companions will be as safe as if you were in St Peter's Church.'

Then I thanked God with all my heart and had no trepidation in going wherever God wished me to go. I said goodbye to my friends in Rome and especially to my confessor who, out of love for our Lord, had kindly sustained and helped me when I was facing my jealous enemies and their storms of wickedness. The clear streams of tears running down our cheeks showed how unhappy our parting made us. Before I left I fell on my knees and received the benefit of his blessing. Charity had joined us together as one, and because of this we trusted that we would meet again, in God's good time, in the ultimate home that awaited us when our exile in this wretched world had come to an end. And after this my companions and I set out for England.

When we were a little way out of Rome, the good priest I had taken as my son, as I have already mentioned, was terrified that we'd be attacked and he said to me, 'Mother, I'm afraid of being killed and slaughtered by enemies.'

'No, Son,' I said, 'by the grace of God everything will go smoothly for you and you'll travel safely.' My words reassured him, for he had great faith in my intuitions and he was as friendly a travelling companion as if he'd been my son by birth.

And so we arrived at Middelburg. My companions wanted to sail to England on the Sunday but the good priest came to me and said, 'Mother, do you mean to go with your companions on this holy day?'

And I replied, 'No, Son, God doesn't want me to leave here in such a hurry.' And I stayed there with the good priest and some of my other fellow travellers until the next Saturday, but most of my companions set sail on the Sunday.

On the Friday, I went out into the open for some fresh air, and some other English people went with me. I did my best to explain God's laws to them, and I warned them in no uncertain terms about swearing oaths and violating God's commandments.

As I was speaking along these lines our Lord Jesus Christ told me to hurry home to my hostel, for severe and dangerous weather was about to break. So I set off homeward with my companions, and as soon as we reached the hostel the weather changed in the way that had been revealed to me.

And it often happened that when I was in the open air or on a journey there were lightning flashes and huge strokes of thunder, so fearful and distressing that I was scared of being struck down and killed; and often there was torrential rain, which oppressed me and filled me with apprehension.

Then our Lord Jesus Christ said to me, 'Why be afraid when I am with you? I have as much power to protect you in the open air as to protect you in the strongest church in the world.'

And after that I was less afraid, for I always had great trust in his mercy. Blessed be his holy name, for he comforted me in all my troubles.

Some time later, an Englishman happened to come where I was, and he swore a great oath. When I heard it I wept, grieved and sorrowed uncontrollably, for I couldn't stop myself weeping and mourning when I heard my brother offending Almighty God without regard for what he was doing.

Chapter 43

Early next day the priest who was like a son to me came and said, 'Mother—good news! Thanks be to God we've a favourable wind.'

And at once I praised our Lord and asked him, of his mercy, to give us favourable wind and weather until we were safely home in England. And God answered me inwardly, and told me that we should set off in the name of Jesus.

When the priest realized that I had made up my mind to leave, come what may, he said, 'Mother, there's no ship here—just a little smack.'

I answered, 'God is as mighty in a little ship as he is in a big one, and he wishes me to go on board.'

Once we were in the little ship the weather began to get very stormy and overcast. We cried out to God for his grace and mercy, and straight away the storms died down and we had fine weather. We sailed all night and all the next day until it was time for evensong, and that is when we arrived at our port.

Once we were on dry land I fell on my knees and kissed the ground, full of thanks to God for bringing us safely home. At that stage I was penniless, but it so happened that we fell in with some other pilgrims, and they gave me three halfpence because in the course of conversation I had told them some uplifting stories.

This pleased me a lot because it meant that when I reached Norwich I could make a devout offering to the Trinity, as I had done in the course of my outward journey. And so, when I got there, I made my offering with a glad heart. And then my companions and I went to see the vicar of St Stephen's, the Reverend Richard Caister, who was still alive at the time. And he took us to a place where he dined and entertained us really well.

And he said to me, 'Margery, it's a wonder that you can be so cheerful after such a long and tiring journey.'

'Sir, it's because I've got every cause to be cheerful and rejoice in our Lord. He has helped me, comforted me and brought me back safely. May he be blessed and worshipped!'

And so we talked about our Lord at length and had a really good time together. And then we left; after which I went to an anchorite—a monk who had come from a far off country. He lived in the Chapel in the Fields and had a reputation for great holiness. He had once had a high opinion of me but evil talk had turned him against me. Because of this I went to him so as to present myself humbly to him and win him round to a kindly disposition towards me.

When I arrived he welcomed me home in a curt way and asked what I had done with the child I had conceived and borne while out of the country, or so he had heard.

And I replied, 'I have brought home the only child God has sent me, for as God is my witness I haven't done anything since I left whereby I could possibly have had a child.'

Nothing I could say would make him believe me, but I humbly and meekly explained to him, out of the trust I had in him, how it was that our Lord desired me to wear white clothing.

And he replied, 'God forbid such a thing!' for by wearing white I would make the whole world wonder at me.

And I rejoined, 'Sir, what should I care so long as God is pleased with my action?'

Then he told me to return to him and accept his guidance and also that of a worthy priest called Father Edward.

I answered that I would first discover whether this was God's will, and with that I took my leave for the time being. And as I went away from him along the road our Lord said to my soul, 'I do not want you to be guided by him.' So I sent him word of the answer I had had from God.

Chapter 44

And then I prayed to God and said, 'Lord, to prove to me that you definitely want me to dress in white, grant me a sign in the form of lightning, thunder and rain (provided it causes no hindrance or harm to anything) so that unworthy as I am I may be all the better able to do as you wish.'

Then our Lord answered and said to his unworthy servant, 'Daughter, have no doubt but that you will have the sign within three days.' And so I did: on the following Friday, as I lay on my bed, I saw great flashes of lightning and heard great rumbles of thunder, but it quickly gave way to fine weather again. Thereupon I firmly resolved to wear white clothes, although I did not have any gold or silver with which to buy them. But our Lord spoke to my soul and said, 'I shall provide for you.'

After this, I went and saw a very respectable man in Norwich who welcomed me warmly and entertained me well. As we sat together telling each other worthwhile stories our Lord kept saying to me inwardly, 'Speak to this man, speak to this man.' So I said to this respectable man, 'Sir, I wish to God that I could find some kind man who would lend me two nobles to buy my clothes—just until I could pay him back.'

And he replied, 'I'll do it with pleasure, madam. What sort of clothes do you want to wear?'

'Sir,' I replied, 'with God's approval I wish to wear white.' So this good man bought me white cloth and used it to make me a gown, a hood, a skirt and a cloak. And on the following day (the Sunday) he brought me all these clothes in the evening and gave me them for the love of God, and for love of our Lord he was good to me in many other ways besides. May Jesus Christ be his reward, and may he have mercy on his soul and on all Christian people.

On the following Trinity Sunday I received communion dressed entirely in white, only to suffer scorn and contempt in various districts, cities and towns. Thanks be to God for everything!

Not long afterwards my husband came from Lynn to Norwich to see how I was getting on and how I had fared, and we travelled home to Lynn together.

A little later I became very ill—so much so that I was anointed in expectation of death. But before I died I wanted to visit the shrine of St James at Santiago, if this was God's will. I wanted to suffer further humiliations because of my love for him, as he had previously promised that I would do.

And then our Lord Jesus Christ spoke to my soul and told me that I would not die yet, though my pain was so bad that I did not see how I could live. But before very long I was fit and well.

As winter drew in I felt so cold that I did not know what to do with myself; I was poor and penniless—in debt, in fact. I had to put up with shame and condemnation because I wore my white clothes, and also because I cried so loudly when our Lord made me think about his passion. It was the pity I felt for our Lord's passion that made me cry so violently. People were all the more astonished because they had never heard me cry before. (As I have already said, it had started in Jerusalem.)

Many people said that no saint in heaven had ever cried as much as I did, and they decided I must have a devil inside me that was making me cry. They declared as much in a forthright way, and they said many other evil things too. For love of our Lord I bore it all patiently, for I knew that the Jews had said so much worse of our Lord himself than the things that were being said about me. I put up with it all the more meekly when I remembered this.

Some people said I had epilepsy because while I was crying my body writhed from side to side, turning all blue and pallid like the colour of lead. Repelled by this illness, people spat at me; others treated me with contempt and said I was howling like a dog. They damned me and cursed me and said that I was a source of evil in the community. Because of the nasty stories which they heard about me, people who had previously given me food and drink out of love for God now sent me away and told me not to come to their homes.

Afterwards, when it was time for me to go to the shrine of Santiago, I went to my closest friends in Lynn and told them that I was hoping to go to Santiago if I could find the wherewithal for the journey, though at the moment I was poor and deeply in debt. And my friends said to me, 'Why have you given your money and other people's away? Where are you going to find what you owe?'

I replied, 'Our Lord God will give me all the help I need. He has never failed me anywhere, so I trust him completely.' And at once a good man approached and gave me forty pence, and I spent part of it on a cheap coat made from animal skin.

And our Lord kept saying to me, 'Daughter, don't be concerned about money; I will see that your needs are met. Your only concern should be to love me and fix your mind upon me. I shall keep the promise I have already made you and accompany you wherever you go.'

After this, a woman—a good friend of mine—came up to me and gave me seven marks to pray for her when I reached Santiago. I then took my leave of my friends at Lynn, meaning to get on my way as quickly as possible, and our merciful Lord reassured me that I would travel safely. 'Daughter,' he said, 'go on your way in the name of Jesus; no thief will be able to lay a finger on you.'

I set out and got to Bristol on the Wednesday of Whit Week. Waiting for me there was the hunch-backed man who had been with me in Rome and whom I had left there on my return to England two years earlier. While in Rome I had borrowed a certain amount of money from him; then at God's command I had given all the money I had to the poor, including, as I have already explained, the money I had borrowed from the man. While still in Rome I had promised to pay him back in Bristol at just this time, and he had therefore turned up to receive his payment. And our Lord Jesus Christ had so ordained it that as I made my way to Bristol people gave me so much money that I could easily pay this man all I owed him. And that's what I did, may God be praised!

At God's command I stayed in Bristol for six weeks while I awaited a ship. This was because there were no English ships that could make the voyage; they had all been requisitioned for the king. Other pilgrims at Bristol wanted to expedite their journeys so they travelled about from port to port, but their trouble got them nowhere and they came back to Bristol, where I'd been staying all along. I'd fared better than them because while they'd been taking all that trouble, our merciful Lord Christ Jesus had visited me with many holy meditations, contemplation of things divine and many sweet comforts.

During my time in Bristol I received communion every Sunday with copious tears and noisy sobs, loud cries and piercing shrieks. As a result, many men and women stared at me, scorned me, despised me, damned me, cursed me, said evil and slanderous things about me, and accused me of saying things which I hadn't said at all. And then I wept my heart out for my sins, praying God to have mercy and forgive me for them.

I said to our Lord, 'Lord, as you hung on the cross you spoke up for those who were crucifying you, saying, "Father, forgive them; they know not what they do." Likewise, if it accords with your will, I beg you to forgive these people for all their scorn and slander and for all their wrongdoings, for I have deserved and warranted far worse than this.'

Chapter 45

On the following Corpus Christi Day, the priest carried the sacrament round the town in a stately procession, with many candles and appropriate solemnity, and I followed behind full of tears and devotion. My mind was occupied with holy thoughts and meditations, and I was weeping and sobbing noisily. A pleasant woman came up to me and said, 'Madam, may God give you the grace to follow in the footsteps of our Lord Jesus Christ.' Her words spoke in my heart and my mind so intensely that it was unbearable, and I had to go into someone's house. In the house I cried, 'I'm dying! I'm dying!' and I roared out so prodigiously that the people were amazed at me, and they were quite bewildered as to what was wrong with me.

In spite of this, our Lord made some people love me and cherish me very much. They invited me to eat and drink at their homes and they were very glad to hear what I had to say about our Lord. In particular, there was a man from Newcastle, Thomas Marchal, who often asked me to meals for the sake of my conversation. He was so attracted and deeply moved by the good words about contrition and compunction, sweetness and devotion, which God gave me to say that he cried like a baby with tears of contrition and compunction, sometimes by day and sometimes by night, at whatever times our Lord chose to visit his heart with grace. Sometimes when he went into the fields he wept so grievously for his sins and his trespasses that he fell to the ground, unable to bear it. He told me that he had lived a dissolute and immoral life and that, God be praised, he now regretted it very much.

From then onwards he blessed the time when he had met me and firmly resolved to live a good life. And he said to me, 'Mother, here are ten marks. I would like you to have it as your own, for by God's grace I will help you to visit Santiago. And whatever you ask me to give to any poor man or woman I will give as you ask. For every penny I keep there will be a penny for you.'

Then it pleased our Lord to send a ship from Brittany to Bristol, and the ship was prepared and provisioned for its voyage to Santiago. This Thomas Marchal then went and paid the captain for his passage and for mine as well.

There was a wealthy man in Bristol who would not let me sail in the ship, for he thought that I was not a good woman. So I said to the rich man, 'Sir, if you turn me out of the ship my Lord Jesus Christ will turn you out of heaven; for I tell you, sir, our Lord Jesus Christ has no liking for a wealthy man unless he is also good and meek.' And I said many other sharp things to the man without any fawning or flattery.

Then our Lord said to me inwardly, 'You will have what you want; you will go to St James as you wish to do.'

And straight after that I was summoned to appear before the Bishop of Worcester, who was staying three miles from Bristol, and I was ordered to answer for myself at that place. On the following day I got up early and went to the place where he was staying, arriving when he was still in bed.

While in the village I came across one of the bishop's most respected colleagues and we talked about God. When he had heard me talk a good while he invited me for a meal and then took me into the bishop's hall. When I entered the hall I saw many of the bishop's men dressed in very ragged and tattered clothes.

Raising my hands, I crossed myself, and they asked me, 'What devil's got into you?'

I replied, 'Whose men are you?'

They answered, 'We're the bishop's men.'

To which I replied, 'Surely you're more like the Devil's men.'

Then they were angry. They took me to task and spoke to me crossly, but I bore it quietly and well. Afterwards I spoke in such a serious way against sin and their own misconduct that they listened silently and by the time I left they reckoned themselves well pleased with my discourse.

After that I went into the church and awaited the bishop's arrival. As he approached I knelt down and asked him what he wanted and why I had been summoned to appear in front of him; it was tiresome and inconvenient for me, since I was a pilgrim and I was bound, God willing, for Santiago.

Then the bishop replied, 'Margery, I have not summoned you, for I know full well that your father is John Burnham of Lynn. Please don't take what has happened badly but be on good terms with me; I mean to be on good terms with you, for I want you to dine with me today.'

'Sir,' I replied, 'please excuse me—I've promised to eat with a good man in Bristol today.'

And he replied, 'Both of you shall eat with me.' So I stayed with him until God sent a favourable wind for my voyage, and the bishop and his household entertained me really well. During this time he asked me to pray that he would die in a state of grace, for a holy man had warned him that he would die within two years (which is what occurred), the holy man having found this out by revelation. So he unburdened himself to me and begged me to pray that he would be in a state of grace when he died.

At last it was time for me to take my leave of him, and he gave me money, blessed me and ordered his followers to see me on my way. He also asked me to visit him when I came back from Santiago. And so I made my way to my ship.

Before I went on board I prayed that God would save and preserve us from vengeance, storms and perils at sea, so that we could travel in safety. My companions had told me that if we suffered any storms I'd be to blame and they'd throw me overboard; they said the ship was the worse for having me on board. So I prayed as follows: 'Almighty God

Christ Jesus, I beg you to show me mercy, and if you wish to punish me spare me until I am back in England. Once I am back, punish me just as you wish to do.' And our Lord granted my request.

So I boarded the ship in the name of Jesus and sailed from Bristol with my companions. God sent us favourable wind and weather. We reached Santiago after seven days, and the people who had been hostile to me in Bristol made a great fuss of me.

We stayed in Spain for fourteen days, and I was richly blessed, both in body and spirit; I felt deep devotion, and at the thought of Christ's passion I cried out loudly and frequently and shed a great many tears of pity.

Our journey back to Bristol took us five days. I did not stay in the city long but set out to see the Blood of Hailes. I was confessed in Hailes, and I cried out loudly and wept noisily. The monks let me stay with them and they entertained me very well, except for their horrible habit of swearing dreadful oaths. By way of rebuke I cited the Gospel, which surprised them a lot. Some of the monks were very pleased with me, even so. God be thanked for his goodness!

Chapter 46

Afterwards, I went on to Leicester, and Thomas Marchal, who I've mentioned before, accompanied me. At Leicester, I went into a beautiful church and saw a crucifix so harrowingly adorned that the sight of it filled me with grief. Looking at it brought our Lord's passion before my mind, and I started to melt and entirely dissolve in tears of pity and compassion. Then the fire of love flared up so keenly in my heart that I couldn't keep it to myself, for whether or not I wished to do so it made me cry out in a loud voice. I yelled so shockingly and wept and sobbed so balefully that quite a number of men and women were amazed at me. When it was over and I was going through the church door a man clutched my sleeve and said, 'Madam, why do you weep so intensely?'

'Sir,' I replied, 'it is something which you cannot be told.'

Then with the good man Thomas Marchal I went and found lodgings and had a meal there. Once we had eaten I asked Thomas Marchal to write a letter to send to my husband asking him to fetch me home. And while we were drawing up the letter the innkeeper came up to my bedroom in a great hurry. He took my bag and told me to come quickly and speak to the mayor. I did as he asked, and the mayor asked me what part of the country I was from and whose daughter I was.

'Sir,' I replied, 'I'm from Lynn in Norfolk, and so is my father. He's been mayor of that fine borough on five occasions, and an alderman there for just as long. My husband's also from Lynn—he's a burgess.'

'Ah,' said the mayor. 'St Catherine used to say what family she was from, yet you and she are not alike. You, you're a cheap whore, a lying Lollard and you have an evil effect on others—so I'm going to have you put in prison.'

To which I replied, 'Sir, my love of God makes me just as ready to go to prison as you are to go to church.'

When the mayor had told me at length what he thought of me and heaped me with insults and affronts, and when, by the grace of Jesus, I had given measured answers to everything he chose to say, he asked his jailer's man to take me off to prison.

The jailer's man, taking pity on my tears, said to the mayor, 'Sir, I have no room for her unless I put her in with men.'

I was moved by the compassion of the man who had taken pity on me. I asked God to show as much grace and mercy to him as he showed to my own soul, and I said to the mayor, 'Sir, I beg you not to put me with men, because I need to preserve my chastity and honour my marriage bond with my husband, as duty requires.'

And then the jailer himself said to the mayor, 'Sir, I will personally undertake to keep this woman in safe custody until you call for her again.'

A man from Boston was present who had spoken to me at the lodging house. 'This woman is certainly thought to be holy and saintly in Boston,' he told the mayor.

Then the jailer took me into his custody and led me home to his own house. He put me into a lovely room, locking the door with a key which he gave to his wife for safekeeping. But he let me go to church when I wanted and had me to eat at his own table, and for love of our Lord he made me really welcome. May God be thanked for it!

Chapter 47

Then the Steward of Leicester, a good-looking man, sent for me to the jailer's wife, but because her husband was not at home she would not release me to anyone, steward or otherwise. When the jailor heard about it he came himself and personally took me in front of the steward. And as soon as he saw me the steward addressed me in Latin, and there were many priests and other people standing around to hear my answers.

I said to the steward, 'Please speak English, because I cannot understand what you're saying.'

The steward replied, 'Well in plain English you're an absolute liar.'

Then I repeated, 'Sir, ask me what questions you like in English, and by the grace of my Lord Jesus Christ I will give you proper answers.'

Then he asked me a lot of questions, and I answered them readily and straightforwardly so that he could not find grounds for any charge. Then the steward led me by the hand to his private room and said all sorts of disgusting things to me, hoping and intending, or so it seemed, to bully me into letting him defile my body. I was very afraid and very upset and begged him to spare me. I said, 'Sir, out of respect for Almighty God, leave me alone—I'm a married woman.'

Then the steward replied, 'You'll either tell me whether you get this talk from God or the Devil or you'll go to prison.'

'Sir,' I answered, 'for love of my Lord I am not afraid to go to prison, for my Lord suffered more out of love for me than I can for him. Please do whatever you think is best.'

Seeing how unafraid I was of going to prison, the steward began to manhandle me, with offensive acts and an evil eye. I was so afraid I told him how my speech and conversation came from the Holy Spirit—I didn't make them up myself. What I said astonished him and he gave up his efforts and his lewdness. He said to me what many men have said before: 'Either you're a thoroughly good woman or else you're a thoroughly wicked one,' and he handed me over to the jailer, who took me back to his home again.

They afterwards arrested two of the people who had accompanied me on my pilgrimage. One was Thomas Marchal, who I have already mentioned, and the other was a man from Wisbech. They put them both in prison because of their links with me. The trouble they were in made me sad and miserable and I prayed to God that they would be freed. Our merciful Lord Jesus Christ then said to me, 'Daughter, out of love for you I shall see to it that far from detaining them the people will be very keen to let them go.'

On the following day our Lord sent such storms—such lightning, thunder and continuous rain—that the people in the town were beside themselves with fear. They were terrified in case it was because they had put my fellow pilgrims in prison. So the town's councillors rushed to the prison and released the two pilgrims who had languished there all the previous night. They took them to the guild hall to be examined in front of the mayor and the leading burgesses. They made them declare on oath whether my faith and beliefs were orthodox or otherwise, and whether I lived a continent and decent life. And they swore that as surely as God would help them at the Day of Judgement I was, to the best of their knowledge, an upright woman whose faith and beliefs were orthodox and who, so far as they knew, was clean and chaste in every way—in spirit, appearance, words and deeds. The mayor then set them free to go wherever they wished.

The storm stopped at once and the weather was fine, may our Lord God be praised! The pilgrims were glad to be set free but they didn't dare to remain in Leicester; instead they went about ten miles away, and they stayed there to hear what was done with me, for when they were both in prison they told me that in their opinion the mayor would have me burnt if he could have his way.

Chapter 48

One Wednesday I was taken into All Saints' church at Leicester. The Abbot of Leicester was seated in front of the high altar, along with some of his canons and the Dean of Leicester, who was a leading churchman. In addition, there were several friars and priests, the Mayor of Leicester and quite a number of other laymen. There were so many people that they were standing on stools to get a good view of me. I knelt and prayed to Almighty God for the grace, wit and wisdom to answer for myself as satisfactorily and respectfully as possible so as to bring my soul the greatest profit and give the people the best example. Then the priest came up to me and led me by the hand to the abbot and his assessors, who were sitting at the altar. They made me swear on a bible that I would give honest answers about what I believed on points of doctrine. They began by considering the holy sacrament of the altar, and I had to say exactly what I believed about it.

I replied, 'Sirs, what I believe about the sacrament of the altar is this: that when a man has been ordained priest then, no matter how evil his life may be, if he duly pronounces over the bread the words of our Lord Jesus Christ when he celebrated the Last Supper among his disciples the bread ceases to have the substance of bread and truly becomes his flesh and blood, and the words, once spoken, can never be taken back again.' And in a similar way I answered on all the points of faith on which they chose to question me, and they were fully satisfied.

The mayor, who was dead set against me, said, 'I'm sure she doesn't believe in her heart what she says with her mouth.'

But the clerks said to him, 'Sir, to our way of thinking she gives an excellent account of herself.'

Then the mayor poured condemnation on me and came out with all sorts of critical and nasty remarks, which are best not repeated.

'Sir,' I said, 'As our Lord Jesus Christ is my witness, whose body is present here and now in the sacrament of the altar, I deny that I have ever in my life had sinful and carnal relations with a man. I have only known my husband's body—the man I'm bound to by the laws of matrimony and by whom I've had fourteen children. I assure you, sir, that there is no one in the world I love as much as God, for I love him above everything else; and, sir, I tell you truly that I love all men in God and for the sake of God.'

I also had some plain words for the mayor himself: 'Sir,' I said, 'you aren't fit to be mayor, and I'll prove as much from the holy scripture; for before he'd punish Sodom and Gomorrah our Lord God said, "I shall come down and see," despite the fact that he knew everything. He did this simply to show men like you that you should never impose a punishment unless you make sure it is called for first. And you've been treating me quite the contrary today, sir, because you've caused me a lot of hurt for things which I have never done. I pray that God will forgive you for it.'

Then the mayor said to me, 'I'd like to know why you go around in white clothes; I'm sure you've come here to lure our wives away from us and lead them off with you.'

'Sir,' I said, 'you won't hear from my lips why I go around in white; you're not fit to be told. But, sir, I will gladly tell these worthy priests by way of confession, and it's up to them whether to pass it on to you or not.' Then the men of the church asked the mayor to withdraw from the chancel, along with the other laymen. And when they had left I knelt on my knees in front of the abbot, the Dean of Leicester and a preaching friar, who was a worthy cleric, and I told the three how, before I'd gone to Jerusalem, our Lord had inwardly advised me and commanded me to wear white clothes. 'I have told my confessors the same thing, and they've ordered me to go round like this because they've too much respect for God to oppose my inner feelings; they'd be more than ready to do so if they felt they could. So, sirs, if the mayor wants to know why I go round in white, you may like to say it's because my confessors tell me to. Then you won't be telling lies but he won't know the full facts.'

The clerks recalled the mayor and spoke to him privately. They said my confessors had told me to wear white clothes and I had accepted this on my obedience. Then the mayor called me to him and said, 'No matter what you say, I will not let you leave here unless you obtain a letter from

the Bishop of Lincoln, since you are in his jurisdiction, discharging me
of responsibility for you.'

I replied, 'Sir, I am more than happy to speak to the Bishop of Lincoln
because in the past he's received me very warmly.'

Then some of the others asked me if I was on good terms with the
mayor, and I replied, 'Yes, and also with all God's creatures.'

And with tears in my eyes I showed my respect for the mayor by asking
him to be on good terms with me and forgive me for anything I had done
to displease him. And this time he spoke to me pleasantly, making me
think that all was well between us; it seemed he was well disposed
towards me, though I afterwards found that this wasn't so. And thus it
was that the mayor allowed me to go to the Bishop of Lincoln and fetch
a letter which would end his responsibility for me.

Chapter 49

So I first of all entered the church of Leicester Abbey, and as soon as the
abbot saw me, he and a number of his brethren kindly came to welcome
me. When I saw them coming, my inner eye at once perceived our Lord
approaching with his disciples, and I was thrilled with sweet and devout
apprehension—so much so that I couldn't stand upright to greet them,
as courtesy required, but leaned against one of the pillars of the church
and clung to it for fear of falling; I was so full of devotion that I couldn't
stand up though I wanted to, and this made me cry and weep intensely.

When I had overcome my tears the abbot asked the brothers to take
me in and comfort me, and they gave me really good wine and made me
feel at home. I then got the abbot to write me a letter to the Bishop of
Lincoln recording the things that had been said while I was in Leicester.
And the Dean of Leicester was ready to go on record and be a witness
too, for he was very sure that our Lord loved me—so much so that he
entertained me well at his own home.

I then took my leave of my so-called son, intending to set out for
Lincoln with a man called Patrick, who had previously been with me at
Santiago. Thomas Marchal had sent him from Melton Mowbray to
Leicester to make enquiries and see how I was faring. This Thomas
Marchal had been terrified that I would be burnt, and had sent this man
Patrick to find out the facts.

Many good people from Leicester came up to Patrick and me and
wished us well. Thanking God for preserving me and giving me the
victory over my enemies, they saw us off from the outskirts of the town

and made a great fuss of us, promising me that if I ever came back again I'd have a far better reception than I'd had this time. But I'd forgotten a piece of Moses' rod which I'd brought from Jerusalem—something I wouldn't have lost for forty shillings. So Patrick went back into the town for my rod and my bag and he happened to meet the mayor, who wanted to clap him in jail. In the end he had to hurry off leaving my bag behind.

Feeling very unhappy, I waited for Patrick in a blind woman's house, dreading to think what had happened to keep him so long. But at last he came riding past the place where I was waiting. When I saw him I cried, 'Patrick, my son, why have you been away from me for such a long time?'

'Oh mother,' he said, 'I've been in great danger on your account. I was nearly put in prison because of you. All because of you the Mayor has given me a hard time, and he has taken your bag away from me.'

'Ah, good Patrick,' I replied, 'don't be annoyed; I shall pray for you and God will reward you well for your trouble. It's all for the best.'

Then Patrick put me on his horse and took me home to his own house in Melton Mowbray, where we found Thomas Marchal, as mentioned above. He helped me down from the horse, thanking God with all his heart that I'd not been burnt. And we rejoiced in God throughout the night.

On the following day I went on my way to Lincoln, where the bishop was in residence. Not being sure just where he was, I went up to an important man with a fur hood. He was one of the bishop's officers, and he said to me, 'Madam, don't you know me?'

'No, sir,' I said, 'I'm sure I don't.'

'And yet you're in my debt,' he said, 'for I've welcomed you warmly in the past.'

'Sir,' I said, 'I hope you did it out of love for God, and I hope he'll reward you really well. But please forgive me; I don't pay much attention to a man's good looks or the features of his face, and because of that I forget him that much quicker.'

And then he told me, in a kind way, where I would find the bishop. And so I got a letter from the bishop to the Mayor of Leicester, ordering him not to trouble me or stop me coming and going as I wanted.

At about this time there was so much thunder, lightning and heavy rain that people thought God was angry with me, and they very much wanted me out of the district. But I was quite unwilling to leave until I'd recovered my bag.

When the Mayor of Leicester received the letter he sent me my bag and let me travel safely where I wanted to. He had held me up for three weeks before allowing me to leave the area and continue my journey. I got Patrick to be my travelling companion and we set out for York.

Chapter 50

When I reached York I paid a visit to an anchoress. She had thought highly of me before I went to Jerusalem and I wanted to hear about her spiritual progress. To make our meeting of minds all the closer I did not want to eat anything with the anchoress that day except bread and water, because it was Our Lady's Eve. But the anchoress did not want to know me, because she had heard so much evil talk about me. So I went and saw other people who were strangers to me, and out of love for our Lord they made me very welcome.

One day, as I sat in a church in York, our Lord Jesus Christ said to my soul, 'Daughter, you have a lot of trouble coming to you.' It made me rather upset and nervous, so I sat there and didn't answer. Then our blessed Lord spoke again: 'Daughter, would you think yourself hard done by to suffer more trouble out of love for me? If you don't want to suffer any more I'll see that you don't.'

I replied, 'No, good Lord, let me be at your disposal, and give me the power and strength to suffer everything you want me to suffer. And let me do so meekly and patiently.'

Knowing that our Lord wanted me to face more difficulties, I accepted whatever he chose to send with a good grace and I thanked him unreservedly for it, because it made my day happy and joyful when I was faced with a problem. And in course of time I found that when I did not have troubles I was not as happy and glad as I was on days when I did.

On a certain occasion I was in York Minster when a clergyman came up to me and said, 'Madam, how long do you mean to stay here?'

'I mean to stay for a fortnight, sir,' I answered—which is what I did. And during that time many good men and women asked me to meals and made me very welcome. They were eager to hear what I had to say, and they marvelled at the value of what I said.

But I also had many enemies who slandered, scorned and despised me. One of these was a priest who came up to me while I was in the minster. He took me by the collar of my gown and said, 'You wolf, what's this cloth that you've got on?' I stood there, unwilling to defend myself. There were children from the monastery going past and they said to the priest, 'It is wool, sir.' The priest was angry because I wouldn't answer him and he came out with a lot of horrid oaths. Then I began to speak fearlessly in the name of God. I said, 'Sir, you should obey God's commandments and not swear in such a casual way.'

The priest asked me who kept the commandments and I replied, 'Sir, those who keep them.'

Then he said, 'Do you keep them?'

I replied, 'Well, sir, I mean to because it's my duty, just as it's yours and everyone else's who hopes to be saved at the last day.'

When he had wrangled with me for a long time he slipped away before I realized that he was going, and I did not see where he disappeared to.

Chapter 51

On another occasion an important scholar came up to me and he asked me how the words 'Crescite et multiplicamini' should be understood.

By way of reply I said to him, 'Sir, these words refer not only to the physical bearing of children but also to the begetting of virtue—the fruit of the spirit. We can do this by hearing God's word, by setting a good example, by meekness, patience, charity and chastity and so forth. As for patience, it is worth far more than the working of miracles.' By the grace of God the scholar was thoroughly pleased with my answer.

And out of his mercy our Lord always ensured that some people loved and supported me. And so it was that in this city of York there were three men who saw eye to eye with me in spiritual matters: a doctor of divinity called John Aclom, a canon of the minster called Sir John Kendal, and another priest who sang masses at the bishop's tomb.

I stayed in the city for a fortnight, as I said I would, and for longer besides; and every Sunday, when I took communion in the minster, I wept profusely, sobbed noisily and cried out loudly so that many people were utterly bewildered as to what was wrong with me.

After one communion a priest who seemed to be a noteworthy scholar approached me and said, 'Madam, when you first arrived you said you would stay for only a fortnight.'

'Sir, with respect, I said I would stay for a fortnight but I didn't undertake not to stay for a longer or shorter time. But as of now, sir, I can definitely say that I'm not going yet.'

Then he set a day when I had to appear before him at the chapter house, and I said I would gladly obey his order. I then went to Master John Aclom, the doctor I've mentioned, asking him to attend in my support. He did so, and they treated him with great regard. Another doctor of divinity had also promised to be there with me, but he held back until he knew which way the case would go—whether for or against me.

On the day in question there were a lot of people in the chapter house of the minster. They wanted to see and hear what they would say to me or do to me. I was in the minster from the start of the day, ready and waiting to answer the charge. And my friends came to me and told me to keep my spirits up, and I thanked them and said I would.

And promptly a really pleasant priest came up to me and took me by the arm to help me through the crowd of people. He led me in front of a noteworthy doctor—the same one who had summoned me to this hearing in the minster chapter house. With them were seated many other respected and noteworthy scholars, some of whom held me in high regard.

The doctor asked me, 'Woman what are you doing here in this district?'

'Sir, I have come on pilgrimage to make an offering at the shrine of St William.'

He replied, 'Have you a husband?'

'Yes.'

'Do you have any letter giving his permission?'

'Sir,' I replied, 'my husband gave me permission by word of mouth. Why are you treating me in this way when you don't do the same with other pilgrims who come here, who don't have letters any more than I have? You let them come and go as they like, in peace and quiet, but you won't leave me alone. Sir, if there are any scholars here among you all who can prove that I've spoken a word out of turn I am ready and willing to put it right. I will not maintain any error or heresy, for I fully intend to hold to the faith of Holy Church, and to please God entirely.'

The scholars then examined me in the articles of the faith and on other points as they saw fit, and I gave them good and honest answers, so that nothing I said gave them grounds to harm me, God be praised!

Then the doctor who was acting as judge and chairman gave orders for me to appear before the Archbishop of York on a certain date in the village of Cawood, and he said that I must be kept in prison until the day for my appearance. But at that the lay people spoke up for me and said I should not be put in prison; they said they would be responsible for me and escort me to the archbishop.

For the time being, the scholars and clerics had nothing more to say to me, so they got up and went their separate ways, and praise be to Jesus they set me free.

Soon afterwards a cleric came up to me—one of the ones who had just been my adversaries. 'Madam,' he said, 'I beg you to forgive me, even though I sat with the doctor who was accusing you; he put me under so much pressure that I didn't dare do otherwise.'

'Sir, I don't bear you any grudge,' I replied.

To which he answered, 'Please pray for me, then.'

'Sir,' I replied, 'I will do, gladly.'

Chapter 52

There was a monk who was going to preach in York, and he had heard a lot of slander and evil talk about me. There was a big crowd to hear what he had to say, and I was among them. During his sermon, he covered a number of issues in such a pointed way that the people were left in no doubt he was referring to me, and my friends, because they cared about me, were sad and upset. But I was all the happier because it gave me a way of showing my patience and charity, which I trusted would please our Lord Jesus Christ.

Once the sermon was over, a lot of people came up to me, including a doctor of divinity who had a high opinion of me. 'Margery,' he said, 'how have you coped with this today?'

'Very well, sir,' I answered, 'God be praised. I have reason to be joyful and glad at heart if I can suffer in any way because of my love for him, for he suffered a great deal more for me.'

Straight afterwards, a man who was well-disposed towards me came with his wife and some other people and led me seven miles from the city to see the Archbishop of York. They took me into a lovely room, and a cleric came in and said to my escort, 'Sir why have you and your wife escorted this woman here? She'll give you the slip and you'll end up looking thouroughly stupid.'

The good man replied, 'I'm sure she'll stay and be more than ready to answer for herself.'

On the following day I was taken into the archbishop's chapel, and many of the archbishop's household arrived. They reviled me, calling me 'Lollard' and 'heretic,' and some swore all sorts of horrible oaths that I would be burned.

By the power of Jesus I said to them, 'Sirs, I'm afraid it's you who'll burn in hell forever unless you give up swearing oaths; you're not obeying God's command. I wouldn't swear as you do for all the wealth in the world.' At this they went away as if they'd been put to shame. Then in silent prayer I asked for God's grace so that during the day I'd conduct myself in the way that would please him most, bring my soul the greatest benefit and give the best example to my fellow Christians. By way of answer, our Lord said that things would work out well.

At last the archbishop came into the chapel with his clerks. 'Why do you go around dressed in white? Are you a virgin?' he demanded.

Kneeling before him I answered, 'No, sir, I'm not a virgin; I'm a married woman.'

He ordered his followers to fetch a pair of fetters. He said I ought to be fettered because I was a false heretic. But I said, 'I'm not a heretic, and you won't be able to prove that I'm one.'

The archbishop went away and left me standing by myself. Then I spent a long while praying to our Lord God Almighty for help and support against all my enemies, both seen and unseen, and I trembled and quivered so amazingly that I had to hide my hands in my clothes so that no one would see how much they were shaking.

After a while the archbishop re-entered the chapel with many notable clerics. Among them was the doctor who had examined me previously and the monk who had preached against me in York not long before. Some of the people asked whether I was a Christian or a Jew; some said I was a good woman and some said I wasn't. Then the archbishop took his seat and the clerics took theirs. (There were numerous clerics, and where they sat reflected their seniority.)

While everyone was assembling and the archbishop was taking his seat I stood at the back, praying so long and fervently for help and support against my enemies that I dissolved into tears. In the end I couldn't help crying out loud, and the archbishop, his clerks and others who were there were amazed to hear me; they had never heard such crying before.

When my crying was over I fell on my knees in front of the archbishop and he said in a really violent manner, 'Why do you cry in such a way, woman?'

I answered, 'Sir, you will one day wish that you had wept as surely as I do.'

The archbishop tested me in the articles of the faith, and God gave me grace to give good, correct answers straight away and without much thinking, so that he couldn't fault me; whereupon he said to the clerks, 'She knows the faith well enough. What shall I do with her?'

The clerks replied, 'We're well aware that she's versed in the articles of the faith, but we don't want to let her stay around here; the populace place a lot of trust in what she says and she may lead some of them astray.'

Then the archbishop said to me, 'I hear bad reports about you; I hear it said that you're a thoroughly wicked woman.'

And I replied, 'And I hear it said that you're a wicked man, sir. And if you're as wicked as people say, you will never enter heaven unless you mend your ways while you're on this earth.'

Then he said, in his violent way, 'Why you!... What do people say about me?'

I replied, 'Others can tell you well enough, sir.'

Then an important cleric with a furred hood said, 'Stop this! Answer for yourself and leave the archbishop out of it.'

Next, the archbishop said to me, 'Place your hand on the bible here in front of me and swear that you'll leave my diocese as quickly as you can.'

'No, sir,' I answered. 'Please give me leave to return to York so that I can say goodbye to my friends.' And he gave me permission to go there for a day or two.

I thought that this was too short a time, so I answered, 'Sir, I cannot leave the diocese in such a rush; I must stay and talk to some worthy men before I go. Also, with your permission, sir, I must go to Bridlington and consult my confessor, a good man who was confessor to the prior who has now been canonised.'

Then the archbishop said to me, 'You must swear that you will not teach the people in my diocese, or stir them up.'

'No, sir, I won't swear that,' I said. 'Wherever I go I shall talk about God and speak out against people who use profane language. I shall do so until such time as the pope and Holy Church decree that no one shall be so bold as to talk about God; because God Almighty doesn't forbid us to talk about him. What's more, the gospel mentions a woman who heard our Lord preach and came up to him and said to him loudly, 'Blessed are the womb that bore you and the breasts that suckled you.' And our Lord replied, 'And equally blessed who are the people who hear God's word and obey it.' So it seems to me, sir, that the gospel permits me to speak of God.'

'Ah, sir,' said the clerks, 'she's talking about the gospel—which shows that she's got the devil inside her.' And straight away a learned clerk brought out a book and cited against me St Paul's prohibition on women preaching.

I answered by saying, 'I don't preach, sir; I enter no pulpits. All I do is talk to people and tell them things that are good for their souls, and I'll do the same for as long as I live.'

Then a scholar who had already examined me said, 'Sir, she told me the worst story about priests that I've ever heard.'

The archbishop asked me to repeat the story.

'Sir,' I said, 'with all due respect, I spoke of just a single priest and I did it in order to make a point. I understand that for the good of his soul God allowed this priest to get lost in a wood. He had no shelter, but as the daylight faded he found a beautiful orchard in which to rest for the night. In the middle was a lovely pear tree all bedecked and adorned with blossom. The flowers were an exquisite sight for his eyes. Then along came a bear. It was big and fierce and hideous and it shook the pear tree and brought down the flowers. This horrible beast then greedily ate and devoured them all. When all the beautiful flowers were gone he turned his tail end in the priest's direction and expelled their substance from his bowel. The priest, repelled by this loathsome sight, began to worry about what it might mean.

'On the following day he was wandering on his way feeling very depressed and preoccupied when who should he meet but an elderly man who looked like a palmer or a pilgrim. This man asked the priest what was getting him down. The priest repeated the whole story. He said he'd been filled with dread and sorrow at seeing the horrible animal making such beautiful flowers and blossoms dirty, then eating them and afterwards expelling them from his bowel in such a repulsive way in front of his eyes—and without his understanding what the meaning might be.

The palmer, showing himself to be God's messenger, addressed the priest in the following way: "Priest, you yourself are the pear tree, and by saying services and administering the sacraments you flourish and flower to a certain extent, though you do your work without dedication, caring little about how you say your matins and your evening office as long as you manage to gabble through them. What is more, you go to your mass without real devotion, and you've very little contrition for your sins. You receive the cup of everlasting life, the sacrament of the altar, in a thoroughly half-hearted way. Then you misuse your time for the rest of the day, devoting yourself to buying and selling, shopping and swapping as if you belonged in the secular world. You sit drinking ale and you give yourself over to greed, gluttony and lust of the flesh, living a life of lechery and uncleanliness. You break God's commandments by swearing, lying, slander, backbiting and other such sins. So it is that your bad behaviour makes you very much like the bear: you devour and destroy the flowers and blooms of virtuous living to your own everlasting damnation and the hindrance of many others besides; and so it will be unless you have the grace to repent and amend your life."'

The archbishop liked the tale a lot; he praised it and said how good it was. But the scholar who had previously examined me in the archbishop's absence said, 'Sir, this tale strikes to my very heart.'

I said to the scholar, 'Ah, good sir, in the place where I live for most of the time is an upright cleric who preaches well and speaks out against the people's wrongdoing. He won't stoop to flatter anyone, and he says from his pulpit, "If my preaching upsets anyone, take good note because it means he feels guilty." And I'm causing you just the same discomfort,' I said to the scholar. 'May God forgive you.'

The scholar was at a loss for words, but afterwards he came and apologised to me for having been so set against me. He also begged me to pray for him specially.

Without more ado, the archbishop asked, 'Where can I get a man who'll take this woman away from me?'

A number of young men jumped up at once, and all of them said, 'My Lord, I'll go with her.'

The archbishop replied, 'You're all too young. I won't have you.'

Then a good, responsible man from the archbishop's household asked his master what he would give him to escort me.

The archbishop offered him five shillings and the man asked for a noble. The Archbishop answered, 'I won't put such a high value on her.'

'Go on, good sir,' I said to the man. 'Our Lord will repay you handsomely.'

Then the archbishop said to the man, 'See—here's five shillings. Get her out of this diocese quickly.'

I knelt down and asked the archbishop to bless me. He asked me to pray for him, gave me a blessing and let me go. I was then escorted back to York, where many laymen and notable scholars welcomed me. They rejoiced in our Lord, who had given me, an illiterate woman, the wit and wisdom to answer so many learned men without suffering any disgrace or blame. Thanks be to God!

Chapter 53

Afterwards, the good man who was escorting me led me out of the city and we headed for Bridlington to see my confessor, whose name was Slaytham. We talked with Slaytham and also with many other people who had previously encouraged me and done a lot for me. But I did not want to stay any longer so I took my leave of them, ready to set out on my way.

My confessor asked me if I was afraid of staying because of the Archbishop of York, and I answered, 'No, of course not.' Then the good man gave me some silver, and he begged me to pray for him. And so we started on the way to Hull.

During our time in Hull we joined a procession, and an important woman used the opportunity to treat me with utter contempt. I ignored her but I had to face many other people who menaced me and said that I should be put in prison. But despite all their malice there was one good man who asked me to a meal and entertained me really well. Then the hostile people - the ones who had treated me with contempt— approached this man and told him not to help me in any way, for they reckoned that I was of bad character.

My host was afraid to let me stay any longer, so at dawn the next day he took me to the edge of the town and saw me off. I headed for Hessle, where I hoped to cross the River Humber. On arriving there I happened to meet two preaching friars and two of the Duke of Bedford's yeomen. The friars told the yeomen who I was and the yeomen arrested me just as I was getting into my boat, and they also arrested the man who was with me.

'Our master the Duke of Bedford has sent for you,' the yeomen said. 'You're reckoned to be the most notorious Lollard around here—and worse than any in London, too. We've been searching for you everywhere; there's a hundred pounds for us if we haul you up in front of our master.'

I said to them, 'I'll gladly go where you take me, sirs.'

They then took me back to Hessle, where people accused me of being a Lollard. Women came running out of their houses with their distaffs and they called to the others, 'Burn this lying heretic.'

As I was being taken to Beverley by the yeomen and friars I have mentioned we met a great many local people. 'Woman,' they said, 'give up the life you're leading; you should spin and card like other women do, and not have all this disgrace and bother. Nothing on earth would make us put up with all that you go though.'

And I said to them, 'I suffer less than I'd like to do for love of our Lord. I suffer nothing but cutting words; but our merciful Lord Jesus Christ— may his name be praised!—suffered vicious blows, cruel scourging and finally a shameful death for me and all humanity. Blessings be upon him! I'm suffering next to nothing compared with what he endured.'

As we proceeded, I told the men some salutary stories until one of the duke's men who had arrested me said, 'I'm sorry I found you; the things you say seem really good.'

Then I replied, 'Sir, don't regret or reproach yourself for having found me. Do as your master wants you to do; I'm sure that everything will work out well. For my part, I'm really pleased that you found me.'

He replied, 'Madam, if you're ever a saint in heaven pray for me.'

'Sir,' I said, 'I hope that you and everyone else who enters heaven will be a saint.'

We carried on until we reached Beverley. In the town lived the wife of one of the men who'd arrested me. They took me to her house and removed my purse and my ring. They provided me with a pleasant room, a decent bed and other necessities. Then they locked the door with the key and took the key away with them.

Afterwards, they took the Archbishop of York's man, who they'd arrested with me, and put him in prison. But a little later that same day we heard reports that the Archbishop of York was on his way to the town where his man had been put in jail. The archbishop was told that his man had been jailed and he had him let out straight away.

The man then came to me and said with an angry look on his face, 'I wish I'd never set eyes on you. I've been put in prison on your account.'

To console him I said to him, 'Be humble and patient, because that will earn you a great reward in heaven.'

Then I stood at the windows, telling moral stories to anyone who would listen to me, and some women cried and said with heavy hearts, 'Why should you be burnt, poor thing?'

I was terribly thirsty, so I asked the good woman of the house if I could have a drink. She said her husband had taken the key of the room, so she couldn't get in to give me one. So then a woman outside got a ladder, put it to the window and gave me a pint of wine in a jug, and also a cup, and they asked me to put the jug and the cup out of sight so the man wouldn't see them when he returned.

Chapter 54

I was lying in bed the following night when a loud voice called 'Margery,' right in my ears. I woke as soon as I heard the voice, feeling very frightened. I lay there, not moving or making a noise, and I prayed as devoutly as I could do under the circumstances. And straightaway our merciful Lord, who is always present everywhere, comforted me—his unworthy servant—by saying to me, 'Daughter, I am better pleased if you suffer contempt and scorn, shame and criticism, injustice and trouble than if you have your head cut off three times a day for seven years. So, Daughter, don't be afraid of anything anyone can say to you. You have good cause to rejoice in my goodness and in the sorrows you have suffered, for when you come to your heavenly home every sorrow will turn to joy.'

On the following day I was taken into the chapter house at Beverley Minster. The Archbishop of York was there, along with many great scholars, priests, canons and laymen. 'What, woman, are you here again?' the archbishop asked me. 'I wish that I could get rid of you.' Then the priest made me stand in front of him and with everyone listening the archbishop said, 'Sirs, I've already tried this woman at Cawood. My clerks and I examined her in respect of her faith and found nothing amiss. What is more, sirs, I have spoken since then with trustworthy men who judge her to be a completely sound and virtuous woman. In spite of all this I gave one of my men five shillings to escort her out of my diocese to restore public order. But as they went they were stopped and arrested, my man was put in prison on her account and her gold, her silver, her rosary beads and her ring were taken away. Now she is brought here and put in front of me again. So is there anyone present who has a complaint against her?'

Then some of the men said, 'Here is a friar who has a lot to say against her.' The friar came forward and said that I vilified men of the church, and he also came out with all sorts of evil talk about me. He said that I would have been burned in Lynn had his order, the Preaching Friars, not saved me. 'And, sir, she says she can weep and feel contrition for her sins at will.'

Then the two men who had arrested me came forward. They agreed with the friar that I was cast in the same mould as [the heretic] Cobham and had been sent to carry letters all around the country. They even said that I hadn't been to Jerusalem or the Holy Land, or on any other pilgrimage, though in fact I had. Like many other people before them they denied the truth and maintained what was false. They went on at length until they eventually ran out of words.

The archbishop then said to me, 'Woman, what have you got to say to this?'

I replied, 'With respect, my Lord, they're coming out with nothing but lies.'

Then the archbishop said to the friar, 'Friar, they're not alleging any heresy; what they're saying is slanderous and wrong.'

'My Lord,' said the friar, 'she is well enough versed in her faith. But the Lord of Bedford is angry with her, and means to have her under arrest.'

'Well, friar,' said the archbishop, 'in that case you can take her to him.'

'No, sir,' said the friar, 'it isn't right for a friar to lead a woman about.'

'But I don't want her to get into trouble with the Lord of Bedford,' replied the archbishop. Then he said to his men, 'Look after the friar until I'm ready to see him again,' and he told another man to detain me, too, until it pleased him to see me again on another occasion.

I begged him to use his authority and see that as a married woman I was not put with men, and the archbishop replied, 'No, you won't come to any harm.'

Then the man who was responsible for me took me by the hand and led me home to his house. He treated me very hospitably, and let me eat and drink at his table. Many priests and other people came to the house to see me and speak with me, and many of them were very sorry that I was having such a difficult time.

Before very long, the archbishop sent for me, and I entered the hall where his household were eating. I was taken into his private room and right to his bedside, where I bowed and thanked him for the gracious way in which he had used his authority over me.

'That's all very well,' said the archbishop, 'but I have now heard worse reports of you than any that reached me earlier.'

I replied, 'My Lord, if you wish to examine me I shall speak the truth; and if you find me guilty I shall accept the punishment you impose.'

There then appeared a preaching friar—the archbishop's suffragan—and the archbishop said to him, 'Now, sir, what you said to me in her absence say again in her presence.'

'Are you sure?' asked the suffragan; to which the archbishop replied that he was.

Then the suffragan said to me, 'Woman, you have visited my Lady of Westmorland.'

'When, sir?' I asked.

'At Easter,' said the suffragan.

Not answering his question, I asked him, 'Well, sir, what if I have?'

And he replied, 'My Lady herself was pleased with you and the things you said, but you advised her daughter, my Lady Greystoke, to leave the baron to whom she is married. You've said enough to be burned alive.' And in front of the archbishop he poured out all sorts of cunningly-chosen words, which it wouldn't be right to repeat.

When he had finished I said to the archbishop, 'My Lord, with respect: I've not seen my Lady of Westmorland for at least two years—not since she sent for me before I went to Jerusalem, sir. If you wish, I will go to her again and get written confirmation that I never gave any advice of the sort.'

'No,' said the people who were there, 'put her in prison and we will write to the worshipful lady. If what she's saying turns out to be true you can let her go free without any misgivings.' And I said that I was more than happy for this to be done.

Then a distinguished scholar who was standing by to the archbishop said, 'Put her in prison for forty days, and then she'll love God all the better for the rest of her life.'

The archbishop asked me what the story was that I'd told the Lady of Westmorland when I'd spoken with her, and I replied, 'I told her a good story about a lady who was damned because she wouldn't love her enemies and a bailiff who was saved because he loved his enemies and forgave them for the wrongs they did him, though he was still considered an evil man.'

The archbishop agreed that the story had merit. Then his steward, and a lot of the others who were there demanded that he should release me at once. 'If she ever comes back we'll burn her ourselves.'

The archbishop replied, 'I don't believe there's ever been a woman in England who's got herself into so much trouble.' Then he said to me, 'I can't think what to do with you.'

I replied, 'My Lord, please grant me your letter and seal to show that—thanks be to God—I have acquitted myself and been cleared of all charges laid by my enemies, without any error or heresy having been proved against me. And may John, your man, conduct me to the river again so that I can make my crossing.'

And the archbishop very graciously granted my wish - may our Lord reward him - and he gave me back my purse, my ring and my beads, which the Duke of Bedford's men had previously taken from me. He was very puzzled as to where I got the means to travel round the country, and I said that good people gave me money to pray for them. Then I knelt to receive his blessing and, taking my leave, I walked from his chamber feeling thoroughly happy. As I did so, the archbishop's men asked me to pray for them, but the steward was angry because I was laughing and talking happily, and he said to me, 'Holy people shouldn't laugh.'

I replied, 'Sir, I have every reason to laugh, for the more shame and contempt I suffer the happier I can be in our Lord Jesus Christ.'

Then I came down the steps into the hall, and there stood the preaching friar who had caused me all this heartache. So I left with one of the archbishop's men, and on me I had the letter which the archbishop had granted me. After escorting me to the River Humber, the archbishop's man took his leave of me, returning to his master and carrying off the letter which I have already mentioned. As a result, I was left by myself without having any introduction to the local people. And all the trouble described above occurred on a Friday. May God be thanked for everything!

Chapter 55

As soon as I crossed the River Humber I was arrested as a Lollard and led in the direction of a prison. There happened to be someone there who had seen me being examined in front of the Archbishop of York, and he gave me permission to go where I wished. He spoke to the bailiff on my behalf and testified that I was no Lollard; and so, in the name of Jesus, I managed to get away.

I then met a man from London, who was with his wife. I travelled with them as far as Lincoln, where I had to put up with a lot of scornful and unkind words, which I unhesitatingly refuted in the name of God.

Many people were impressed by my astute and clever replies. There were lawyers who said to me, 'We have studied for many years but we haven't the capability to answer as you do. Who teaches you such quickness of mind?'

And I replied, 'I receive it from the Holy Spirit.'

Then they asked, 'Do you have the Holy Spirit within you?'

'Yes, sirs,' I answered, 'no one can utter a single good word without the gift of the Holy Spirit, for our Lord Jesus Christ said to his disciples, "Don't worry about what you're going to say, for it won't be your spirit that speaks inside you but the spirit of the Holy Ghost."' Thus it was that our Lord—may his name be worshipped—gave me the grace to answer them.

On another occasion, some men employed by a great lord approached me. Using a lot of profane language, they said to me, 'We're given to understand that you can tell us whether or not we'll be saved.'

I said, 'Yes, I certainly can. Because as long as you swear such horrible oaths in wilful disobedience to God's command and choose to carry on in your sin I can say without hesitation that you will be damned. But if you follow the path of contrition and absolution, undertake penance willingly and do your best to give up your sin and avoid it in future, I am just as sure that you will be saved.'

'What, is this the best you can tell us?'

'It seems perfectly good to me,' I replied; whereupon they went away from me.

I then travelled homeward until I arrived at West Lynn. Once I was there I sent into Lynn for my husband, Master Robert my confessor and Master Aleyn a doctor of divinity, and I told them some of the things I'd been through. I also explained that I couldn't come home to Lynn until I had gone to the Archbishop of Canterbury for his letter and his seal: 'Because I didn't have his letter and seal, the Archbishop of York wouldn't take me seriously when we had our meeting. So I promised him that I wouldn't return to Lynn Bishop without them.'

I asked the priests for their blessing, then I said goodbye to them and set off with my husband for London. When I arrived there I soon succeeded in getting my letter from the Archbishop of Canterbury, but I stayed in the city for a long time and was warmly received by many good people.

Later, on my way home to Lynn, I was three miles short of Ely when a man came riding after me and arrested me and my husband too, with the idea of taking us both to prison. He criticized us spitefully and poured contempt on us, using all sorts of cutting words. In the end I asked my husband to show him the letter from my Lord the Archbishop of Canterbury. When the man had read the letter he addressed us in a pleasant, agreeable way, asking why we hadn't shown him the letter before.

With that, we parted from the man and arrived in Ely, and from there we travelled home to Lynn. Once in Lynn I had to put up with a lot of contempt, criticism, scorn and slander, and many people damned me and cursed me. On one occasion a stupid man, with little thought for his own shame, purposely threw a bowl of water over my head as I walked down the street. In no way upset, I thanked God for it—as I did on all sorts of other occasions—and said, 'May God make you into a good man.'

Chapter 56

Afterwards, God punished me with various serious illnesses. I had diarrhoea for such a long time that I was anointed in expectation of death. I was so weak that I couldn't hold a spoon in my hand. Then our Lord Jesus Christ spoke in my soul and said that I would not die yet, after which I recovered for a short while. Next, I got such a terrible pain, first in my head and then in my back, that I thought it was going to drive me mad. And when I had got over all these illnesses another illness quickly followed. This one affected my right side on and off for seven years and ten months. Sometimes I had it once a week, and it might last for thirty hours, twenty, ten, eight, four, or only two. It was so intense and sharp that I couldn't help bringing up the contents of my stomach, which were as bitter as gall. During an attack I was quite unable to eat or drink; all I could do was groan till it went. At those times I used to say to our Lord, 'Ah, blissful Lord, why did you choose to become a man and suffer all that pain for my sins and the sins of everyone who shall be saved when we are so unfilial to you, and I —the worst wretch of all— can't bear this minor discomfort?

'Ah, Lord, out of your mighty pain have mercy on my little pain; do not give me as much of the dreadful pain you suffered as I deserve, for I cannot bear as much as that. But if you wish me to bear that much send me fortitude, Lord, because I cannot bear it otherwise. Ah, blissful Lord, provided it hindered no one's soul I would rather, out of love for you, suffer all the spiteful words that people could say about me—and that all the clergy could preach against me—than endure this pain. It is nothing for me to suffer spiteful words for your sake, Lord. All that the world can take from me is reputation and property, and I set no store by worldly renown. I pray you, Lord, to deny me all kinds of worldly possessions, honours and desires—in other words, all the worldly desires and pleasures which could detract from my love for you or lessen my merit in heaven. And I pray you, of your mercy and for your everlasting glory, to grant me every kind of desire and possession which will increase my love for you.'

Sometimes, despite my physical illness, the passion of our merciful Lord Jesus Christ so possessed my soul that I was temporarily unaware of my own sickness. At the apprehension of our Lord's passion I wept and sobbed as though I could see him suffering his pain and passion in front of my eyes.

When my illness had run its course I ceased to have weekly attacks of pain, as I had done before, but my crying and weeping increased so much that priests didn't dare to give me the sacrament publicly in the church; instead, they gave it to me privately, in the prior's chapel at Lynn, where no one could hear. And in the chapel I was so intensely aware of our Lord and his conversation, having been turned out of church because of my love for him, that when it was time for me to receive the sacrament I cried as if my soul was about to part from my body. Two men had to hold me in their arms until my crying had ceased, because I couldn't bear the abundant love that I found in the precious sacrament, which I firmly believed was very God and very Man in the form of bread.

Then our blessed Lord said to me inwardly, 'Daughter, I don't want the grace that I've given to you to be hidden away. The more people try to impede it and stop it the more will I make it public and known to all the world.'

Chapter 57

It was the monks' custom to change their posts at a certain date, and a different monk duly arrived in Lynn who didn't like me and wouldn't let me enter their chapel as I'd always done before his arrival. Then the Prior of Lynn, Thomas Hevyngham, met with me and Robert Spryngolde, who was then my confessor, and apologized for the fact that I could no longer receive the sacrament in his chapel. 'One of my fellow brothers has just arrived,' he replied, 'and he won't go into the chapel while you're there. So please find somewhere else for yourself.'

Master Robert replied, 'Sir, we must see that she receives the sacrament in St Margaret's church. We've no choice in the matter, because she's got a letter from my Lord the Archbishop of Canterbury— it bears his seal—and it commands us on our obedience to hear her confession and give her the sacrament whenever she requires us to.'

So from then on I was given communion at the high altar of St Margaret's church, but when it was time to receive the blessed sacrament our Lord visited me with so much grace that I could have died with all the crying I did. I cried so loudly that it could be heard in every part of the church, and outside it too, and I couldn't receive the sacrament from the priest's hands. Until my crying was over, the priest had to turn and face the altar again with the precious sacrament; then he finally turned and gave me the sacrament in the normal way. Though this often occurred when the time came for my communion there were also times when I received the precious sacrament weeping softly and quietly, without any violence; it depended on how our Lord chose to visit me with his grace.

One Good Friday, as I watched the priest kneeling in front of the Easter Sepulchre and other townsmen standing there with lighted torches in their hands, following the custom of Holy Church and devoutly enacting the grievous death and shameful burial of our Lord Jesus Christ, my heart was suddenly filled with the thought of the sorrows which our Lady suffered at the sight of his precious body hanging on the cross and then being buried in front of her, and my mind was entirely absorbed in the passion of our Lord Jesus Christ. My inner eye, the eye of my soul, beheld him as palpably as if I was there in person to see his precious body beaten, scourged and crucified. By the grace of God this sight and inner vision stirred my mind so intensely that I was struck with pity and compassion: I sobbed, roared, cried, flung out my arms and yelled aloud, 'I'm dying! I'm dying!' so that many people stared at me, wondering what the trouble was. And the more I tried to prevent myself from crying the louder it was. I just wasn't able to cry or desist from crying at will; it was all in God's hands. Then a priest took me in his arms and carried me into the cloister of the priory to let me get some fresh air; I was in such a state that he didn't think I'd survive otherwise. At that stage I turned all pale and blue, like the colour of lead, and I sweated profusely. And this sort of crying lasted for a span of ten years, as I've already indicated.

And every Good Friday throughout this time I wept and sobbed for five or six hours on end, and as I did so I kept crying out, though it sapped my strength and left me feeling drained and weak. Sometimes on Good Fridays I wept for an hour for people's sins; I was sorrier about their sins than I was about my own because our Lord had forgiven me my own sins before I went to Jerusalem. Even so, I wept copious tears for my own sins when our Lord chose to visit me with his grace. Sometimes I wept for another hour for the souls in purgatory, another for those in trouble, poverty, or any sort of suffering and another for the Jews, the Saracens and all the heretics; I prayed that God of his great goodness would open their eyes so that through his grace they should come to the faith of Holy Church and be heirs of salvation.

Often when I was ready to pray our Lord said to me, 'Daughter, ask what you like and you shall have it.'

I replied, 'I ask absolutely nothing, Lord, except what you can easily give me: the mercy which I ask you to have on people's sins. In the course of a year you often tell me you've forgiven my own sins; so now instead of asking you to have mercy on my sins I ask for your mercy on the sins of others. For Lord, you are pure loving-kindness; it brought you into this wretched world and led you to suffer dreadful pains on account of our sins. Why should I not be concerned for others and want you to forgive their sins? Blessed Lord, it seems to me that you've shown a great deal of goodness towards me, even though I'm an unworthy wretch. You're as good to me as if I were the purest virgin in the world and had never done wrong. Lord, how I wish I had a spring of tears to stop you imposing on man's soul the ultimate punishment of eternal separation from you, for it is hard to accept that any mortal could suffer perpetual separation from your glorious face. And, Lord, may I ask you to give people contrition and tears, just as you give them to me for my sins and those of others. I would fill people's hearts with contrition to make them give up their sins as readily as I would give away a coin from my purse.

'Lord, I marvel at the fact that I who have been a sinful woman—the most unworthy creature who has ever enjoyed your mercy on earth— should feel such concern for the souls of my fellow Christians; because it seems to me that even if they had condemned me to the most shameful death which anyone could possibly suffer on earth I would forgive them out of my love for you, Lord, and see that their souls were saved from everlasting damnation. So, Lord, as long as I can weep I shall carry on shedding abundant tears on their behalf, succeed as I may. And, Lord, if you wish me to cease from weeping I beg you to take me out of this world, for what would I do on earth if I could do no good? Even if it were possible for all this world to be saved by the tears which fall from my eyes I would not deserve thanks, since all praise, all honour, all worship are due to God alone. If you wished it, Lord, I would show my love for you and glorify your name by being cut up as small as meat for the cooking pot.'

Chapter 58

Once, as I was meditating, I craved to hear more of God's word. 'Lord,' I said, 'you have so many scholars in this world, and how I wish you'd send me one of them to fill my soul with your word and with readings from holy scripture. My soul always seems so hungry all the while, and filling it is more than all your clerics can ever do by their preaching. If I had enough money I would give a noble every day in order to hear a daily sermon; your word is worth more to me than all the wealth in the world. So, blessed Lord, take pity on me, because you've taken away the anchorite who was a special comfort and help to me and often refreshed me with your holy word.'

Then our Lord Jesus Christ gave me an answer in my soul: 'Someone who comes from a long way off will help you in the way you want.'

Many days after God gave me this answer a priest who had never known me before came to Lynn for the first time. When he saw me walking in the streets he was very keen to speak with me and he asked other people to tell him about me. They said they trusted to God that I was a really good woman.

Soon afterwards, the priest sent for me to go and talk with him and his mother. (He'd rented a room where he and his mother could live together.) So I went to find out what he wanted. I talked with him and his mother and they both entertained me very well. Then the priest took a book and read from it how our Lord had wept on seeing the city of Jerusalem and had spoken of the troubles and sorrows that would fall upon it, though the people did not know the hour or day when this would occur.

When I heard him read of how our Lord had wept, I wept in great sorrow and cried out loudly, and the priest and his mother had no idea of why I was weeping. And when my crying and weeping were over we were filled with gladness and rejoiced in our Lord.

Once I had said goodbye and left, the priest said to his mother, 'I'm at a loss to make out why this woman weeps and cries so much, but she seems to be a good woman, and I very much want to meet her again.' His mother felt exactly the same and advised him to do so.

In the days that followed, the priest grew to like and trust me a lot, and he blessed the day when he'd first met me, for he found that I gave him great spiritual comfort. I also caused him to study many worthwhile texts and the work of many illustrious scholars, which he would have passed over had it not been for me. He read me many good books of deep devotion and other books too, such as the Bible with scholarly commentaries, St Bridget's book, Hilton's book, Bonaventura's *Stimulus Amoris* [The Spur of Love], the *Incendium Amoris* [The Fire of Love] and others like them.

This showed that the spirit which had answered my complaint about not hearing enough good reading had come from God. The spirit had told me that someone who came from a long way off would help me in the way I wanted, and the spirit had proved to be thoroughly truswothy.

The priest read me books for the best part of seven or eight years, and it greatly increased his wisdom and goodness, but he suffered a great deal of slander because of his friendship with me, and because he read me so many books and defended my practice of weeping and crying. He afterwards gained a benefice and had a great many souls in his care, and he was thoroughly glad that he had previously done such copious reading.

Chapter 59

Listening to all these holy books and listening to sermons steadily deepened my ability in meditation and the contemplation of things divine. It would be impossible to record all the holy thoughts, holy intimations and sublime revelations I received from our Lord. Some concerned myself and other men and women and some concerned the souls of the dead—the saving of some and the damning of others—but this was a torment and a painful lesson for me to bear. It filled my heart with gladness and joy to hear of those who were going to be saved, since I dared to wish that salvation would be for everyone; and when our Lord showed me any who were doomed to damnation I suffered great pain. I didn't want to hear about it; I could hardly believe that God could show me such a thing, and I did my best to put it out of my mind. Our Lord reproached me for doing this; he told me to accept that it was only out of his lofty mercy and goodness that he was showing me his secret decisions and he said to my mind, 'Daughter, you must hear of the damned as well as the saved.' But I wouldn't believe what God was telling me; I preferred to believe it was some evil spirit trying to deceive me.

Because of my presumption and disbelief our Lord deprived me of all my good thoughts, the ability to hear his holy speech and conversation and the contemplation of things sublime to which I had been accustomed before. Instead, he let me have as many evil thoughts as I had previously had good ones. This affliction lasted for twelve days on end; and whereas I had had four hours of holy speech and conversation with our Lord each morning, so now I had as many hours of foul thoughts and evil, lecherous desires, inclining to any and every vice as though my body was public property. And so it was that the Devil deluded me, whispering damnable thoughts to me just as our Lord had previously filled my mind with his holiness. And just as I had previously had many glorious visions and holy thoughts about our Lord's manhood, about our Lady and many other holy saints so now, no matter what I did to try and prevent it, I witnessed vile and appalling sights. Along with other, similar abominations I found myself staring at men's penises.

I truly believed I was seeing priests and all sorts of other men of religion, and laymen too, both heathens and Christians, coming up to me so that I couldn't ignore them or avoid seeing them and showing me their uncovered organs. And while this was happening the Devil spoke within my mind and asked me to choose which man I'd have first, for I had to be their common property. He told me I fancied one of them more than all the others, and I thought it was true; I couldn't withstand him; I had to do what he told me to do. For all this world I wouldn't have done it if I could have helped it, but it seemed to me that I had to comply—that these terrible sights and evil desires were delectable to me in spite of myself. It made no difference where I went or what I did; these evil thoughts continued to haunt me. Whenever I was about to see the sacrament, say my prayers or do any other virtuous deed, this blight was allowed to afflict my mind. I made confession and did all I could to stop it happening but I gained no relief, and the problem brought me near to despair. I cannot express the pain I was in and the sorrow I suffered.

'Lord,' I said, 'you used to say you would never forsake me. What has become of your promise now?'

And straight away his angel came to me. 'Daughter,' he said, 'God has never forsaken you, and will keep his promise never to do so; but you refuse to believe that it's God's spirit who speaks in your soul and tells you his secrets about some people being saved and some being damned. Because of this, God has punished you in this shape and form, and the punishment will last for twelve days until you accept that it is God, not a devil, who is speaking to you.'

Then I said to the angel, 'Oh, I beg you to pray for me to our Lord Jesus Christ. May he mercifully rid me of these cursed thoughts and speak to me as he used to do; and I shall vow to God to accept that the voice I heard before was his, for I cannot bear this dreadful affliction any longer.'

My angel replied, 'Daughter, my Lord Jesus Christ will not remove it from you till you have suffered it for twelve days, for he wants you to learn from it which is better—to hear God's voice or to hear the Devil's. Although he lets you suffer this pain it doesn't mean that he's angry with you.'

And so I had to endure that torment till the twelve days were over, and then my thoughts, inclinations and desires, and the speech and conversation of our Lord Jesus Christ, were as holy as they had ever been, and our Lord said to me, 'Daughter, rest assured that I am not a devil.'

I was overjoyed to hear our Lord speaking as he had done in the past, so I said to him, 'I shall regard every good thought as the speech of God. Lord, may you be blessed for deigning to restore my peace of mind. Lord, I wouldn't for the world go through such torment again as I've suffered for these twelve days; I thought I was in hell and I bless you for the fact that it's over. So, Lord, I will now be at peace and obey you. Say in my heart whatever you think it's best to say.'

Chapter 60

The good priest mentioned above who used to read to me became very ill. I was inwardly moved to care for him on God's behalf. When I found myself short of anything he needed I went round visiting good men and women to get whatever was necessary for him. His illness was so long and serious that people began to despair of his life.

On one occasion I was in church hearing mass and praying for the priest when our Lord told me that he would survive and get completely better. This prompted me to go to St Stephen's church at Norwich where the good vicar who had died only shortly before that time is buried. On the strength of the vicar's merits God had shown his people a great deal of mercy, and I wanted to go there to thank God for the priest's recovery.

I took my leave of my confessor and travelled to Norwich. As I entered St Stephen's churchyard the fire of love burned so ardently in my breast that I cried, I roared, I wept, I fell to the ground; then, getting up, I entered the church in tears and went to the high altar, where I sank to the ground beside the grave of the good vicar. I sobbed noisily, wept and cried out loudly, for my spirit was completely overwhelmed at the thought of our Lord's goodness in performing so many acts of grace for his servant, the man who had been my confessor and had often heard me confess all the details of my life and given me the precious sacrament of the altar. It increased my devotion to know that our Lord was working such special acts of grace for a creature I had been close to during his time on earth.

I had such holy thoughts and such holy feelings that my weeping and crying were indescribable. People were amazed at me, thinking I must be weeping because of some physical or worldly attachment. 'What's wrong with you, woman?' they wanted to know. 'Why are you in such a state? We knew the vicar as well as you did.'

Then priests arrived there who knew how things affected me. They were very kind and took me to an inn where they got me to drink and treated me royally. Also, there was a lady who wanted to invite me for a meal. Out of politeness I attended a service at the lady's church, where I saw a beautiful statue of our Lady called a *pietà*. Gazing at the *pietà* totally filled my mind with the passion of our Lord Jesus Christ and the compassion felt by our Lady, St Mary, and it drove me to cry out loudly and weep in great sorrow as if my heart was about to burst.

The lady's priest came up to me saying, 'Madam, Jesus has been dead for a long time.'

When I'd stopped crying I said to the priest, 'Sir, his death is as fresh to me as if he had died this very day, and it seems to me that it ought to be like that for you and for all Christian people. We should always remember his goodness and think of the pitiful death that he died for us.'

The good lady heard what I said and remarked, 'Sir, this is a good example to me, and to others too, of the acts of grace God performs in her soul.' And so it was that the lady spoke up for me and answered for me. Soon afterwards she had me to her home for a meal and as long as I wanted to stay there she treated me kindly and well.

A little later I returned home to Lynn, and the priest who had read to me for about seven years and for whom I had particularly made my visit to Norwich recovered and was up and about again. May Almighty God be thanked for his goodness!

Chapter 61

There arrived in Lynn a friar who was regarded as a holy man and a good preacher. His reputation and the excellence of his preaching were known far and wide. Good, kind people came and said to me, 'Margery, you'll hear plenty of sermons now that one of the most famous friars in England has arrived in the town to live with the brothers.' I was really pleased, and I thanked God with all my heart at the thought of such a good man living among us.

Soon afterwards, he delivered a sermon in St James's Chapel in Lynn, and a lot of people gathered there to hear what he said. Before the friar entered the pulpit the local parish priest went up to him and said, 'Sir, please don't let it annoy you but there'll be a woman at your sermon who weeps, sobs and cries out when she hears about our Lord's passion or anything else that excites deep devotion. She doesn't carry on for long, sir, so if she makes any noise during your sermon accept it patiently and don't be put off.'

The good friar began to deliver his sermon and what he said was very holy and very devout, and he had so much to say about our Lord's passion that after a while I could no longer bear it. Having stopped myself crying for as long as I could, I shouted out loudly and burst into tears. The good friar put up with it patiently and didn't say anything about it at the time.

Soon afterwards the friar preached another sermon in the same place. I was there again and my soul rejoiced when I saw how eagerly people came running to hear the sermon. I thought to myself, 'Ah, Lord Jesus, if you were here to preach in person I'm sure they'd be more than happy to hear you. Lord, may your holy word dwell in their souls as I hope that it will do in mine; and may as many be saved by his voice as would have been saved by your voice if you had been preaching yourself.' Full of such holy thoughts and feelings I asked God to bless the people there; and the holy sermon and my own meditations caused such a ferment of grace and devotion within my mind that I couldn't stop myself weeping noisily.

The friar declared, 'I want this woman out of the church; she's upsetting everyone.'

'Sir, you'll have to excuse her,' answered friends of mine. 'She can't help it.' However, many people came out against me; they were thoroughly glad of the good friar's opposition to me, and some said I had a devil inside me. They had often said as much before, but now they felt more sure of themselves because they sensed that this friar supported their views. And he wouldn't let me hear his sermons unless I would give up my crying and sobbing.

There was a certain good priest who had read me a lot of worthwhile books and knew why I cried. He spoke to another priest, who had known me for many years, and told him his plan. What he meant to do was to go to the friar and see if he could soften his heart. The other good priest said he would gladly go with him to win the friar round if he possibly could. So they went together and did their best to persuade the good friar to let me attend his sermons unobtrusively, and to bear with me—as other good men had done in the past—if I happened to sob or cry. He answered curtly that if I entered any church where he was preaching and made any of my habitual noise he would denounce me in no uncertain terms; there was no way that he would put up with my yelling.

In response to this, an eminent doctor of divinity and a bachelor of law went to see the friar as the good priests had already done. The doctor of divinity was a white friar—an elderly, serious-minded and well-respected scholar who had known me for many years of my life and believed in the acts of grace that God was performing within me. The bachelor of law was my confessor, and he had a great deal of grounding and experience in interpreting scripture.

When they visited the friar they sent for wine to put him in a good mood and they appealed to him to look with favour on the way the Lord was working in me and be kind enough to put up with it if I happened to cry or sob while he was delivering his sermon. These worthy clerics also told him that what I did was a gift from God. I could only do it when God bestowed the gift upon me, and at such times I had no power to resist it. What was more, God had revealed to me that he could withdraw the gift from me whenever he wished - a fact that the friar had not been aware of.

For all of this, the friar was quite unmoved by what the doctor of divinity and the bachelor of law had to say to him. He set more store by the good opinion of people in general, and he said he wouldn't indulge my crying no matter what anyone said or did, because he couldn't believe that it came from God. In his opinion, if I couldn't resist the attacks they must be due to a heart disease or some other illness, and if I'd only acknowledge this he'd treat me gently and encourage everyone to pray for me. Thus he'd tolerate me and let me cry in moderation provided I put it down to some sort of physical illness. But I knew from God's revelations and from practical experience that it wasn't a matter of any disease and I wouldn't for the world say other than what I believed. As a result, no agreement was reached.

To my great regret, the eminent doctor of divinity and my confessor advised me not to attend the friar's sermons. Then someone else—a leading burgess who became mayor of Lynn a few years later—went to the friar and appealed to him as the clerics had done, but he got the same answer. My confessor then commanded me to stay away when the friar was preaching; if he was preaching in one church I should go to another. I was so upset I didn't know what to do, for hearing a sermon brought me more comfort than anything else on earth, and now I was stopped from doing so; and the converse was that nothing on earth brought me greater pain than not being able to hear a sermon.

I might be all by myself in one church while he was preaching in another, but my cries were as loud and astonishing as they were when I was among the people. I was excluded from his sermons for years because I cried so much when our Lord chose to fill my mind and my sight with his bitter passion. But, as I have already said, I was only excluded from the friar's preaching and not from that of any other clerics. This was the case even though many notable doctors of divinity and other scholars, both religious and lay, preached in Lynn during that period and I often cried loudly and sobbed violently during their sermons. In spite of the noise they accepted it patiently, and some who had previously spoken with me and understood how I lived my life stood up for me when they heard any murmuring or grumbling about me.

Chapter 62

On St James's Day the good friar—who was at that time neither bachelor nor doctor of divinity—preached in the grounds of St James's chapel in Lynn. There were a great many people to listen to him because of his popularity and his reputation for holiness. Some people took such delight in his preaching that if they heard he was going to preach in the surrounding area they would accompany him or follow him from town to town. May God be praised for such holy and devout preaching! However, on St James's Day his preaching was largely aimed against me. He didn't refer to me by name but he expressed himself in such a way that people were left in no doubt as to who he meant. This caused a stir because there were many men and women who trusted me and held me in high esteem. They were very upset and unhappy to hear him speaking against me in the way he did and they wished that they hadn't gone to hear him on that occasion.

When the friar heard the congregation murmuring and grumbling, he was afraid my supporters would pit themselves against him at a future date, so he banged his hand on the pulpit and said, 'If I hear any further talk of these matters I'll speak out so plainly that all her followers will be put to shame.' At that, many of those who pretended to be my friends turned coat; they were needlessly rattled by what he had said, and hardly dared to speak with me.

The priest who afterwards wrote this book was one of the people who turned against me. He made up his mind to stop placing any faith in my insights. However, our Lord soon brought him back again, and he came to regard me more highly and trust my weeping and crying more firmly than he had done before. This came about when he read a book about a woman called Mary of Oignies, her way of life, the wonderful sweetness with which she heard the word of God and the wonderful sorrow she had when she thought about his passion. And he read of the copious tears she wept, which made her so weak and feeble that she couldn't bear to see the cross or hear our Lord's passion recounted—she dissolved into tears of sorrow and pity.

The book's eighteenth chapter, beginning 'Bonus est, domine, sperantibus in te' [Lord, it is good to hope in you], deals especially with the plenteous grace of her tears, and the nineteenth chapter tells of how, at the request of a priest who didn't want her weeping and sobbing to trouble or distract him during mass, she left the church, crying out loudly that she couldn't stop herself from doing it. And during mass, at the reading of the Holy Gospel, our Lord visited the priest with so much grace and devotion that he wept profusely, wetting his vestments and the sacred vessels. His weeping and sobbing were so abundant that he couldn't restrain himself; he could hardly manage to stand at the altar. He hadn't had much regard for the woman, but this experience taught him that she couldn't help weeping, sobbing and crying out, for the grace that filled her was incomparably greater than ever he felt inside himself. He also learned that God bestows his grace where he chooses.

At the prompting of a well-known cleric (a bachelor of divinity) the priest who set my story down looked into the case I have mentioned above in far more depth and detail than is recorded here. (The above is only the gist of it, because by the time the priest set pen to paper he couldn't remember it very well, so he wrote comparatively little about it.) Whereas the friar's preaching had made him abandon me and shun me, the details of Mary's case reconciled him to me and made him take me more seriously.

The priest went on to read, in the second chapter of a treatise called *The Prickynge of Love*, that Bonaventura wrote about himself as follows: 'Ah, Lord, what shall I call and cry out now? You delay your coming; weary and overcome with desire, ruled by love and not by reason, I begin to go mad. I dash wherever you want me to, Lord, in total submission. The sight of me makes people angry and sad, because they don't know that I am drunk with your love. They say, 'Look, that madman is crying in the streets,' but they cannot perceive how much my heart is yearning, Lord.' As well as reading it in chapter two of *The Prickynge of Love* he read the same thing in *Stimulus Amoris*. In *Incendium Amoris* he also read a similar account relating to the hermit Richard of Hampole, and this, too, encouraged him to take me seriously. Elizabeth of Hungary was another who cried out loudly, as her book records.

Beside the priest, there were many others who had abandoned me because of the friar's preaching but a lot of them regretted it and turned to me again, though the friar stuck to his opinion. His sermons always included something aimed against me, irrespective of whether I was present or not, and there were people who believed the worst of me for days on end. Some said there was a devil inside me; they told me to my face that the friar should have driven it out. So it was that I was subject to widespread slander and backbiting—and all because God gave me the gifts of contrition, devotion and compassion which led me to weep and sob and cry out intensely in spite of myself. I had no choice; I would rather have wept quietly in private than out in the open, had it been under my control.

Chapter 63

Some of my friends came and told me it would be easier for me to leave the town than stay there because so many people were opposed to me. I told them that I would stay for as long as God wished me to. 'This town is where I've committed my sins,' I told them, 'so it's the place where I should suffer to make up for them. But as someone who has sinned against God I am not suffering the sorrow and shame I deserve. I thank Almighty God for everything he sends me, and I pray to him that whatever evil anyone in the world says about me may help towards the remission of my sins; and if anyone praises God's works of grace within me, may it be to the glory of God and may it help to praise and magnify his holy name everlastingly. Every honour belongs to him, whereas I have fully deserved to suffer every kind of despite, shame and condemnation.'

On another occasion my confessor came to me in a lady chapel called the Chapel of the Lying In. He said to me, 'Margery, what are you going to do now? Apart from the moon and the seven stars there's no one left to turn against you. There's hardly anyone on your side apart from me.'

I said in reply, 'Sir, rest assured that everything will turn out well in the end. I can tell you for a fact that my Lord Jesus Christ gives me great inner comfort; without it I would be in despair. My blessed Lord Jesus Christ won't let the friar drive me to despair, despite his reputation for holiness. My Lord tells me that he is very displeased with him and that it would have been better if he'd never been born because he despises the things God is doing within me.'

Our Lord also said to me, 'Daughter, if a priest despises you, knowing why you weep and cry, he is accursed.'

I was once in the prior's cloister, having left the church for fear of upsetting the people with my noise, and our Lord said to me, in a tone of great sadness, 'Daughter, I want you to go back into the church. I am going to stop you crying out so that even if you want you won't be able to yell in that particular, noisy way in future.'

Telling my confessor all about it, I did as our Lord commanded, and it was just as I'd been led to expect: I never again cried as loudly as before, nor in the same way, though I still sobbed and wept as feelingly as ever I had done, sometimes aloud and sometimes silently, just as God controlled it himself. Many people thought that I daren't cry out any longer because the good friar had preached against me and was determined not to put up with me. They hailed him as a holy man and regarded me as a dishonest, deceiving hypocrite. And whereas some people had slandered me for crying out, I was now being slandered for not crying out. And so it was that slander and bodily anguish beset me on every side, but everything served to increase my sense of inner peace.

Then our merciful Lord said to me, his unworthy servant, 'Daughter, I must comfort you, for you have now found the proper way to heaven. It is the way to heaven which I and my disciples trod. You will now know all the better the sorrow and shame I suffered out of love for you, and your pity will be all the more intense when you think of my passion.

'Daughter, I have often warned you that the friar would speak evil of you. Now I am warning you not to tell him the secret that I am about to reveal to you, as I do not want him to hear it from you. And I tell you, Daughter: he is destined to suffer severe retribution. His name will be cast in the mud and yours will be as his is now. And I will make as many people love you out of love for me as have hitherto despised you out of love for me. A time will come, my Daughter, when the Church will accept you and shut him out.

'Here in this church you have suffered a great deal of scorn and criticism because of the gifts I have given you and the grace and goodness I have filled you with, but one day people in this church and district will worship me for my presence within you, and agree that I obviously love you dearly. Daughter, I shall do so many gracious things on your behalf that everyone will marvel and wonder at my goodness.'

Then I said to our Lord with great reverence, 'I don't deserve to have you show me so much grace. Lord, it's enough for me if you save my soul from everlasting damnation by your great mercy.'

'Daughter, what I am doing is for my glory, so I want your will to accord with mine. The less regard you have for yourself the better will I esteem you and love you. Daughter, see you don't fret over worldly goods. I have put you to the test of poverty and chastened you as I wanted to do—both within your soul and outwardly through the slander you've suffered. So, Daughter, I have granted you your heart's desire, for you will know no other purgatory than what you are facing here on this earth.

'Daughter, you often say to me in your thoughts that rich men have every reason to love me well. What you say is perfectly true, because it's plain to see that I've given them plenty of wealth with which to serve me and love me. But love me with all your heart, good Daughter, and I shall see that you have sufficient riches to love me with, for heaven and earth would fail before I failed towards you. And you will not fail, even if other people should do so.

'I would never forsake you even if all your friends abandoned you. There was once a time when you made me the steward of your household and the executor of all your good works, and I will be a faithful steward and a faithful executor, carrying out your will and desire in every respect. And I'll provide for you, Daughter, as if you were my own mother and my own wife.'

Chapter 64

I said to my Lord Jesus Christ, 'Ah, blessed Lord, I wish I knew how best to love you and please you—and I wish my love seemed as pleasing to you as yours seems to me.'

Then our sweet Lord Jesus said in reply, 'Daughter, if you knew how pleasing your love is to me you would love me with all your heart unceasingly. Daughter, you can rest assured that your love is even more pleasing to me than mine is to you.

'Daughter, you have no idea how much I love you, for no living soul can conceive such love, or feel it as it is; it would give you such unbearable joy that you'd die, you'd burst. It's because of this that I measure it out to you as I do—it's to give you the greatest ease and comfort. But, Daughter, you will truly know in another world how much I loved you on this earth, and then you will have great reason to thank me. There, before your perpetual sight, will be all the good days you spent in this world—days of contemplation, devotion, and great loving kindness, given to you to the benefit of your fellow Christians. It will be your reward when you come home to heaven.

'Daughter, there is no scholar in all this world who can teach you better than I can do. Serve me as I wish and I shall serve you as you wish. What better sign of love can there be than to weep for your Lord? Daughter, you know full well that the Devil is devoid of love; he is angry with you and may perhaps do something to hurt you, but he won't harm you much—he'll hurt you a little in this world just to frighten you sometimes, and that will make you pray all the more intensely for grace, and cause you to love me all the more.

'No scholar can condemn the life I teach you. If he does he isn't on God's side, he's on the Devil's side. I can tell you for a fact that if any living soul is prepared to suffer as much contempt out of love for me as you have done, clinging to me as firmly and loyally as you, no matter what people do or say to him, I shall treat him with every kindness, and favour him both in this world and the world to come.'

Then I said, 'Ah, beloved Lord, you should teach religious men and priests to live like this.'

Our Lord replied, 'No, my Daughter, no, because they don't love the thing which I love best—humiliation, contempt, scorn and public condemnation. Because of this I shall not bestow this grace upon them. Let me tell you, my Daughter, that anyone who is afraid of suffering worldly shame cannot truly love God. Daughter, the garb of holiness covers a great deal of evil. If, like me, you could see all the wickedness that's done in the world you'd be amazed that I don't take vengeance once and for all, but I refrain from it out of my love for you. You weep so much for mercy each day that I cannot do other than grant it to you, but people still refuse to believe that I give you such goodness on their account. Even so, Daughter, a time will come when they will be more than ready to believe in the grace I have given you for them. I shall say to them, when they have passed from this world, "See: I caused her to weep for your sins and though you held her in great contempt, her loving concern for you never ceased."

'And so it is that the virtuous will thank me greatly for the grace and goodness that I have given you, while the wicked will sneer and grudge the fact that I give you such grace. I shall punish them for it as if their sneering and grudging had been directed at me.'

'No, beloved Lord Jesus,' I implored, 'don't punish any living soul because of me. You know, Lord, that far from wanting vengeance I ask you to show your mercy and grace to everyone if you're willing to grant it; but punish us as you wish, Lord, if it saves us from being parted from you for evermore. My soul knows how full of love you are, Lord, for you say that you don't want sinners to die; you want everyone saved. Lord, since you want the salvation of all it must also be my own desire. You tell me to love my fellow Christians as I love myself. Lord, you know that I have wept and sorrowed for many years for my own salvation. I must do the same for my fellow Christians.'

Chapter 65

Our Lord Jesus Christ said to me, 'Daughter, once you're in heaven with me you will clearly see that no one is damned unless he fully deserves to be damned, and you will find yourself more than satisfied with all that I do. So, Daughter, you should give me great thanks for stirring so much love in your heart. I am Almighty God, and I make you weep each day for your sins because I move you with pity for my bitter passion and my mother's earthly sufferings—the anguish she went through and the tears she wept. And I also make you weep for the holy martyrs in heaven. When you hear about them you cry and weep out of gratitude for the grace I have shown them; and when you see any lepers your compassion makes you thank and praise me for treating you more kindly than them. And you also cry because you feel great pity for everyone, wishing that you could give them the ease, both in body and soul, that you'd like for yourself. What is more, you weep out of pity for the souls in purgatory, fervently wanting an end to their pain so that they can praise me for ever more.

'All that I give you springs from my goodness, and you owe me a great debt of gratitude for it. Even so, I thank you for loving me so much and for having such a keen desire for all men and women to love me dearly. It is right and proper for everyone—both lay and holy—to want to meet their material needs but, as you've seen, they aren't as concerned about loving me as they are about getting worldly goods.

'Daughter, I thank you for the way you long to regain my blessed presence when we are apart, and thank you for trying to stop people breaking my commandments or swearing in my name. If you can't stop them swearing you suffer great pain and your love for me makes you denounce their behaviour. This has brought you many cutting, hostile words—and has earned you many delights in heaven.

'Daughter, I once sent St Paul to you to give you the strength and reassurance to speak boldly in my name from that day onwards. And St Paul told you that you had suffered a great deal of tribulation because of his writing, and he promised you that just as loving him had brought you shame and scorn, it would also bring you the grace to withstand it. He also told you about many of the joys of heaven and about my great love towards you. And, Daughter, I have often told you that if you want to speak with any of the saints in heaven they are ready to bring you comfort and speak to you in my name. My angels are ready to offer me your holy thoughts, your prayers and the tears of your eyes, for your tears are what the angels drink; to them they are spiced and honeyed wine. So, darling Daughter, don't grow tired of sitting all alone on the earth and thinking of me in solitude; I don't tire of you and my merciful eye is always upon you.

'Daughter, you can boldly say to me, "*Ihesus est amor meus*,"—"Jesus is my love." So, Daughter, let me be your consuming love and the joy of your heart. Just think, my Daughter: you've every cause to love me supremely for the gifts I have given you in the past. You also have another important reason to love me, because although your husband is alive and well, you are living in chastity like a widow, just as you want. Daughter, I have drawn the desire of your heart from men's hearts to my heart. There was once a time, my Daughter, when you thought it was all but impossible for this to happen; that was when your heart was afflicted with the dreadful torment of fleshly desires. No wonder you cried to me, "Lord, by all your painful wounds, draw the love of my heart entirely to your heart." Daughter, for all these reasons (and the many blessings and favours I've shown you at home and abroad) you've every cause to love me well.'

Chapter 66

'Daughter, I want you to eat meat again as you used to do. You must bow to my wishes and abandon your own, telling your confessors to let you do as I require. The grace you receive won't be any the less—it will be much more. You'll enjoy the same reward in heaven as if you'd still been fasting as you were inclined to do. Daughter, I did once tell you to give up meat and for many years you've obeyed my advice and gone without it, so now I am telling you to eat it again.'

With deep reverence I said in reply, 'Oh, blessed Lord, the people know that I've been going without meat for all these years. If they see me starting to eat it again they'll be very surprised and I think they'll probably treat me with contempt and scorn.'

Our Lord replied, 'Let them say what they like—ignore their jibes.'

I went at once to my confessors and told them what our Lord had said to me. And as soon as they knew what God required they commanded me on my obedience to eat meat again as I had done many years earlier, though doing so brought me a great deal of scorn and criticism.

For many years, I had kept a vow to fast on one day a week for as long as I lived in honour of our Lady. But our Lady appeared to my inner sight and told me to go and tell my confessor that she wanted me released from my vow so that I would have the strength to endure my spiritual labours; unless I kept up my bodily strength they'd be more than I could bear.

After careful thought, my confessor judged that a relaxation was necessary, so he told me on my obedience to eat as often as everyone else, but in moderation, as and when God wished me to. And far from ebbing away, the grace I enjoyed increased because if only it had been the will of God I would rather have fasted than taken food. What is more, our Lady said to me, 'Daughter, weeping and crying are wearing you out— you're completely exhausted. I'd be pleased if you showed me your love by not fasting, because eating will help you to sustain your special accomplishment, which is the shedding of tears.'

Chapter 67

There was once a huge fire in Lynn Bishop which destroyed the guildhall belonging to the Guild of the Trinity. It was so severe and destructive that it seemed almost certain to consume the magnificent and beautifully adorned parish church—the church of St Margaret— along with all the rest of the town, had it not been for God's miraculous intervention. I was present at the scene and witnessed the danger and harm that was threatening the town, and throughout the day I cried aloud and wept freely, asking God to show his grace and mercy on all the inhabitants.

At other times the townspeople wouldn't put up with my wailing and crying although they showed God's abundant grace within me, but on this occasion they wanted to stave off the physical danger they were in so they let me carry on wailing and crying for all I was worth. No one told me to stop; in fact they asked me to keep it up because they believed that through my wailing and crying our Lord would show them his mercy.

My confessor came to me and asked me whether it would do any good to carry the sacrament towards the fire. 'Yes, sir, yes,' I answered, 'because our Lord Jesus Christ told me that everything would be all right.' So my confessor, who was the parish priest of St Margaret's church, took the precious sacrament and approached the fire with it as devoutly as possible and then returned it to the church—by which time the sparks were flying around the building.

Wanting to follow the precious sacrament to the fire, I had gone out through the church door. But on seeing the hideous flames I had cried out loudly through my tears, 'Good Lord, may everything be all right.' I was struck by these words because our Lord had previously told me that everything would be all right, so I cried again, 'Put everything to rights, good Lord. Mercifully send some rain or other weather that will quench this fire and calm my heart.' Then I went back into the church and saw the sparks coming into the choir through the lantern windows. This renewed my anguish and amid all my tears I cried out again for God's grace and mercy.

Suddenly three leading citizens came up to me. Their clothes were white with snow and they said to me, 'Look at this, Margery—God has shown his mercy on us and sent us a good fall of snow to smother the flames. Cheer up and thank God for what he has done.' At that I let out a great cry and I praised and thanked God for his mercy and goodness. In particular I thanked him for having told me that all would be well at

a time when this seemed extremely unlikely except through a miracle
and special grace. When I saw how good the outcome was I felt that I
had every reason to thank our Lord.

At this point my confessor came up to me. He said he believed God
had saved us from the danger because of my devout prayers; there was
no other way of explaining how a bright clear sky could be filled so
quickly with heavy clouds and huge flakes of snow which had robbed
the fire of its natural power. May our Lord be praised!

In spite of the mercy which God had shown because of me there were
some who, as soon as the danger was over, slandered my crying. Some
of them said to me, 'Our Lady never cried, so why should you cry in such
a way?' I told them I couldn't help it and I hurried off into the cloister
of the priory. Once I was there my mind was filled with the passion and
precious wounds of our Lord Jesus Christ and the price he had paid for
my redemption, and I cried and roared so prodigiously that people could
hear me from a long way away and I couldn't stop myself.

I marvelled at how our Lady could bear or endure the sight of Christ's
precious body being scourged and nailed up on the cross. I remembered
people's comments about how our Lady—Christ's own mother—had
never cried like me, and I said through my tears, 'Lord, I am not your
mother. Rid me of this unbearable pain. Your passion will kill me.'

A distinguished scholar—a doctor of divinity—happened to be
passing and he said, 'I'd give twenty pounds to feel such sorrow for our
Lord's passion.' Once he had reached his lodgings this scholar sent for
me to go and pay him a visit there. I went straight to his room, still in
tears, and this excellent scholar gave me a drink and made me thoroughly welcome. Afterwards, he took me to an altar and asked me what
special gift I had that enabled me to cry and weep so intensely. I told him
a lot about why I wept but I didn't tell him about any of the revelations
I received. He told me that I could do no other than love our Lord, who
had given me so much evidence of his love for me.

Afterwards, there came a parson—a man with a university degree—
to preach in the morning and afternoon. As he preached his sermon in
a very devout and holy way I was moved by religious feeling until I
finally gave a loud cry. The congregation began to complain about my
noise—for this was the time when the friar was preaching against me,
as I have already said, and before the time when our Lord took my crying
away from me (which I've mentioned above though it actually happened after this).

The parson paused in his preaching and said to them, 'Friends, be
quiet. Don't complain about this woman, because if you do you may

be committing a deadly sin and it won't be her fault—you'll be the authors of your own damnation. You may think her way of carrying on is a mixed blessing but it's up to you to give her the benefit of the doubt in your hearts. As for me, I'm sure her crying is thoroughly good. I'd go as far as to call it a gracious gift from God, May his name be praised!' The people thought well of the parson for saying such salutary things, which increased their belief in his piety and holiness.

Afterwards, once the sermon was over, a good friend of mine met the friar who had preached against me so vehemently. My friend asked the friar what he thought about me and the friar gave a sharp reply: 'She's possessed by a devil.'

Chapter 68

Shortly afterwards, the Preaching Friars met in chapter at Lynn. Many of the order's leading members came to the town, and one of them was expected to preach a sermon in the parish church. Among the men who attended the chapter was a renowned doctor of divinity called Master Custawns, who had known me many years earlier. When I heard people say he was coming to town I went to see him and told him why I cried and wept so intensely; I wanted to know whether he thought there was anything wrong with the way I cried and wept. The scholar said to me, 'Margery, I've read about a holy woman who'd received from God the same gift of weeping and crying as you. She lived at a church but the priest did not have time for her tears and he agitated against her until she was forced to leave. Consigned to the churchyard, she prayed that the priest would have some understanding of the grace she felt, for she certainly didn't have the power to cry or weep except when God ordained. And as the priest was saying mass our Lord overcame him with devotion so suddenly that he couldn't control himself. After that, far from despising the woman he gave her encouragement.' Thus it was that the doctor endorsed my crying and weeping; he said that God should be highly praised for giving me such a gracious and distinctive gift.

This doctor then went to another doctor of divinity—the one who had been chosen to preach to everyone in the parish church—and asked him not to be put off but accept it quietly and uncomplainingly if I cried or wept during his sermon.

When the time came for this scholar to preach he was led to the pulpit with great respect. He began to preach devoutly and reverentially on our Lady's Assumption and what he said uplifted my mind with the sweetest devotion, making me yell at the top of my voice and weep profusely. The worthy doctor stood silently and waited very patiently until I had finished, then he carried on to the end of his sermon.

That afternoon he sent for me to go to his lodging. He treated me in a friendly way and I thanked him for the patience and kindness he had shown in putting up with my crying and weeping during his sermon that morning.

The scholar replied, 'Margery, I wouldn't have said a word against you even if you had cried till the evening. If you'd like to come to Norwich I'd make you welcome and entertain you to the best of my ability.' And by the grace of God—may his name be praised!—this worthy scholar took me in hand and supported me against my enemies.

Afterwards, at Lent, a good Augustinian friar preached in his priory at Lynn, and I was among the large congregation that gathered to hear him. God, of his goodness, inspired the friar to preach about his passion with so much feeling and devotion that I couldn't bear it. I fell to the ground weeping and crying so intensely that people there were astonished. They condemned me and cursed me viciously, thinking (in line with what the hostile friar had preached, as I've explained) that I could have desisted if only I'd wanted. And then the good friar who was giving the sermon said to everyone, 'Friends, be quiet. You've practically no idea what she's feeling.' So the people fell silent. The turmoil stopped and they heard the rest of the sermon in peace.

Chapter 69

On a certain Good Friday the Prior of Lynn was due to preach at his church, St Margaret's. He took as his theme, 'Jesus is dead.' I was deeply pierced with pity and compassion and I cried out and wept as if I was seeing our Lord lying dead in front of me. The worthy prior—a doctor of divinity—bore with me quietly and patiently and made no move to have me stopped.

On another occasion the Bishop of Norwich, John Wakering, preached at St Margaret's in Lynn and I cried and wept really loudly during the course of the sermon. Like many other God-fearing clergy, both regular and secular, he accepted it kindly and patiently, the grey friar whom I've mentioned being the only one who ever spoke out against my crying.

So our merciful Lord kept his promise to me: he cared for me at all times and he stirred the spirits of two good scholars who had known my speech and accomplishments for many long years. He gave them the courage and strength to speak up for me on his behalf and they did so both in the pulpit and anywhere else where they heard any stirring against me, and they proved their points by citing scripture. One of these scholars was a white friar, a doctor of divinity, and the other was a bachelor of canon law, who was well versed in scripture.

It came about that some envious people complained to the provincial of the white friars that the doctor of divinity was having too much to do with me in that he encouraged me in my weeping and crying and told me anything I wanted to know about the scriptures. As a result he was ordered on his obedience not to speak with me any more and to stop explaining the scriptures to me. He found this very painful and he told a number of people that he would rather have lost a hundred pounds— if he'd had a hundred pounds to lose—than have lost the chance to speak with me, for my conversation was so uplifting and beneficial.

When my confessor discovered that the worthy doctor was under orders not to speak or communicate with me he guarded against any chance of its happening by charging me on my own obedience not to go to the friars again, not to speak with the doctor and not to ask him any more questions. I was denied a great deal of spiritual comfort and this made me very sad and unhappy. I would rather have relinquished my worldly possessions than his conversation, which had helped to make me a much better person.

Some time later, I happened to meet the doctor of divinity in the street. Neither of us spoke a word, but I let out a cry and burst into tears. Later, when I was meditating, I said in my heart to our Lord Jesus Christ, 'Lord, why should I not have this scholar to help me? He has known me for so many years and has done such a lot to make me love you more. Lord, you have already taken the anchorite from me—the most precious and special comfort I have ever had in the world. I trust his soul to your mercy, Lord. He loved me out of his love for you and while he drew breath he would never have failed me, no matter what anyone said or did. And now Master Aleyn and I are barred from seeing each other. Sir Thomas Andrew and Sir John Amy have benefices which keep them from Lynn, and Master Robert scarcely dares to speak with me. So I now have absolutely no one—neither adult nor child—to comfort me.'

Our merciful Lord Christ Jesus answered me in my mind and said, 'Daughter, I have more to offer your soul than the anchorite or any of those you've mentioned or any living soul in the world. I will comfort you myself—I'd like to speak to you more often than you would let me.

And I promise you, Daughter, that you'll speak to Master Aleyn again as you have in the past.'

And then, through the action of the Prior of Lynn, our Lord put a priest in charge of the lady chapel of St Margaret's church. (It is called the Chapel of Lying In.) This priest often heard my confession in place of my main confessor, and I told him as accurately as I could about my whole life from early childhood onwards. I told him about my sins, my efforts, my troubles, my meditations and the revelations and gifts of grace that God had given me through his mercy. As a result, the priest felt sure that God was bestowing his grace upon me in great abundance.

Chapter 70

God visited the doctor of divinity, Master Aleyn, with such a serious illness that no one who saw him expected him to live. When I was told how ill he was I was very upset, particularly as I had understood by revelation that I would speak with him again as I had done in the past. If he died from the illness my inner sense would be proved incorrect. I rushed into the choir of St Margaret's church, knelt in front of the sacrament and spoke as follows, 'Lord, by all the goodness you've shown and in the certainty of your love I beg you to spare this worthy scholar until I can speak with him as you have promised me that I would do. And, glorious Queen of Mercy, remember what he used to say about you in his sermons. He used to say, Lady, that anyone was blessed indeed who had you as a friend because when you prayed the whole company of heaven prayed with you. So, by your sublime love for your son, let Master Aleyn live until we're free to speak to one another, since at present we are under orders to stay apart.'

In accordance with our Lord's will the worthy scholar recovered shortly afterwards and went about his business again in excellent health. What is more, his provincial gave him permission to speak to me and my confessor gave me permission to speak to him.

It happened that this doctor was going to dine in town with an excellent woman who had taken the mantle and the ring, and he sent for me to go and see him. I was very surprised but I set off and went there.

When I arrived I was too overcome with tears to speak—too grateful to our Lord for vindicating my feeling that we'd be free to talk to each other again. The doctor said to me, 'Margery, it's good to see you after being kept away from you for such a long time. Now our Lord has sent you here so that I can talk to you. Praise be upon him!'

Our meal was a time of great joy and gladness. We enjoyed it far more with our spirits than with our physical senses, since tales from holy scripture provided the sauce and the seasoning. And then he gave me a pair of knives as a sign that he would stand beside me in God's cause, just as he had done in the past.

Chapter 71

One day, a priest came to see me who placed great faith in my inner feelings and revelations. He wanted to test them in various ways and he asked me to pray to our Lord for insight as to whether the Prior of Lynn, who was a good patron to him, would be removed from his office. I was to give him a true report of whatever I felt in the matter. I prayed about it and, on receiving God's answer, I told the priest that his master the prior would be recalled to Norwich and one of his brothers would be sent to Lynn to take his place. This came about, but the man who was sent to Lynn only stayed for a little while before being called home to Norwich again. The previous prior was then sent back to Lynn, and he stayed until he died about four years later. During that time I often fancied that the man who had been recalled to Norwich after staying only briefly in Lynn would return to be Prior of Lynn again. However, I didn't believe it because he'd arrived there once and had been recalled home soon afterwards.

Once, as I was wandering up and down in the white friars' church in Lynn, I detected a scent so wonderfully sweet and heavenly that I felt I could have lived on it without any food or drink for as long as it lasted. And at the same time our Lord said to me, 'Daughter, this sweet smell is a sign to assure you that there will soon be a new prior in Lynn, and it will be the man who was last called home from here.' This was shortly before the old prior died, and when he did so our Lord said to me as I lay in my bed, 'Daughter, reluctant as you are to believe my promptings, you will see the man I told you about taking up his office as Prior of Lynn this very week.' He told me the same thing every day that week until I was forced to believe it, and I was overjoyed to think that my inner feeling had been correct.

This excellent man—an outstanding scholar, a doctor of divinity—duly came to Lynn, but he had only been there a little while when he and some of England's other leading clerics were chosen to go abroad to join the king in France. Then a priest who had held a position under this prior came and begged me to help him: he wanted me to remember the prior next time God ministered his holy speech to my soul, and find out whether he'd actually have to go abroad. I prayed for an answer to his question and I was told that the prior would not be going, though he himself expected to do so. He was fully prepared for the journey and had even said a very sad goodbye to his friends—he was frail and weak and did not expect to come back again. However, the king died before he was due to set out and the prior stayed at home after all. This meant that my feeling had been correct and I hadn't been deceived in the slightest. Also, it was being said that the Bishop of Winchester had died, yet I felt that he was still alive—and that was the case. Besides the examples recorded here, our Lord of his mercy gave me insights into many other things as well, though I did not deserve it by any merits of my own.

Chapter 72

In the course of time my mind and thoughts became so closely joined to God that I could never forget him. I was thinking about him constantly and I saw him in all created things. And the more I grew in love and devotion the more I grew in grief and contrition, in humility, meekness and holy awe. I became more aware of my own shortcomings, and if I saw an animal being punished or beaten severely it would occur to me that for being so unfilial towards God I deserved an even harsher punishment. Then I wailed, wept and sobbed for my sins and out of pity for the animal I could see being punished and beaten.

If I saw a prince, a bishop or any man of rank and degree who commanded respect and deference my mind was at once freshly turned to our Lord. Knowing how much regard a mortal man can enjoy on this earth I imagined the joy, the bliss, the adoration and reverence God must enjoy in heaven among his blessed saints. Above all, when I saw the precious sacrament carried around the town with candles and devotion and the people all kneeling I had a great many holy thoughts and meditations, and I often wailed and roared fit to burst, such was the faith and trust I had in the precious sacrament.

Many people wanted me with them when they were dying. They had not been keen on my weeping and crying during their lives but they wanted me to weep and cry—and pray for them, too—when they were dying, and so I did. When I saw people being anointed I had all sorts of holy thoughts and conceptions, and if they died in my presence I felt I was seeing our Lord or our Lady dying, depending on how God chose to illumine my inner eye. At this, I cried, wept and sobbed amazingly, just as if I had actually witnessed the death of our Lord or the death of our Lady.

It seemed to me that God took many people from this world who would rather have lived. I would much rather come to his breast, but he seemed to have no desire for me. Thoughts like this made me weep and sob all the more intensely.

A wealthy woman once sent for me so we could talk together. In the course of our conversation she showed a tendency to flatter me and praise me. I hated being praised, and crying out loudly and shedding tears of adoration, I immediately offered it up to our Lord, wanting no one to praise me but him. No worship or praise, love or affection, shame or despite could draw my love away from God. I lived according to the words of St Paul: 'To them that love God all things turn to goodness.' Whatever I saw or heard, my love and inner feeling for God always increased. May his name be praised, who gave me so much grace for the sake of so many people.

On another occasion another wealthy lady sent for me. She had a large household and enjoyed great respect and adulation. When I saw her with all her retinue round her, waiting on her hand and foot, I burst into tears and wept my heart out. A priest heard me wailing and crying, and being a man with little taste for spiritual things, he condemned me on the spot and said to me, 'What devil is plaguing you? Why are you crying in such a way? May God make you sorry!' I sat there and didn't say anything. Then the lady took me aside into a garden and asked me to tell her why I cried so bitterly. Thinking that it was the best thing to do, I gave her some idea of the reason, though it made her annoyed with her priest for having criticized me in such a way. She took a great liking to me and asked me to stay with her longer, but I excused myself and said that I couldn't agree with the extravagant dress and bad behaviour I saw among her followers.

Chapter 73

I was once in the Holy Thursday procession when my soul perceived our Lady, St Mary Magdalene and the twelve apostles. And I saw with the eye of inner perception how our Lady took her leave of her blessed son, Jesus Christ, and how he kissed her and all his apostles and also the woman who truly loved him, Mary Magdalene. It struck me as both a sorrowful parting and a joyful parting. And when I saw this sight in my soul I collapsed in the field with the people all round me. I yelled, I roared and I wept as if I was going to burst. I couldn't curb or control myself, and many people were astonished at the way I was crying and roaring. However, my mind was preoccupied with our Lord and I took no notice of what they might be saying or doing.

I experienced many holy thoughts at that time but I couldn't describe them afterwards. All earthly things had fled from my mind, which was fixed entirely on things of the spirit. I thought that all my joy had departed, for I saw my Lord ascend into heaven and I couldn't bear to live without him. I wanted to go with him, since all my joy and bliss were centred on him; I knew that I would never again have joy or bliss until I had entered into his presence. I was weeping because of these holy thoughts and holy desires, but the people did not know what was wrong.

On another occasion I was with our Lady, who seemed to be dying. All the apostles were kneeling in front of her and asking her to give them her blessing. This made me cry and weep intensely, and the apostles asked me to stop and be quiet. I said in reply, 'Do you want me to see God's mother dying and not shed tears? It isn't possible—I'm so full of grief I cannot help myself. What else can I do but weep and cry?'

And then I spoke inwardly to our Lady: 'Ah, blessed Lady, pray to your son and ask him to let me come to you now, without being kept from you any longer. Lady, it is altogether too painful for me to witness your son's death and yours as well and not be with you, just living alone without a companion or comforter.'

Then our gracious Lady answered my soul, promising to pray for me to her son. 'Daughter,' she said, 'all these sorrows you've had over me and my blessed son will become your everlasting joy and bliss in heaven. My Daughter, you can be sure that it will be more than good when you come to us, and that when you come you'll be warmly received. You must wait until the time is right; you cannot come yet. And, Daughter, you'll certainly find I'm a true mother to you, giving you the help and support a daughter deserves from her mother and obtaining grace and virtue for you.

'The plenary remission you received [in Jerusalem], which was confirmed [in Ramleh] on St Nicholas' Day, is granted not only to you but to all who believe (from now until the end of the world) that God loves you, and give him thanks for your life. If they turn from their sins, fully intending never to slip back into them and ready to undertake penance with a sad and regretful heart, they shall have the same pardon that was granted to you at Jerusalem and Ramleh.' (I have already mentioned this pardon earlier.)

Chapter 74

One day I was hearing mass and wondering when I would finally die. I was sighing and grieving because I seemed to be waiting so long, and I said, 'Oh, Lord, how long shall I go on weeping and mourning for your love and because I yearn so much to have you near me?'

Our Lord answered within my soul and said, 'For a whole fifteen years.'

Then I replied, 'Lord, that will seem like thousands of years.'

Our Lord answered me, 'Daughter, think of my blessed mother, who remained on earth for twenty-five years after my death. You should also think of John the Evangelist and Mary Magdalene, who loved me so much.'

'Ah, blessed Lord,' I answered, 'I wish I deserved to be assured of your love as much as Mary Magdalene did.'

Our Lord replied, 'Daughter, I truly love you as much as I loved her, and the same peace that I gave to her I give to you. For, Daughter, none of the saints in heaven is displeased if I love a creature on earth as much as I love them. They want nothing but what I want myself.'

In ways like this our merciful Lord Christ Jesus drew me to his bosom and made me contemplate his passion. As a result, I couldn't bear to see a leper or other sick person, especially if there were open sores to be seen on their body. It made me cry and weep as if I was seeing our Lord Jesus Christ and his bleeding wounds—which is what my inner eye perceived, since my mind was transported to our Lord Jesus Christ when I saw a sick man. I then suffered dreadful sorrow and grief because I couldn't express my love for Jesus by kissing the lepers when I saw them or met them in the street.

I now began to love what I had previously hated most intensely. During my years of worldly prosperity nothing had seemed more loathsome or abominable to me than the sight of a leper, but now, through our Lord's mercy, I wanted to hug them and kiss them for the love of Jesus at any suitable time or place.

I told my confessor how keen I was to kiss lepers, and he warned me that I should not kiss any men; if I had to kiss anyone I should just kiss women. I was pleased to think I could kiss sick women, so I went to a place where they lived—women who were riddled with disease—and I fell on my knees in front of them, begging them to let me kiss their mouths for the love of Jesus. I kissed two of the women, and I had many holy thoughts in my mind and I shed many tears of devotion. After kissing them I told them things that were good for their souls and urged them to be patient and long-suffering so that they would not resent their sickness. Rather, they should thank God for it so that they would have great joy in heaven through the mercy of our Lord Jesus Christ.

One of the women was tempted to commit so many sins that she did not know what to do for the best. Her unseen enemy was tormenting her so severely that she did not dare to bless herself or offer any worship to God for fear that the Devil would kill her. She was beset with foul and dreadful thoughts - more than she could ever describe - despite the fact that she claimed to be a virgin. I paid her a lot of visits to try and comfort her, and I prayed for her. I especially prayed that God would give her the strength to withstand her enemy, and we have to believe and trust that he did so. May his name be blessed!

Chapter 75

Once, when I was making my devotions in St Magaret's church, a man came and knelt behind me, wringing his hands and showing signs of great distress. Noticing the state he was in, I asked him what the trouble was. He said he was having a difficult time because his wife had just given birth to a child and had become insane. 'Madam,' he said, 'she doesn't know me or any of her neighbours. Her roaring and yelling terrify people, and because she's liable to lash out and bite, her wrists have been put in manacles.'

I asked the man if he'd like me to go with him and see his wife, and he answered, 'Yes, madam, for the love of God,' so we left the church and set off to see this unfortunate woman who'd lost her mind.

When we got to the house the woman immediately spoke to me in a serious and pleasant way and said that I was thoroughly welcome. She was pleased I'd come and my presence was quite a comfort to her. 'You're a really good woman,' she told me, 'and I can see throngs of beautiful angels around you. Please don't leave me—having you here is such a big help to me.'

When other people went to see her she cried out and showed her teeth as if she was going to eat them. She said she could see lots of devils all round them and she wasn't prepared to let them touch her.

Night and day, she roared and yelled nearly all the time. People couldn't stand the noise and they wouldn't have her living near them. As a result, she was consigned to the farthest-flung part of the town and put in a room where no one could hear her yells. She was bound hand and foot with iron chains to stop her hitting anyone. But I went to see her at least once or twice a day, and while I was with her she was perfectly calm and happily heard what I had to say without roaring or yelling.

I prayed for this woman every day, asking God to restore her sanity if that was his will, and our Lord replied to my soul that she would be perfectly well. This made me all the more ready to pray for her recovery than I had been before. I continued to pray for her every day, with tears and sorrow, till God gave her back her wits and her intelligence. She was then brought to church and purified, like other newly-delivered women. May God be praised!

Those who knew of it thought that it was a mighty miracle. The man who wrote this book considered that he'd never before seen a man or a woman as totally deranged as this woman had been, or as hard to control or keep in order, who afterwards so completely regained her composure and judgment. May God who is always ready to help us in time of need be worshipped and praised everlastingly for his mercy and goodness.

Chapter 76

My husband was getting on in years—he was over sixty—and as he was coming down from his bedroom with nothing on his feet and legs he slipped or missed his footing and fell from the ladder onto the ground. He landed on his head, and it was so badly cut and bruised that for several days he had to have five linen plugs in it while it healed.

By the grace of God, some of his neighbours knew straight away that he'd fallen from the ladder, perhaps through hearing the noise and clatter. They came and found him lying in a heap only half alive. He was covered in blood and it seemed unlikely that he'd have the chance to talk to a priest or a cleric except through a miracle or some special grace.

His neighbours sent for me, his wife, and I came at once. We helped him up and we had some stitches put in his head, but he was laid up for such a long time afterwards that some people thought he was sure to die. They said that if he did die I would deserve to hang for neglecting him up to the time of his fall.

We didn't live or sleep together because, as I have already explained, we had taken a vow of chastity—something we'd both done freely and by our common consent. After taking our vows we had lived apart as a way of avoiding all temptation, and to prevent people suspecting us of any lapses. We had carried on living together at first, but people had slandered us and said that we were still gratifying our lust and desires without regard for the vows we had taken. When we went on pilgrimages or to meet and consult with other spiritually-minded people there were those who shamefully failed in their duty to fear and love our Lord Jesus Christ and accused us of going off to woods, thickets or secluded hollows where we could put our bodily lusts into practice without anyone seeing or knowing about it. We realized how ready people were to think evil of us and as far as possible we wanted to avoid creating suspicion, so we gladly agreed to live apart, eating in different places and having separate accommodation. This was why I was not living with him, coupled with the fact that I did not want anything to stand in the way of my meditation.

As I have already indicated, it was being said that if my husband died because of his fall and serious injury I deserved to be held responsible for it. I therefore asked our Lord to let my husband survive for a year and to spare me from slander, if it was his will.

Our Lord said to my mind, 'Daughter, I shall grant your request and let him live. I have already worked a great miracle for you by sparing his life. Now I am asking you to take him home and care for him out of love for me.'

I answered, 'No, good Lord, because in that case I shall not be able to devote myself entirely to you as I do at the moment.'

'Daughter,' said our Lord, 'your reward for taking care of him and helping him in his time of need will be as great as if you were saying your prayers in church. You have often said how much you would like to look after me, so show how you love me by caring for him. In the past he has done as both of us wanted—he has released your body to me so that you could serve me and live in chastity and cleanliness. Now, in turn, I release you so that in my name you can help him in his time of need.'

'Ah, Lord,' I said, 'be merciful to me and give me the grace to obey your wishes and carry them out. May my unseen enemy never be able to stop me doing what you want.' I then took my husband into my home and nursed him for the rest of his life. It was very hard work because towards the end he became like a little child again. His mind had gone and he never seemed to relieve himself in the proper place. Wherever he was—by the fire, at the table, it made no difference—he soiled his linen like a child. Because of this I had much more work than I would normally have had, what with washing things and wringing them out, and much more expense in maintaining fires. So badly did these things interfere with my meditations that I could easily have resented all my labours, but I remembered how in my younger days my mind had been filled with voluptuous thoughts, sexual lust and overwhelming desire for his body. I was glad for this to be redressed in the shape of that same body, so I took it much better than I would have done and I served him and helped him as I imagined I would have served Christ himself.

Chapter 77

Soon after my amazing cries began, I was communing with my sovereign Lord Christ Jesus and I said to him, 'Lord, why do you make me cry out so that people marvel at me? They say that my soul is in great danger for provoking so many people to sin against me, and you know, Lord, that I would never give anyone cause or occasion to sin if I could help it. Lord, rather than inciting anyone into wilful wrongdoing I'd prefer to be sentenced to spend my life in a dungeon twenty yards under the ground, where I'd cry and weep for my own sins, the sins of others and above all, out of love for you.

'Lord, the world won't let me do as you want or obey your promptings, so if it's your will please stop me crying out during sermons when your holy word is being preached; instead, let me do my crying when I'm all by myself so that I'm not turned out and prevented from hearing the preaching and reading of your holy word. Being made to miss it is the greatest pain I could suffer in the world—the worst torment of being in prison. Good Lord, if, in spite of everything, you want me to carry on crying out, please have me do it as much as you like when I'm alone in my room but consider sparing me from doing it in public.'

Our merciful Lord Christ Jesus answered me in my mind and said, 'Daughter, don't pray for that. Even if my mother and all the saints in heaven pray for you, this wish of yours is something which I will not grant. Instead, I shall make you obedient so that you cry when and where I want you to, sometimes loudly and sometimes quietly. I have already told you that you are mine and I am yours and so shall we be eternally.

'Daughter, you see how the planets obey my will, and you know I sometimes send thunderclaps that terrify people, flashes of lightning that set fire to churches and houses, and sometimes gales that blow down steeples and houses and uproot trees and do serious damage far and wide.

'Just as you cannot see the wind but can easily feel it so it is, my Daughter, with the power of my Godhead: no human eye can see it but it can be clearly felt in a humble soul where I choose to perform my acts of grace, as I do in yours. I enter your soul as suddenly as a flash of lightning and set it ablaze with love. I sustain the fire of love until it rids it completely of all worldly filth.

'Sometimes, Daughter, I send earthquakes to frighten people and put them in awe of me. And, Daughter, I have done the same thing in your soul and other chosen souls who I mean to save, for I overturn the firm ground of your hearts and frighten you so that you're terrified I shall avenge myself on you because of your sins. When you first turned towards me, Daughter, you were afraid in this way, as all young novices need to be. But now, Daughter, you have every reason to love me well; the perfect love that I give you dispels all fear from your heart.

'Other people have little regard for you but I prize you all the more highly. And just as you know when the sun is shining on you, so you can tell that the love of God is always upon you.

'Daughter, you know that I sometimes send heavy rain and sudden downpours, while at other times my raindrops fall on you gently and lightly. And when I choose to speak to your soul I treat you in just the same way, my Daughter. Sometimes I make you weep and cry gently as a mark of my love. At other times I make you cry out and roar so that the grace I give you frightens people. This is also a mark of my love, because I want to make them aware through you of the sorrows my mother suffered for me, and thus increase their compassion towards her.

'As a third mark of my love I give you this assurance: whoever grieves as much for my passion as you have done on many occasions, and gives up their sins, will have everlasting bliss in heaven.

'The fourth mark of my love is this: anyone on earth, no matter how dreadful a sinner he is, need never despair if he takes your life as his example and follows it as best he can.

'Daughter, as the fifth mark of my love I want you to know in your heart that the dreadful pain you feel inside you when you cry so sorely out of love for me will ensure that you suffer no pain when you have left this life and also that you will suffer less at the time of your death. This is because you have so much compassion on my mortal flesh that I must surely have the same compassion on yours. So let people say what they want about your crying, Daughter—you are not in any way to blame for their sin. Daughter, the people sinned against me and yet I did not cause their sins.'

Then I replied, 'Lord, blessed may you be, for it seems to me that you yourself do everything that you ask of me. In holy scripture you tell me to love my enemies, Lord, and I'm sure I've never in my life had such an unpleasant enemy as I've been to you. Lord, even if I could show you my love by dying a hundred deaths a day I could never repay the goodness that you have shown to me.'

Our Lord replied, 'Daughter, I ask you to give me nothing but love.

You can never please me better than to give me your love; no penance that you could do on this earth could please me as much as to have your love. Daughter, think about me as much as you can. Do not forget me when you sit at your table; always remember that I reside in your heart and know every good and evil thought you have within you. I know your slightest whim and I know each time you blink your eye.'

I replied to our Lord, 'Truly, Lord, I wish I could love you as much as you would like me to love you. If only I could love you as much as all the saints in heaven and all the creatures on earth! Lord, out of love for you I'd let myself be put naked on a hurdle so that everyone stared at me (provided it didn't endanger their souls) and pelted me with mud and slime, and I'd have myself drawn from town to town every day of my life if you were pleased and no one's soul suffered any harm. But your will must be done, not mine.'

Chapter 78

Each year, when I was in the Palm Sunday procession in the churchyard with the other people, I watched the priests performing the ceremonies and I saw how they and everyone else knelt down in front of the sacrament. And it seemed to my inner vision as if, at that very moment, I was seeing our Lord in his human form being hailed by the people of Jerusalem, just as he had been during his lifetime here on earth. The sweetness and devotion I felt were more than I could bear, and I wept, sobbed and cried aloud. I had all sorts of holy thoughts about our Lord's passion and I saw him with my inner eye as clearly as if he'd been standing in front of me. I couldn't help my weeping and sobbing. I just had to weep and cry out and sob when I saw my saviour suffering so much pain because of his love for me. All I could do was pray that every living soul would worship and adore our Lord both then and forever, and that they would be worthy to hear, understand and humbly obey God's holy words and carry them out to the best of their ability.

In Lynn someone usually preached a sermon on Palm Sunday. In the course of his sermon, the learned preacher would generally quote the following words from the pulpit: 'Our Lord Jesus is pining for love.' When people spoke of the perfect love of our Lord Jesus Christ for humankind, when I heard of how dearly he redeemed us by his bitter passion, shedding his lifeblood and suffering such a shameful death for our salvation, these words affected my mind so much that I couldn't contain the fire of love within my breast. Whether I liked it or not, what had been pent up inside me insisted on coming out into the open. And so it was that I cried aloud, and wept and sobbed in anguish as though I was going to burst, such was the pity and compassion I felt at our Lord's passion. Sometimes I cried so loudly and noisily that the exertion made me break out in sweat, and many people were shocked and condemned me out of hand, thinking that I was putting it on. But our Lord was quick to reassure me: 'Daughter,' he said, 'I'm very pleased, because the more shame and condemnation you suffer out of your love for me the more joy you'll have when you're with me in heaven, and that is exactly how it should be.'

Sometimes my ears were filled with sounds and melodies that made me think of the joys of heaven, and I grieved in my heart as I yearned and longed to go there myself. And our Lord Jesus Christ often said to me, 'Daughter, there are many people alive today who will be dead within a year from now,' and he told me in advance what disease would strike them. I saw things happen as I was expecting, which greatly strengthened my love for God. Our Lord also used to say to me, 'Daughter, there are those who, during their lives on earth, refuse to believe in my goodness and grace towards you, but I shall make sure they know the truth when they have departed from this mortal world.

'Daughter, your love is so intense that you want everyone to be saved, and so do I. There are people who say as much themselves, but it's obvious that they won't be saved. They're sometimes prepared to hear God's word but they're not always willing to do as it says; they neither grieve for their sins nor let anyone else do the grieving for them. Even so, my Daughter, I have ordained you to be a mirror among them, sorrowing so that they can follow your example and have some contrition in their hearts and gain salvation. They have no interest in contrition or sorrow, but do your duty and pray for them while you are in this world; in heaven your reward and payment will be as great as if your goodness and prayers had brought salvation to everyone.

'Daughter, I have often told you that your prayers will save many thousands of souls. Some who lie on the point of death will receive grace through your merits and your prayers, because your tears and your prayers are thoroughly sweet and pleasing to me.'

Then I gave our Lord Jesus Christ my unspoken answer: 'Oh, Jesus, may you be blessed forever. I have every reason to thank you and love you with all my heart, since it seems to me that you pour out your love for the profit and welfare of people's souls. Oh, Lord, I believe that anyone who is parted from you eternally must be thoroughly wicked, neither wishing for good nor doing good nor desiring good. So I thank you, Lord, for all the goodness you've shown to me, a thoroughly unworthy wretch.'

On Palm Sundays, the priest used to use the shaft of the cross to strike the church door and have it opened, and he then bore the sacrament into the church with all the people following. On these occasions I remembered how our Lord had rebuked the Devil and opened the gates of hell, confounding him and all his host. I also thought of all the grace and goodness he had shown to those souls, freeing them from perpetual prison, the Devil and all his host notwithstanding.

I had many holy thoughts and holy desires which I could never tell or recount, nor could my tongue ever express the overflowing grace that I felt. May our Lord be blessed for all his gifts!

As the procession entered the church I could see the priests kneeling in front of the cross: and, as they chanted, the priest who was conducting the service on that particular day raised the cloth that covered it. He did it three times, raising it higher on each occasion, so that in the end the cross was in full view. At this, my mind was completely distracted from the things of this world and focused entirely on things of the spirit, and I begged and prayed that eventually, in heaven, I'd be able to see the one who is both God and man in a single Person. And throughout the whole of the mass that followed I wept and sobbed profusely, letting out some passionate cries, for I thought that with the eye of faith I could see our Lord Christ Jesus in my soul as clearly as I had previously seen the crucifix with my natural sight.

Chapter 79

Then, with my inner vision, I saw our blessed Lord Christ Jesus on the road to Calvary; and before he proceeded he knelt to receive his mother's blessing. His mother said to him, 'Oh, my dear son, how can I bear such sorrow? You're the only joy I have in the world.' And she fainted and collapsed in front of him.

'Dear Lord,' I said, 'if you still mean to die let me die first. Don't make me go through this day of sorrow, because I wouldn't be able to bear the grief your death would cause me. Son, to save you from dying I would like to die on your behalf, so long as the soul of humankind would still be saved. Dear son, if you don't have pity on yourself have pity on your mother; you know for a fact that apart from you there is no one in all this world who can comfort me.'

Then our Lord raised his mother in his arms and kissed her tenderly and said to her, 'Oh, blessed mother, take heart and be at peace with yourself. I've often told you that unless I die no one will be saved or enjoy the bliss of heaven. Mother, this is what my Father wants and I beg you to make it your own desire too; my death will bring me great honour, and it will bring great joy and benefit to you and to all who trust in my passion and live accordingly.

'Blessed mother, you must stay in this world when I am gone because Holy Church will place its faith entirely in you and its faith will grow by the strength of yours.

'Beloved mother, please stop grieving. You won't be left without help or comfort; my cousin John will remain in this world to sustain you on my behalf, and I shall also send my holy angels to support you during your life on earth. And I shall come in person to reassure you in your soul; for remember, mother, I've promised you the bliss of heaven—it's yours by right.

'Beloved mother, what more could you ask than to be queen in the place where I am king, and for all the angels and saints to obey you? Whatever favour you ask of me I shall grant your wish. I shall give you dominion over the powers of darkness so that they shall be afraid of you, though you will not be afraid of them. And, blessed mother, I have already promised to come for you myself when you pass from this world. All my heavenly host of angels and saints will be with me and I shall conduct you to the Father with every kind of music, melody and joy. And there I shall set you in peace and repose for ever more, and you will be crowned as the Queen of Heaven, the Sovereign Lady of All this World and the Empress of Hell.

'So, darling mother, I beg you to give me your blessing and let me go and do my Father's will, for that is why I entered this world, taking flesh of your flesh and blood of your blood.'

When I saw this glorious sight in my soul—how he and his mother blessed each other, how his holy mother was too overcome to speak any more but fell to the ground, how he went on his way with his blessed mother lying there as if she was dead—then it seemed to me that I grasped our Lord Jesus Christ by the clothes and fell at his feet. I implored him to bless me, cried out loudly and wept in anguish, and my soul cried out to him, 'Oh, Lord, what will become of me? I would rather you killed me than let me stay in the world without you. How can I stay here without you?'

Then our Lord answered me, 'Be at peace, my Daughter. Stay here with my mother and repose yourself in her, for she must endure this suffering too. But, Daughter, I shall return to comfort both of you and turn all your sorrow into joy.' And it seemed to me that our Lord then departed on his way, and I went to our Lady and said, 'Oh, blessed Lady, get up and let's follow your blessed son for as long as he stays in sight; I want to see him as much as I can before he dies. Dear Lady, how can your heart endure the sight of your blessed son having all this torment? Lady, I cannot bear it myself although I'm not his mother.'

Our Lady replied, 'Daughter, you've heard for yourself that it can't be changed. I have to accept it out of love for my son.'

Then it seemed to me that we set out to follow our Lord; we saw how he prayed to his Father on the Mount of Olives, heard the gracious answer his Father gave him and the gracious answer he gave in return. After this our Lord went and told his disciples to rouse themselves because his enemies were near. A crowd of people arrived with torches, and also a lot of men armed with staves and swords and poleaxes. They were looking for our Lord Jesus Christ, and when he asked them, as meekly as a lamb, 'Who are you seeking?' they answered savagely, 'Jesus of Nazareth.'

Our Lord replied, 'Ego sum [I am he].'

At this, I saw the Jews fall to the ground—they were so afraid that they couldn't stand upright. However, they were soon on their feet again, searching as they had done before.

Our Lord asked, 'Who are you looking for?' and again they answered, 'Jesus of Nazareth.'

'I am Jesus of Nazareth.' our Lord replied.

Judas then came up to Jesus and gave him a kiss, and the Jews grabbed him roughly. Our Lady and I suffered intense sorrow and pain when we saw the lamb of innocence being contemptuously handled and pulled around by his own people—the ones to whom he'd been specially sent. And just at that moment my inner eye perceived how the Jews put a blindfold over our Lord's eyes and beat him and struck him about the head and punched his sweet face amid spiteful yells of 'Now tell us who hit you.' They didn't hesitate to spit in his face as disgustingly as possible, and our Lady and I (for at the time I was her unworthy servant) wept and sighed in deep sorrow at the foul and poisonous way the Jews were treating our blessed Lord. They had no compunction about pulling his blessed ears and tugging out the hairs of his beard. After that I saw them pulling his clothes off and driving him ahead of them, completely naked, like the worst wrongdoer in the world.

As naked as the day he was born, Jesus meekly let them drive him as far as a pillar of stone, never protesting but letting them do and say whatever they wanted. They tied him to the pillar as tightly as they could and beat his lovely white body with rods, whips and scourges, and I inwardly sensed the anguish of our Lady's tears. I couldn't help weeping and crying too, when I saw such visions in my soul. They were as vivid and real as if everything was happening there and then in front of me, and it seemed to me that our Lady and I had always been together to witness our Lord's suffering.

For years on end I had such visions every Palm Sunday and every Good Friday and also at many other times, though they made me cry and weep intensely and brought me a lot of contempt and criticism in all sorts of places. But my Lord said to me inwardly, 'Daughter, out of love for you I suffered all these torments and pains and others besides— more than anyone on earth can tell. You have every reason to love me dearly, my Daughter, since I've bought your love at such a high price.'

Chapter 80

On another occasion when I was meditating in church I had a vision of our Lord Jesus Christ with his body bound to a pillar and his hands bound to it above his head. There were sixteen men with sixteen scourges, each of which had eight balls of lead at the ends of its thongs, all bristling with barbs like the rowels of spurs. The men with the scourges agreed that each of them should give our saviour forty strokes. At this piteous sight I wept and cried out as if I was going to burst with all my sorrow and pain.

When our Lord had been thoroughly beaten and scourged the Jews untied him from the pillar and gave him his cross to carry on his shoulders. It seemed to me that our Lady and I went another way so as to meet him later, and when we did so we saw that the heavy cross was giving him a lot of pain. It was so big and heavy that he could hardly carry it, and our Lady said to him, 'Ah, my sweet son, let me help with that heavy cross.' But she was so weak that all she could do was faint and fall to the ground, where she lay as still as death. Then I saw our Lord stoop down by his mother and do his best to comfort her with soothing words. When I heard what he was saying and saw their sympathy for one another I wept and sobbed and cried aloud. I felt as though I would die of compassion and pity at seeing such a poignant sight and having all the holy thoughts it brought to my mind, which were so exquisite that afterwards I could never convey how they had felt at the time.

Afterwards, by the mercy of our Lord Jesus Christ my vision took me to the place where our Lord Jesus Christ would be nailed to the cross.

And I saw the Jews violently snatch a silken cloth from our Lord's precious body. Sadly, the cloth was so firmly stuck and congealed to his body with his precious blood that it tore the skin from his blessed flesh and reopened his precious wounds and made the blood stream down all over him. Then his precious body looked to me as raw as an animal freshly flayed—a most pitiful and sorrowful sight for my eyes. This was a new cause of sorrow and it made me weep and wail intensely.

Next, I saw how the cruel Jews, putting his precious back to the cross, took a nail—it was long and rough and spiteful-looking—and held it to his hand and drove it right through in a very violent, cruel way. As we watched, his blessed mother and I saw his precious body crumple and contort as all his sinews and veins responded to his pain and agony, and we grieved and mourned and sighed for him with all our hearts.

Then, with the eye of inner vision, I saw how the Jews tied ropes to Jesus's other hand, for his sinews and veins had shrunk so much with anguish that the back of his hand wouldn't reach the nail-hole they'd marked on the cross. They pulled on the ropes to make it reach, and my pain and my sorrow increased all the while. They hauled on his feet in the same way, and it seemed to me that within my soul I heard our Lady say to the Jews, 'Oh cruel Jews! Why are you treating my son like this when he never did you any harm? You're breaking my heart!'

It seemed to me that the Jews answered back in a surly way and pushed our Lady away from her son.

Then I saw myself shouting at the Jews and saying, 'You evil Jews, why are you killing my Lord Jesus Christ? Kill me instead and let him go.' (I was so distraught that I really did start weeping and yelling, and many of the people in the church stared at me in astonishment.)

Next, I saw the Jews raise the cross with our Lord hanging from it. With a great hue and cry they raised it a certain way from the ground then let the shaft drop into its socket. This jolted and jarred our Lord's body; all his joints were broken and dislocated, and rivers of blood from his precious wounds rained down on every side of the cross, so all the time I had more and more reason to weep and mourn.

At this point I heard our Lord, as he hung there on the cross, speak to his mother in the following way: 'Woman, behold your son—St John the Evangelist.' And it seemed to me that our Lady collapsed to the ground in a faint, and that St John raised her up in his arms and spoke to her as reassuringly as he possibly could.

And I had the impression of saying to our Lord, 'Oh, Lord, the mother you're leaving behind is so unhappy. What can we do? How can we bear to mourn you when we love you so much?'

And I heard the two thieves addressing our Lord and our Lord replying to one of them, 'Today you'll be with me in paradise.' I was glad to hear our Lord say this, and I appealed to his mercy and asked him to be as gracious toward my soul whenever I departed this life as he was to the thief, since I reckoned myself to be worse than any thief could be. At that point it seemed that our Lord commended his spirit into his Father's hands and passed away, whereupon our Lady fainted and lay there as if she was dead too.

At this, I saw myself running about and crying and roaring as if I was mad, but when I came to our Lady I fell on my knees in front of her and said, 'Lady, I beg you to stop grieving now, for your son is dead and out of his agony, and I think you've already grieved enough. Lady, let me mourn on your behalf, for our sorrows are one.'

Next, I thought I saw Joseph of Arimathea taking our Lord's body down from the cross and placing it in front of our Lady on a marble slab. When her son was taken down from the cross and placed on the slab our Lady seemed to experience a sort of joy. She bent down over her son's body and kissed his mouth and wept so profusely over his blessed face that her tears washed the blood away from his features.

And I thought I heard Mary Magdalene say to our Lady, 'Please, Lady, let me touch his feet and kiss them—they give me grace.' Straight away our Lady let Mary Magdalene and everyone else who had gathered round worship and revere the Lord's precious body in whatever way they wanted to. Mary Magdalene took our Lord's feet and our Lady's sisters took his hands. (One sister took one hand and the other took the other hand.) They wept intensely as they kissed his hands and his precious feet. As for me, I seemed to keep running around in a frenzy. I fervently wished that I could have had the precious body all to myself and wept my heart out in its presence; it seemed to me that I loved him so much I could have died of weeping for him and mourning his death.

I saw St John the Evangelist, Joseph of Arimathea and other friends of our Lord approaching. They wanted to bury our Lord's precious body and they asked our Lady to let them do so. Our sorrowful Lady said to them, 'Sirs, how could you take my son's body away from me? During his lifetime I could never see enough of him; please let me keep him now he is dead—don't separate me from my son. If you really mean to bury him bury me with him, because I can't live without him.' It seemed to me that they pleaded so beguilingly that she finally let them bury her dear son with all due worship and reverence.

Chapter 81

When our Lord was buried, our Lady fainted and collapsed as she was leaving the tomb. St John helped her up and Mary Magdalene went on the other side of her, and they did their best to console her and comfort her. I wanted to stay at our Lord's tomb, and the tenderness and compassion I felt for his death and the God-given yearning that was filling my mind made me grieve and sob and mourn and cry out. (The people stared at me; they wondered what was wrong with me, for they had very little idea of the cause.) I wanted to stay there until I died and then be buried beside our Lord.

A little later, I thought I saw our Lady walking towards her home, and as she did so a lot of good women came up to her and said, 'Lady, how sorry we are that your son is dead and that people of ours have treated him with so much contempt.' Our Lady was too upset to speak, but by way of reply she lowered her head and gently thanked them with her looks and expression.

Once our Lady was home and resting on her bed it occurred to me to make her a nice hot drink, but when I took it to her she told me to throw it away: 'My own child is the only sustenance I can accept.'

Then St John came to our Lady and told her that Peter was too ashamed to come in. Our Lady told St John to go straight back to St Peter and get him to come and see her. At that, my inner vision perceived St Peter coming right to our Lady, falling on his knees and saying, amidst his tears and sobs, 'Lady, I beg you to forgive me. I've forsaken your beloved son—the sweet master who loved me so well. Have mercy on me, otherwise how can I dare to look at either of you?'

'Ah, Peter,' said our Lady, 'don't be afraid. Although you forsook my sweet son he never forsook you, Peter, and he's coming back to comfort us all. Peter, I know this because he promised that he would come again on the third day to give me strength. Ah, Peter,' said our Lady, 'three days seems a long while to wait to see his blessed face.'

Then our Lady lay still on her bed and listened as Jesus's friends poured out their sorrow to her. Our Lady just lay there mourning and weeping, her face full of grief, till in the end Mary Magdalene and our Lady's sisters took their leave of our Lady and went to buy ointment with which to anoint our Lord's body.

Left alone with our Lady, it seemed to me like a thousand years till the third day came. But at last it arrived and I found myself in a chapel with our Lady, and our Lord Jesus Christ appeared to her saying, 'Hail, holy parent.' I thought I heard our Lady ask, 'Are you my sweet son Jesus?'

to which he replied, 'Yes, blessed mother, I'm your own son Jesus.'

He helped his blessed mother up and kissed her tenderly. And it seemed to me that our Lady touched and felt our Lord all over his body, his hands and his feet to see if there was any soreness or any pain. And I heard our Lord say to his mother, 'Dear Mother, my pain is entirely gone, and now I shall live for ever more. And, Mother, your pain and your sorrow will also be turned to great joy. Mother, ask me anything you want to know and I shall tell you.' And when he had let his mother ask the things she wanted and answered her questions he asked if he could go and speak with Mary Magdalene.

Our Lady replied, 'That would be good. She has grieved a lot for you while you've been gone. But please don't leave me for very long.'

(These inner sights and apprehensions made me weep and sob and cry out loudly. I couldn't control the intensity of it or stop myself from doing it. It happened to me on Easter Day and other days when our Lord bestowed his grace upon me. May his holy name be blessed and worshipped!)

In my mind's eye I was suddenly at Jesus's tomb, where I found myself mourning him and seeking him with Mary Magdalene. I saw how our Lord Jesus Christ appeared to her looking like a gardener and said, 'Woman, why are you weeping?'

Mary didn't know who he was. She was burning with the fire of love and she answered, 'Sir, if you've taken my Lord away tell me and I'll fetch him back.'

Then our merciful Lord was filled with pity and sorrow for her. 'Mary,' he said.

When she heard that word she recognized Jesus. Calling him Master, she fell at his feet, wanting to kiss them.

'Don't touch me,' said Jesus.

Then it seemed to me that Mary Magdalene said to our Lord, 'Lord, I can tell that you don't want me to be as friendly with you as I used to be,' and she looked upset.

'Mary,' said our Lord, 'I won't forsake you; I'll stay with you for ever more. Go and tell my brothers and Peter that I have risen.'

Mary left looking overjoyed, which astonished me because if our Lord had spoken to me as he had done to her—saying 'Don't touch me' when she wanted to kiss his feet—I wouldn't have been happy in the slightest. His words made me so upset and unhappy that on the many occasions when I heard them in sermons my love and desire to be with our Lord made me weep and sorrow and cry as though I was going to die.

Chapter 82

On the Day of the Purification—otherwise known as Candlemas Day—when I saw the people in church with their candles, my mind was thrilled with a vision of our Lady offering her blessed son our saviour to the priest Simeon in the Temple. It was as real to my mind as if I'd been there in person to make the offering with our Lady herself. This inner contemplation of our Lord Jesus Christ, his blessed mother, Simeon the Levite, Joseph and all the others who were there when our Lady was purified affected me so deeply that I was hardly able to take my candle up to the priest, as the others did when the time came to make the offering. Instead, I staggered from side to side as if I was drunk, and I wept and sobbed so intensely that I was hardly able to stay on my feet, such was the fervour of love and devotion God incited within me by giving me such sublime visions. Sometimes I couldn't stand at all but collapsed and cried out loudly, and a lot of the people standing round me wondered what was wrong with me. My spirit was in such a ferment that my body gave out—it was too much to bear.

I often had similar holy thoughts and meditations when I saw women being purified after giving birth, for it seemed to my soul that I was seeing our Lady's purification. My inner vision was also stirred at the sight of women coming to make an offering with the women who were being purified. My mind was drawn completely away from earthly sights and considerations and focused instead on things I could see with my inner eye. They were so exquisite and holy that when this ravishment happened to me I couldn't help weeping, sobbing and crying, though it cost me a lot of unwanted attention, mockery and scorn.

And when I saw weddings, where men and women were joined together in accordance with the laws of the Church, my inner eye saw how our Lady was joined to Joseph, and I also saw the mystical union of human souls with Jesus Christ. I prayed to our Lord that my love and affection should join me to him and to him alone for ever more, and that I should have the grace to obey him, love him and hold him in awe, worshipping him and praising him and loving only the things he loved and desiring only the things he desired. I prayed that day and night I would be ready to do as he wanted with a joyful heart, not grudgingly or reluctantly.

I had far more holy thoughts than I could ever repeat. They did not arise from my own study or my own mind; I received them from the one whose wisdom can only be understood by favoured souls, whom he enlightens to a greater or lesser extent as he decides. His will is subject to no constraints; it is his to exercise as he likes.

Sometimes these thoughts and desires were accompanied by heartfelt tears and sobbing and sighing, sometimes with noisy screams (if that's what God ordained) and sometimes with gentle, private tears which did not cause any disturbance at all.

I could only weep, whether noisily or silently, when God gave me tears. I was sometimes devoid of tears for half a day or even a whole day, and my longing for them caused me such torment that if this world had been mine I would gladly have given it up in exchange for a few tears, or else have suffered great bodily pain.

At times when I was barren of tears neither food, drink nor conversation would bring me pleasure or comfort, and I felt and looked unhappy until God restored them to me, which cheered me up again.

Although our Lord sometimes took away my abundant tears he did not withdraw my holy thoughts or my wish to be with him for years to come, for he was always the centre of my thoughts and desires. But I felt no relish or sweetness except when I could weep because that's when I felt most able to pray.

Chapter 83

There were two priests who were strongly inclined to take my crying and weeping seriously, although they sometimes had real doubts about it. Since my crying occurred when people were there to see it happen they secretly agreed, without my knowledge, to test whether I was crying just so people would hear.

One day, the priests came and asked me to go two miles from my home on a pilgrimage to a chapel dedicated to God and the Archangel Michael. It stood in open fields, well away from any houses.

I said I was very happy to go and we set off along with one or two children. Once we were there we prayed for a while, and I was so overcome with sweetness and devotion that I couldn't keep it to myself but burst out with tears and sobs and yells that were just as loud as when I was among the people in Lynn—or louder, in fact. There was nothing I could do about it, yet no one was there but the two priests and the one or two children.

As we were on our way home we met some women with babies in their arms and I asked if any of the babies were boys but they said they weren't. My mind was so full of the childhood of Christ that I couldn't bear my desire to see him, and I fell down and wept and cried so intensely that it was amazing to hear. Having heard me crying in a private place as well as in a public one, in the countryside as well as in town, the priests had all the more faith in my integrity. As well as the priests, there were several nuns who wanted to know about me in the hope that this would increase their devotion.

I was once in my usual church at midnight hearing matins when our Lord filled me with so much devotion, such lofty meditations and such inner strength that I was set ablaze with the fire of love, and it reached such a pitch that I cried out aloud. This was so that God's servants should praise his name all the more—his servants being those simple, unassuming souls who trusted the goodness of our Lord Jesus Christ, who blesses whomever he wants to bless. My crying did most for the people who took my calling seriously, for it greatly increased their merit and virtue, though it possibly gained very little merit and virtue for doubters. Even so, whether people believed in my crying or not, my grace never dwindled but grew all the while.

And our Lord visited me as often by night as he did by day, and with just as much blessing. He came to me when he wanted, how he wanted and where he wanted; I never lacked grace except when I doubted or mistrusted God's goodness, thinking or fearing that it was my unseen enemy using his cunning to mislead me and do some harm to my soul. People and evil spirits sometimes sowed ideas like this in my mind, and they could easily have made me abandon my path of righteousness but for the mighty hand of our Lord's mercy, which frustrated their malice. At times like these I lacked grace and devotion and any worthwhile thoughts or ideas until by the mercy of our Lord Jesus Christ I was firmly convinced that God was definitely speaking inside me for my good and the good of other people, and wished to be worshipped for the blessings he gave me.

Once I was sure it was God and not an evil spirit that stirred me to so much devotion, contrition and holy contemplation my mind was filled with so much holy thought and discourse as to how I should love God, and worship and serve him, that I could never repeat more than a small part. These things were so sublime and holy that I was nervous of telling them to anyone; in any case, they so transcended the power of my mind that my tongue could never express what I felt in my soul, which understood far more than I could put into words. If one of my confessors had come to me when I was just getting up from contemplating or meditating I could have told him a lot of what our Lord had said to me inwardly, but within a short time I'd forgotten most of it, if not all.

Chapter 84

The Abbess of Denny, a house of nuns, kept sending for me to go and speak with her and the sisters. I wanted to put it off until another time because I felt that the effort would put me under a lot of strain. However, when I was meditating and had a strong sense of sweetness and devotion, our Lord commanded me to go to Denny for the sake of the ladies who wanted to meet me. He said to my soul, 'Daughter, in the name of Jesus set out and go to the house at Denny because I want you to strengthen them in their faith.'

I was reluctant to go because there was an epidemic of plague at the time and the last thing I wanted was to die while I was there. However, our Lord spoke to my mind again and told me that I would come back safely.

I immediately went and saw the wife of a leading burgess and told her that I was going to Denny. This woman had a high opinion of me. Her husband was lying seriously ill so she was relying on me and she didn't want me to go to Denny. 'I'd give forty shillings rather than have my husband die while you were away,' the woman explained.

But I replied, 'I wouldn't stay at home, even if you gave me a hundred pounds.' I'd been inwardly told that I had to go and I wouldn't do otherwise. Come what might, I was definitely going. After all, I wouldn't have dreamed of going out if God had told me to stay at home.

God then informed me that the burgess wasn't going to die, so I went back and told his wife to take heart: her husband was going to live a while yet; he wouldn't die in the near future.

The good wife was very pleased indeed. 'May what you say be the gospel truth,' she said.

I wanted to get on my way in accordance with God's command but on reaching the quay I found that all the boats for Cambridge had already left. I was very concerned because I couldn't see how to do God's will, but he straight away told me not to be unhappy or downcast; he would provide for me perfectly well and see that I travelled there and back safely—which is how it turned out.

Then our Lord thanked me because during my meditations and visions I'd helped to look after him from the time of his childhood to the time of his death. 'Daughter,' he said, 'when you're with me in heaven your reward and payment for the service and deeds you've performed in your mind during meditation will be as great as if you'd actually carried them out. And, Daughter, when you supply yourself, your husband, your confessor or anyone else you receive in my name with food, drink or other necessities your reward in heaven will be just the same as if you'd done it for me or my blessed mother, and I shall thank you for what you've done.

'Daughter, you say that I deserve to be called All Good, and you'll find that I am all good to you; and you say that it's also fitting for me to be called All Love, and you'll find that I am all love to you. I know every thought that's in your heart, and I know you've often said to yourself that if you'd had any number of churches piled high with money you'd have given it all away for my sake. And it's gone through your mind that if you'd had sufficient wealth your love for me would have led you to found many abbeys for religious men and women, and you'd have given each of them a hundred pounds a year to serve me. You've also wished to have many priests in the town of Lynn who could serve me day and night by singing, reading, worshipping and praising me and thanking me for all the goodness I have shown you in this present life. Daughter, I promise to give you the same payment and reward in heaven for your good intentions and good desires as if you'd actually carried them out.

'Daughter, I know the way you feel towards all kinds of people including lepers and prisoners; I know how much money you'd give them each year to be my servants and I regard it as having been actually done.

'Daughter, I thank you for the goodness you show to all lecherous men and women; you pray for them and weep many tears for them, wanting me to free them from sin and be as gracious to them as I was to Mary Magdalene so that they will love me as much as Mary Magdalene did. If only they'd love me you'd want them all to have twenty pounds a year to sustain them in their love and praise. Daughter, I'm very pleased indeed with the goodness you show to them in your prayers.

'I also thank you for the goodness you show when you pray that all Jews, Saracens and heathens should adopt the Christian faith to the greater glory of my name; and I thank you because you weep and shed holy tears for these people, fervently hoping that if it's my will and if any prayer can bring them to grace or Christian faith I should hear your pleas on their behalf.

'And thank you, Daughter, for your loving-kindness to everyone now alive in the world and to all who shall live till the end of time. You love them so much that you'd be chopped up as small as meat for the cooking pot if only your death would induce me to save them all from damnation. You often say to yourself that there are plenty of souls in hell and you don't want anyone else to earn damnation.

'So, Daughter, all your good inclinations and good desires have earned you honour and reward in heaven. Be sure of this and never doubt it in the slightest, because all your spiritual gifts come from me and I give you them so that your reward in heaven will be all the greater. I assure you, Daughter, that every good thought and desire in your soul is the voice of God. Sometimes you cannot hear me but at other times you understand clearly.

'Daughter, I am like a God who has hidden in your soul; sometimes I take away your tears and devotion so that you realize you have no goodness of yourself but only the goodness that comes from me. I also do it so that you can truly know how painful it is to be without me and how sweet it is to feel me again. I want to make you all the more eager to seek for me when you do not have me and I want you to know how others suffer when they yearn for my presence. For there are many people in the world who, given just a single day of their lives enjoying what you enjoy so often, would never stop loving me all the more and thanking me for it. As for you, Daughter, you can't go without me for a single day without great pain. You have every reason to love me well, because it's not out of anger that I sometimes deprive you of your sense of grace and your fervent devotion; I do it to make it clear to you that there cannot be any falsehood in your weeping, crying, sweetness, devotion, sense of my passion or in any of your other gifts of grace. They aren't from the Devil; they are graces and gifts which I myself give or send to you. They are special gifts for those chosen souls who I knew from before the beginning of time would live with me forever in a state of grace.

'If you so desire, you can make a pretence of understanding, constant prayer, lengthy fasts and harsh penances. All these things you can put on display for all to see; you can let them see you reaching into your pocket in great acts of charity or uttering high-sounding words with your mouth. You can do all these things for show if you want—or, if you choose, you can do them in a good and holy way.

'But, Daughter, I have filled you with so much love that you can't pretend where that is concerned; nor can you waste your time while your mind is occupied with it, since as long as your thoughts are good you cannot commit any sin. The Devil has no idea of the holy thoughts I give you, and no living soul knows how good and holy your thoughts of me are. Even you can't describe the sense of grace and goodness I give you. So, Daughter, you and your holy thoughts are more than the Devil and the world can ever understand, and living souls are greatly deceived when they judge your heart, which no one can know but God alone.

'Daughter, I assure you that you have as much reason to be glad and have a joyful soul as any woman or girl in the world. I love you so much that I cannot take my love away from you. Daughter, no heart can conceive and no tongue can tell how much I love you, and I call on my blessed mother, my holy angels and all the saints in heaven to witness to this, for in heaven all of them worship me out of their love for you.

'People on earth will do the same, my Daughter, because I mean to make everyone know of the grace I have shown you in this present life. Everyone will be struck by my goodness and marvel at the special favours I've shown to you, a woman who knows what it is to do wrong. Because I have been so gracious and merciful to you, living souls will not despair, no matter how sinful they may be. They too can have mercy and grace if they want it.'

Chapter 85

Once, when I was kneeling in front of an altar of the cross and saying a prayer, my eyes kept closing as if I was going to fall asleep. In the end I couldn't help dropping off, and there straight away appeared to me an angel clothed entirely in white. The angel looked like a little child carrying a huge book in front of him. I said to the child, or rather the angel, 'Ah, this must be the Book of Life.'

In the book I saw the name of the Trinity all in gold. And I said to the child, 'Where is my name?'

The child replied, 'Here is your name; it comes just after the Trinity.' And with these words he disappeared—I didn't know how.

Straight afterwards, our Lord Jesus Christ spoke to me and said, 'Daughter, because your name is written in heaven in the Book of Life you must be true and steadfast and strong in faith. It was an angel that gave you this reassurance so, Daughter, you've every cause to be glad. I am working morning, noon and night to draw your heart ever closer to mine. You should focus your mind entirely on me, since that will do more than anything else to increase your love for me. Daughter, if you want to do God's will you must shun wrongdoing; God requires submissiveness, self-sacrifice and chastity.'

On another occasion I was meditating in a chapel of our Lady when the person of our Lord Jesus Christ filled my mind, and to all appearances he stood before me in his human form with his wounds bleeding as freshly as though he'd just been scourged in front of me. At this, I wept and cried for all I was worth. If my sorrow for Christ was great before I had this vision it was very much greater afterwards and so was the love I felt for our Lord. Moreover, I was amazed that our Lord had chosen to become a man and suffer such torments for me—a woman who had treated her creator so ungratefully.

On yet another occasion I was in the choir of St Margaret's Church. Overcome with sweetness, devotion and tears, I asked our Lord Jesus Christ how I could please him best and he said to my soul, 'Daughter, think of your wickedness and consider my goodness.'

In response to this I said over and over again, 'Lord, out of your goodness have mercy on all my wickedness. I can't have been as wicked as you are good; I could never be that bad even if I tried, since your goodness is absolute. But that makes it hard to believe that you could dismiss anyone from your presence forever.'

I remained motionless in the choir, weeping and mourning because of my sins, and I suddenly fell into a sort of sleep. The eye of my soul straight away saw our Lord's body lying in front of me. It seemed to me that his head was right by me and his blessed face was looking up. He was the most beautiful man you could see or imagine. Then someone came along with a dagger and slit that precious body open right down the chest. It made me cry in great distress, for I now had greater feeling, pity and compassion than before for the way our Lord Jesus Christ had suffered.

So it was that my understanding and love for our Lord grew day by day—may his name be blessed!—and the more I loved him the more I grieved over people's sins.

There was also a time when I was in a lady chapel weeping at the thought of our Lord's passion and other good and blessed things with which our Lord was filling my mind. I don't know how soon it happened but a sort of sleep seized me, and straight away my mind perceived our Lord standing over me. He was standing so close that I imagined I took his toes in my hand and felt them, and they had the feel of real flesh and bone.

I gave thanks to God for all these visions, which focused my thoughts and feelings on the manhood and passion of Christ until the time when our Lord was ready to show me some of the mysteries of his ineffable Godhead.

As I've already said, I had feelings and visions like these soon after my conversion, when my mind was set on serving God as wholeheartedly as I was able. Having left the world entirely behind I used to spend my days in church, especially during Lent when after much insistence and begging my husband allowed me to remain undefiled by sex. I was also doing great bodily penance in preparation for my journey to Jerusalem.

Later, after my husband and I had mutually agreed on taking a vow of chastity, as I've already explained, and I'd been in Rome and Jerusalem and suffered a lot of contempt and criticism because of my weeping and crying, our Lord of his mercy drew my affections into his Godhead, and this brought me keener love and desire and deeper understanding than his manhood had done. Thus the fire of love burned hotter within me, my understanding became more lucid and my devotion more fervent than when my meditation and contemplation had been focused on his manhood alone. Even so, my crying wasn't as intense as it had been earlier; it was gentler, softer and more easeful for my spirit to bear, though my tears continued to flow just as freely.

Once, when I was in the lady chapel in the house of the Preaching Friars, my eyelids drooped as if I was half asleep. Suddenly, in the most beautiful vision I ever had, I seemed to see our Lady holding a lovely white cloth in her hand. 'Daughter,' she asked, 'would you like to see my son?' And straight away I saw that our Lady had her blessed son in her hand. In front of me, so that I could see what she was doing, she gently placed the cloth around him. This was a new source of joy and comfort to my soul, so marvellous that I could never explain how much it meant to me.

Chapter 86

On a certain occasion when our Lord addressed my soul, he said to me, 'Daughter, I will give you new joys and comforts in heaven to reward you for all the times you have received the blessed sacrament of the altar with more holy thoughts than you could repeat. And, Daughter, you will know in heaven just how many days of high contemplation you have had on earth. I've given them to you freely as a gift and a blessing, but they will bring you the same grace and reward in heaven as if they'd been due to your own merits.

'Daughter, I offer you many thanks for letting me do as I wished in your heart and for letting me be so intimate with you. Daughter, you couldn't have pleased me more than to let me speak within your soul, for in that way I came to know your will and you came to know mine.

'You call to my mother to enter your soul; you ask her to take me in her arms, put me to her breast and feed me. And, Daughter, I know the holy thoughts, the goodwill and kindness you feel for me as your soul receives my precious body; and I know how you invite Mary Magdalene into your soul to make me feel at home—for I'm well aware of all your thoughts. Apart from my mother, you think of Mary Magdalene as the worthiest person to have in your soul, and the one whose prayers are most to be trusted, and certainly in the bliss of heaven her intercession on your behalf is very powerful.

'Daughter, you sometimes think that your soul is broad and wide enough for the whole court of heaven. You summon them there to welcome me, and I know what you say to them: "Come to my soul, all you twelve apostles who God so dearly loved on earth, and receive your Lord." And you ask Catherine, Margaret and all the holy virgins to welcome me in your soul. Then you ask my blessed mother, Mary Magdalene, all the apostles, martyrs, saints, Catherine, Margaret and all the holy virgins to strew the bedchamber of your soul with beautiful flowers and sweet spices ready for me to take my rest.

'What is more, Daughter, you sometimes imagine that in your soul you have cushions made of gold, red velvet and white silk. The cushion of gold would be for my Father, in accordance with his might and power. The red velvet cushion would be for me, the second Person, your love and your joy. I am always in your thoughts because I paid for you so dearly, and you think you could never repay me for the love I have shown you, even if you could show me your love by dying a thousand deaths a day. Daughter, you think I deserve to be seated on the red cushion in your soul in memory of the red blood I shed for you. As for the Holy Spirit, he is full of love and purity so you picture him sitting on the white cushion. It is right that he should do so, since all holy thoughts and chastity proceed from him.

'Daughter, I know everything that goes through your mind: you think you can only worship the Father if you worship the Son and that you can only worship the Son if you worship the Holy Spirit. And sometimes, Daughter, you say to yourself that if the Father is all-powerful, all-knowing, all-gracious and all-good then the Son must be all-powerful, all-knowing, all-gracious and all-good. And then you reflect that since the Holy Spirit proceeds from the Father and the Son he must have just the same properties as they do. What is more you believe that each of the three Persons of the Trinity contains in his Godhead all that the other Persons have; so you rightly believe there are three distinct Persons yet one divine substance. Each Person knows what the others know, each can do what the others can do, and each desires what the others desire. Daughter, this is the true and proper faith and you only have it because I've chosen to give it to you.

'So, Daughter, you can see that you've every reason to love me with all your heart so that I can make it my home whenever I choose. Daughter, if you let me live in your soul on earth you can be certain of living in heaven with me for evermore. Don't be surprised that you weep so much when you go to the altar and receive my blessed body in the form of bread. Before receiving communion you silently pray to me, "Lord, as surely as you love me cleanse me from the stain of sin and give me grace to receive your body in a fitting way, with all due worship and reverence."

'Daughter, I promise I hear your prayer, for there's nothing you could say to make me happier than when I hear you speak of my love for you. At that, I fill you full of my grace and put so many holy thoughts in your mind that you cannot possibly recount them all. You feel me so close that you've no hesitation in asking me to bless you, your husband and your children, and you inwardly make all Christian men and women your children and you ask me to bless them accordingly. You also ask for my mercy on your husband's soul; you are grateful to me for having given you such a man—one who puts up with living chastely despite enjoying good physical health. You are certainly right to be struck by this and to love me for it all the more.

'Daughter, if you knew how many wives in the world would love me and serve me devotedly if only they could be as free from their husbands as you are from yours you would see how much cause you have to be grateful. However, because such women are prevented from doing as they would like, and suffer great pain, they will have a sublime reward in heaven. When people mean well, I treat their intentions as if they had put them into practice.

'Sometimes, Daughter, I make you especially sad about your confessor's sins; you want them forgiven as completely as you want your own to be. And sometimes, when you receive the precious sacrament, I make you pray that your confessor's preaching shall save as many men and women as you hope will be saved by the tears of your eyes, and that my holy word shall disturb their hearts as much as you want it to disturb your own. You ask the same grace for all the good men who preach my word throughout the earth - that they shall do good to every sentient being. And often on the day you receive my precious body you ask me to show my grace and mercy to all your friends and to all the enemies who ever humiliated you, condemned you, scorned you or mocked you because for the sake of young and old I perform such works of grace within you. Your tearful, heartfelt sobbing and weeping have brought you a great deal of shame and criticism, but they will also bring you great joy in heaven.

'Daughter, don't be ashamed to receive my grace when I wish you to have it; I shall not be ashamed to receive you into heavenly bliss to reward you for all your virtuous thoughts and words and deeds and for every day you have spent in holy contemplation and for all the good inclinations that you have had in this life. You will be with me everlastingly, my beloved darling, my blessed spouse, my holy wife.

'So don't be afraid, Daughter, even though everyone wonders why you weep so poignantly when you receive me; if they knew the grace I was giving you at that very moment they'd be more inclined to wonder why your heart doesn't burst—and it would do if I didn't hold back some of my grace. But, Daughter, you yourself can see that once you've received me into your soul your peace and quiet return to you and your sobbing stops. The people wonder at that as well but it shouldn't be a surprise to you, since you know that I treat you like a man who is going to take a wife. Once he has married her he feels perfectly sure of her; he knows no one will come between them because they can now sleep easily in their bed without any shame or fear of disgrace. Things are the same for you and me, Daughter: every week, and especially on Sundays, there's fear and anxiety in your soul as to how best to make yourself sure of my love. You are full of reverence and holy dread as you wonder how to receive me, to your soul's salvation, with all due meekness, humility and grace. But any lady in the world is concerned about how to receive her husband when he comes home after a long time away.

'Beloved Daughter, thank you for all the sick people you've cared for in my name, and for all the various kind and helpful things you've done for them. When you're with me in heaven your reward will be the same as if you'd cared for me in person when I was on this earth. And, Daughter, I thank you for all the times when you've been at home in your bedroom and bathed me in your soul as if I'd been there in the flesh; I'm well aware of all the holy thoughts about me that have gone through your mind. And, Daughter, I thank you for all the times when you have made your bed a haven for me and my blessed mother. For these and all the other good thoughts and actions which you've entertained or carried out in my name and out of your love towards me you will have all manner of joy and everlasting bliss with me and my mother, my holy angels and apostles, my martyrs, confessors, virgins and all my holy saints.'

Chapter 87

I remained completely motionless in the church, hearing and understanding these lovely words that were being spoken inside my soul. The voice was as clear as the voice of a friend. When I heard our Lord Jesus Christ making me such promises I wept and sobbed, and holy and reverent thoughts filled my mind. I gave him thanks and said in my heart, 'Lord Jesus, may your name be blessed. I have never deserved all this from you, and I only wish I were in that place where I wouldn't displease you ever again.' With thoughts like these—far more than could ever be written down—I worshipped and magnified our Lord Jesus Christ for his holy visitations and for giving me such inner comfort.

Through visitations and holy contemplation of the sort which I have described above, but incomparably deeper and more sublime than those, our saviour had enabled me to persevere in my way of life for over twenty-five years by the time this account was put in writing. These things were a weekly or daily occurrence unless I was busy helping the sick or preoccupied by other things that I had to do for myself or my fellow Christians. At times like that they were often withdrawn, since they only come to a soul that is stilled by lengthy spiritual exercise.

The kind of speech and conversation which I enjoyed made my love for our Lord intense and strong; it did a lot to confirm my faith and it made me humbler and kinder, and better in other ways too. I firmly believed it was God who was speaking in my soul, not an evil spirit, since his words did so much to increase my confidence, strength and virtue. May his name be praised!

I was often so ill I thought I was dying, and other people thought so too, but I was inwardly told that far from dying I'd soon be completely well again, and so it turned out. Sometimes our Lady spoke words of comfort during my illness. At other times, St Peter, St Paul, St Mary Magadalene, St Catherine, St Margaret or one of the other saints in heaven—whichever of the saints God chose to let me call to mind—spoke to my inner understanding and told me how I should love God and how I should please him best. They answered the questions I asked them, and their way of speaking showed which saint was addressing me and giving me comfort.

Our Lord poured out his mercy on me with so many plenteous visitations of holy speech and talk that I often didn't know how the day had slipped away. Sometimes five or six hours passed when I would have said less than an hour had gone by. It was so sweet and holy—just as if

I was visiting heaven. It never seemed long or tedious—I just didn't know where the time had gone. I would rather have spent a hundred years—if I'd lived that long—serving God like this than a day in the sort of service I'd given him when I first began.

I often said to our Lord Jesus Christ, 'Oh, Lord Jesus, since it's so sweet to shed tears of love for you in this world I'm sure it must be joy indeed to be with you in heaven! So I pray you, Lord, may I have no other joy on earth than to mourn and weep out of love for you. Lord, it seems to me that if I were in hell it would not be a torment but a sort of heaven if only I could weep and mourn out of love for you as I do on this earth. Love of you dispels all dread of our unseen enemy, and to please you I would rather be in hell for as long as you chose than stay in this world and cause you displeasure.'

Chapter 88

When this book was being written down I was concerned with getting the writing finished, so I said fewer prayers than I had done in previous years and spent more time at home with my scribe. When I went to church to hear mass I intended to say my matins and other accustomed devotions but I found that I couldn't concentrate on them. I was much more inclined to meditate but I feared that this would displease our Lord. However he spoke to my soul and told me not to worry: 'However many prayers you'd like to say, I accept them as though you'd actually said them. I'm very pleased by your efforts to make a written record of the gifts of grace I've given you, and I'm also very pleased with your scribe. Nothing could please me more than your writing—not even if you were both in church and weeping together as much as you've ever done in your life. Daughter, this book of yours will cause many people to turn to me and believe in me.

'Daughter, how better can you pray than to pray to me with your own heart or your own mind? When you pray with your mind you yourself understand what you're asking and what I say in reply; you understand what I promise to you and those you love and all your confessors. As for your confessor Master Robert, I have granted your wish to give him the benefit of half your tears and half the gifts of grace I've granted to you. As a result, he'll have the reward for your weeping as though he'd done it himself. Daughter, rest assured that when the time comes you'll rejoice together in heaven and you'll bless the day when you met each other. What is more, you'll bless me forever for giving you such a good confessor; although he's sometimes been strict with you it's been all for the good, because otherwise you would have felt too much personal liking for him. When he was strict the whole of your being fled to me, saying, "Lord, who can I trust but you alone?" And then, from the depth of your heart you cried to me, "Lord, by the power of your painful wounds draw all my affections into your heart"—and that's what I've done.

'You often think that I've done a lot for you—that I've worked a special miracle in drawing all your affection to me. That's because there are times when you were so attached to a certain individual that you thought it was almost impossible to direct your affections anywhere else. But you loved me so much that you would have been glad for that person to forsake you if I'd wanted him to, though without his support you couldn't have expected many people to take you seriously. If he'd forsaken you you'd have thought it the greatest public humiliation you'd ever suffered, but for that very reason you were ready to endure it out of love for me if I'd so desired. The thought of suffering makes you love me all the more, so I treat your willingness as if you had put it into practice.

'I'm well aware that you're still very attached to Master Robert, and I've often said that it's right for him to return your feeling and accept that it's God and not a devil who speaks inside you. Moreover, Daughter, I'm very pleased that he and Master Aleyn have used their sermons to excuse your weeping and crying. Because of this they'll both have great rewards in heaven.

'Daughter, I've often said that I'd support your weeping and crying by means of sermons and preaching. What is more, I want you to know that Master Robert, your confessor, pleases me very much when he assures you that I love you. I know you place a lot of faith in the things he says because he refuses to flatter you. I'm also very pleased with the fact that he tells you to be silent and dwell and meditate inwardly on the holy thoughts I put in your mind. I have often told you to do so myself but you only obey me very grudgingly.

'Daughter, as I've often reminded you, I shall approve of you whether you pray aloud or ponder inwardly, read or listen to others reading. But if only I could convince you that contemplation is the best thing for you, and that nothing could foster your love for me more: surely it's right and proper that the closer you let me be to your soul in this earthly life the closer I'll be to your soul in heaven. So, Daughter, if you won't obey me obey your confessor, who gives you the same advice as I do.

'Daughter, when your confessor tells you you're displeasing God you're ready to believe him; you're sad and upset and you weep your eyes out until you're back in a state of grace. At times like that I can't bear to let you suffer for long without putting it right, so I frequently come in person to reassure you and tell you how much I love you. You hear from my lips that my love is as real as my Godliness, that there's nothing you can see or touch in the world that's as sure as my love.

'Blessed Daughter, love me just as I love you and always keep me in your thoughts. I don't forget you, for my merciful eye is always watching over you. My merciful mother knows that it's so; she has often remarked on it, and so have many of my other saints. You've every reason to love me with all your heart and affections; I shall give you my whole heart in return. And, Daughter, you can rest assured that if you obey my will I shall do as you desire.'

Chapter 89

In the period while I was busy having this treatise written I frequently wept and shed holy tears, and a hot and delectable tongue of fire often lapped round my chest. There were also times when my scribe was unable to stop himself crying. Often, when I went to the church between our sessions, our Lord Jesus Christ, his glorious mother and throngs of saints came into my soul and thanked me, saying they were very pleased I was writing this book. I frequently heard a bird singing sweetly in my ear, along with other sounds and melodies that went beyond my powers of description.

During the writing I was often ill, but as soon as I set to work I was suddenly restored to perfect health—and I often had to be ready for work at very short notice.

On one occasion—it was the season of Advent, just before Christmas—I was praying in church when I thought to myself that I'd like it if God, of his goodness, made Master Aleyn preach the finest sermon he possibly could. No sooner had I had this thought than I heard our Sovereign Lord Jesus Christ say to my soul, 'Daughter, I've clearly heard what you're just now thinking about Master Aleyn, and I promise that he will deliver a truly holy sermon. You must take his words as seriously as if I'd preached them myself, because I shall be speaking through his mouth and what he says will be full of comfort and consolation for you.'

As soon as I had heard God's answer I went and repeated it to my confessor and to two other priests I trusted a lot. Having told them, I was sick with fear as to whether he'd preach as well as I had felt he would, because revelations are sometimes hard to understand. Things people think are revelations sometimes turn out to be tricks and illusions, and rather than giving credence to every intuition it's better to keep a level head and find out whether it's sent by God. Nevertheless, on this occasion things turned out exactly as I had been led to expect, and my apprehensions and misgivings gave way to great inner comfort and happiness.

Sometimes, when I didn't know how to interpret them for days on end, my feelings oppressed me; I was afraid of being deceived and deluded—so much so that while I waited for God, of his goodness, to tell me what they meant, I would rather have had no head on my shoulders.

I sometimes took things literally that were meant to be taken in a spiritual sense, and my fear of my inner feelings was the greatest scourge I suffered on earth, especially when I first started having them. My fear made me very cautious because I couldn't rejoice in my feelings until experience showed me whether they were well-founded or not. But may God be blessed for evermore, for he steadily increased the power and the strength of the love and awe I felt towards him, and as I persevered he helped me to grow in virtue too.

This account ends here, for God took to his mercy the man who wrote the text from which it is copied out. Although he didn't write lucidly or clearly, if we judge his work by our everyday speech, his writing and spelling did make sense, and with God's help and mine (for I felt and did everything in the account) the original text is correctly reflected in this little book.

THE BOOK OF
MARGERY KEMPE

Second Book

Chapter 1

After our sovereign saviour had taken the person who first wrote the above book to his abundant mercy, and after the priest, already mentioned, had copied it out as best he could, this priest thought it right that people should hear of God's other holy works whenever God wished them to do so, to the honour of the blessed Trinity and the worship of his holy name. In the year of our Lord 1438, at the feast of St Vitalis the Martyr, he therefore began to record, at my dictation, some of the favours—not all of them—which our Lord had bestowed on his simple creature in the years that had passed since the writing of the first account.

To start with, here is an important matter which it fails to mention. The affair began soon after I'd given up worldly concerns and was mentally joined to God as far as my human frailty allowed. I had a son, a tall young man, who lived with a well-respected burgess in Lynn and sailed overseas for the purpose of trade. I wanted to save him from the perils of this wretched and unpredictable world if only I could find a way. I did what I could, and whenever we met and had time to talk I advised him to abandon worldly pursuits and follow Christ, till in the end he used to hurry away if he ever saw me coming.

Despite his efforts to avoid me, my son and I one day bumped into each other. I did as I had done before and advised him to avoid the snares of the world and not be so preoccupied with worldly matters. He didn't agree and answered back sharply. I was getting a little angry myself so I said to him, 'Well, if you won't take my advice to give up worldly things I'm telling you by the power of my prayers to at least keep your body free from commerce with women until you marry according to the laws of the Church.'

My son and I went our separate ways, and shortly afterwards he went abroad on a trading mission. While he was there, other people's bad influence and his own lack of discipline led him into the sin of lechery. Before very long his skin changed colour and lumps and pustules covered his face as if he'd got leprosy. When he came back to Lynn and returned to the master he'd been living with his master dismissed him, not for anything he'd done wrong but perhaps assuming from the state of his face that he was a leper.

My son went round telling everyone that his mother must have cursed him, causing God to give him this dreadful punishment. Someone who knew what he was claiming took pity on his suffering and came and told me I'd done a really evil thing, because thanks to my prayers God had punished my child. I didn't let it bother me, and I let it be known that I wouldn't lift a finger to help until he came and asked me himself. In the end he realized that was the only answer. Coming to see me he told me about his misdeeds and he promised to obey God, do as I wanted and make amends for what he'd done wrong. He also said that with God's help he'd try as hard as he could to avoid all wrongdoing in future. He begged me to give him my blessing, and he especially begged me to pray to our Lord to have mercy on him and forgive him for sinning, and to take away the horrible illness that made people shrink from his company and friendship as if he was a leper. He supposed my prayers must have brought this punishment down upon him, and he thought my prayers could cure him as well if only I'd be good enough to offer them on his behalf. I was sorry for him to have such an illness but was sure he'd recover. I sharply told him to mend his ways and promised to secure his recovery if God would grant it.

When I was ready to meditate I didn't forget my own flesh and blood; I asked God to forgive him for what he'd done wrong and free him from the illness our Lord had given him (provided this was our Lord's will and would help my son's soul). I prayed until he was completely healed, and he lived for many more years and had a wife and child, having married in Prussia. May God be praised!

I was overjoyed when news arrived from overseas that my son had got married. I thanked God with all my heart, fully believing that he'd live a wholesome, continent life in accordance with the laws of matrimony. When God blessed them with a child—a beautiful little girl—he sent home to England and let me know how wonderfully he and his wife had been blessed.

I was in a chapel of our Lady thanking God for the grace and goodness he had shown my son and longing to see them if only I could when suddenly God replied in my mind that I'd see them all before I died. I was very surprised and I wondered how it could possibly happen, since they and I were on opposite sides of the sea and we had no plans to make the crossing. Even so, I knew perfectly well that nothing was impossible for God, and I trusted that my inner sense would prove to be justified in God's good time.

Chapter 2

A few years after my son had got married he came home to England to see his father and myself, and we found that he was completely changed in dress and outlook. In the past, his clothes had been showily cut and his talk had been frivolous. Now his clothes were straight and una-dorned at the hems and his conversation was full of virtue.

I was amazed at this sudden change. 'God bless us all!' I said. 'What's come over you, son?'

'Mother,' he answered, 'it seems to me that thanks to your prayers our Lord has called me, and by the grace of God I mean to pay more attention to your advice in the future than I have in the past.'

Seeing the marvellous way in which our Lord had called him to himself, I gave God all the thanks I could, and I watched how my son conducted himself, afraid that he was putting on an act. The longer I observed him the more sober and reverent to God he appeared. Once I was sure he was being drawn by our Lord's mercy I was overjoyed— I couldn't stop thanking God for his goodness and his grace.

To spur him on and make him all the keener to follow where our Lord was leading, I opened my heart to him, disclosing and explaining how our Lord, by his mercy, had once called me. I revealed the way in which he had done this, and I also informed him of all the favours he had shown me, though he told me he wasn't worthy to hear it.

To gain his pardon, my son went on many pilgrimages to Rome and other holy places, but he always returned to his wife and child as duty required. He told his wife so much about me that she wanted to leave her father and mother and her own country in order to come to England to meet me. This pleased him a lot and he sent word to England to let me know what his wife was wanting. He asked my advice as to whether he should come all the way by sea or whether he should take the overland route. (He relied on my advice because he believed it came from the Holy Spirit.)

On receiving his letter and hearing his request I set about praying in order to find out what God advised us or asked us to do. In the course of my prayers I was told that my son would travel safely whether he made his journey by land or sea. I then wrote him letters saying that by the grace of God his method of travel would make no difference: he'd get here safely in either case.

Once he had my advice he enquired when ships would be sailing to England and he booked a ship (or part of one) for his belongings, his wife, his child and himself, intending them all to cross to England together. As soon as they had gone on board there was such a storm that they were afraid to set sail, so he, his wife and child all disembarked again. They left the child in Prussia with some of his wife's friends and then took the overland route to England to visit me and his father. When they arrived I rejoiced in our Lord because I'd been right in thinking they'd travel equally safely, no matter how. May God be praised!

When they arrived on the Saturday they were in good health but the next day, Sunday, we were having a midday meal with close friends when my son was taken ill, and he had to leave the table and lie on a bed. The illness and incapacity lasted about a month, at the end of which he passed to the mercy of our Lord. He had mended his ways and embraced the true faith, so it's certainly true that he travelled home safely, not only in the physical sense of returning safely to home to die but also in the spiritual sense of going to the land of immortal life, where death is unknown.

Not long afterwards his father also went the way of all flesh. My daughter-in-law (who was German) stayed on with me (this book's main subject) for a year and a half, but her friends wanted her to go back home and they wrote her letters from Germany urging her to return to her native country. Not wanting to upset her friends, she told me what they were asking of her. She said she felt that she ought to comply, and she asked if I minded her going home to Germany.

I didn't want to stand in her way and she prepared to leave as soon as there were any ships going in that direction. Before long we learned of a German ship that was due to sail [from Ipswich] with some Germans on board, and we felt that it would be nicer for her to sail with them than with anyone else. She went to her confessor to receive absolution and while she was making her confession I wandered up and down in the choir thinking, 'Lord, if you wished I would ask my confessor to let me accompany her on her voyage.'

Our Lord answered me inwardly saying, 'Daughter, I know that if I told you to go you wouldn't hesitate, so I don't want you even to broach it with him.' That made me really cheerful and glad because it led me to think that I wouldn't be going overseas. I had once been in serious danger at sea and I'd made up my mind that I wouldn't go to sea again by choice.

When my daughter-in-law had received absolution the good man who was at that time confessor to both of us came up to me and said, 'Who'll see your daughter-in-law safely to the port to find her ship? It isn't right for her to make such a long journey by herself with one young

man. They'll be strangers in a foreign country.' He said this because a
foreigner had come to fetch her. Neither of them was very well known
in the area and because of this her confessor was all the more concerned
about her safety.

'Sir,' I replied, 'I'll see her to Ipswich myself if you like. Her ship will
be there and also some fellow Germans who'll look after her on the
voyage.'

My confessor replied, 'How can you go with her? You've only recently
hurt your foot and it isn't completely better yet. In any case, you aren't
as young as you used to be. You mustn't go.'

'Sir,' I replied, 'I'm sure God will take good care of me.'

Then he asked who I'd have to go with me and see me back home.

'Sir,' I replied, 'what about the hermit attached to this church? He's
a young man and surely for love of our Lord he'll accompany me there
and back, if only you'll let me go.'

So I got permission to escort my daughter-in-law to Ipswich and make
my way back to Lynn again. It was Lent when we embarked on our
journey and when we arrived at a church only five or six miles from Lynn
we went inside to hear mass. While we were there I felt an urge to shed
tears of devotion but none were forthcoming, and my heart was filled
with repeated commands to go abroad with my daughter-in-law. I tried
to put it out of my head but the idea returned so insistently that I
couldn't recover my peace of mind—I was constantly being pressed and
commanded to join the ship.

I thought it would be an onerous undertaking for me, and I inwardly
made excuses to God, saying, 'Lord, you know that I'm bound to
obedience and I don't have my confessor's permission. I can't do this
unless he's willing and gives his consent.'

The answer I received in my mind was, 'I, Jesus, am asking you to go
in my name. I have more authority than your confessor and I excuse you
from asking his permission. I shall see that you have a safe journey in
each direction.'

I still wanted to get out of it if I possibly could so I said in reply, 'I
haven't as much gold or silver as I need for the journey. Even if I had
enough, and wanted to go, I'm sure my daughter-in-law would prefer
it if I stayed at home. And perhaps the crew won't let me on board to
make the crossing.'

Our Lord replied, 'If I am with you who can be against you? I shall
provide for you and see that you have friends to help you. Do as I tell
you and no one on the ship will try to stand in your way.'

I realized that there was nothing for it but to make the journey as God

required, so I decided to go to Walsingham first and make an offering
to the glory of our Lady. On my way there I heard that a friar was going
to preach a sermon in a little village slightly out of my way. I turned aside
and went to the church, and I found that the friar who was preaching
was a famous man who'd attracted a very large audience.

Time and again he repeated the words, 'If God is with us who can be
against us?' These words made me all the more inclined to obey God's
will and do as he wanted, so with my daughter-in-law and the hermit
I went to Walsingham and then to Norwich.

At Norwich I met a grey friar who was a leading cleric and a doctor
of divinity. He had already heard about my way of life and the inner
sense of God that I had. This scholar treated me very well and conversed
with me as he had done before. As for me, my repeated sighing and the
sadness in my face and mood led the doctor to ask me what was wrong.

'Sir,' I said, 'when I had my confessor's permission to leave Lynn I was
planning to see my daughter-in-law to Ipswich so that, God willing, she
can make the crossing to Germany. As for me, I was meant to be going
back to Lynn as soon as I reasonably could. A hermit is travelling with
me for the very purpose of escorting me home, and there's no other
thought in his mind but to do so. But, sir, when I was about six miles
out of Lynn praying in a church I was inwardly commanded to go
overseas with my daughter-in-law. I'm sure she'd rather I stayed at
home—and so would I if only I dared. I was moved in my soul to make
the journey, and I couldn't calm my spirits or make my devotions until
I'd agreed to obey this call, but it's giving me a lot of worry and bother.'

The cleric replied, 'You must do as God wants. I believe it's the Holy
Spirit who is speaking within you, so follow your inclinations in the
name of Jesus.'

These words did a lot to reassure me, so I left and headed for the sea
along with my companions. We arrived as the ship was ready to sail, and
I asked whether I could make the crossing to Germany with them. The
captain said I was welcome on board, and the other passengers had no
objection. No one stood in my way as much as my daughter-in-law, who
should have been the person most on my side. I then said goodbye to
the hermit who'd been my travelling companion. I gave him something
for his trouble and asked him to give my confessor and my other friends
in Lynn my apologies when he got back home, because at the time I'd
parted from them I didn't have the slightest thought or intention of
making a sea crossing for as long as I lived. 'But I've got to obey the will
of God,' I told the hermit.

The hermit left looking very fed up and returned to Lynn. He passed on my apologies to my confessor and my other friends and he told them about my sudden and unexpected departure, saying he'd had no idea we were going to part so abruptly.

When they heard the news they were very surprised and they all came out with different opinions. Some put it down to the workings of the female mind; they said it was stupid for an elderly woman to risk her life at sea for the sake of her daughter-in-law, visiting a foreign country where she'd never been and not knowing how she'd ever get back. Others thought I was very kind to help my daughter-in-law to return to the homeland and friends she'd left when she and her husband had come to visit me here. There were also those who knew more about the way I lived, and they thought and believed that it must be the will and action of Almighty God for the greater glory of his name.

Chapter 3

My companions and I embarked on the Thursday of Passion Week, and God sent us good wind and weather on that day and the Friday, but on the Saturday and the Palm Sunday our Lord, acting as he saw fit, tested my faith and endurance by sending such terrible storms and high seas that we all thought we'd die. The storms raged night and day, and they were so severe and horrendous that the ship was completely out of control. All we could do was commend ourselves and our vessel to our Lord's command. The crew gave up trying to exercise their craft and their skill and we let our Lord propel us wheresoever he wished.

I don't think I'd ever gone through so much anguish and torment before. I cried to our Lord for mercy and asked him to save me and everyone else on board. I thought to myself, 'Lord, I came here out of love for you, and you've often promised that I wouldn't die on the road, at sea or in a storm. People have often damned me and cursed me because of your acts of grace within me. They've wished me a dreadful, tormented death, and it seems as if it's coming true. Lord, make haste to withdraw these storms and show us mercy or I'll be robbed and cheated of the promise you've made so often. I'm a worthless wretch but I've always trusted in your mercy and goodness; now if my enemies have their way and I'm deceived, they'll be gloating over my distress.

'Blessed Jesus, remember your abundant mercy and keep the promise you've given to me. You've brought me here to face the perils of the open seas, so prove that you are truly God and not a devil. For years I've trusted and obeyed your advice, and by your mercy I'll do the same for years to come if you save us from these dreadful dangers. Lord, help and sustain us before we die or give up hope; we can't remain in this plight for long without your mercy and your support.'

Speaking inside me, our merciful Lord reproached me for my cowardice. 'Why are you terrified? Why are you so frightened?' he asked. 'I'm as powerful here at sea as I am on dry land. Why don't you trust me? I'll never deceive you and I'll honour all my promises to you. Rely on my mercy and suffer patiently for just a while. Be firm in your faith, otherwise how can you hope to please me? If you'll trust me completely and dispel all your doubts, you'll find inner strength. Instead of being full of dread and apprehension, you'll be able to reassure all your fellow passengers.'

By talking to me in that way, and in ways far higher and holier than I could ever describe, our Lord brought me comfort. May his name be blessed! And when I prayed to holy saints, our Lord allowed them to talk to my soul in words of great comfort. Finally, our Lord came and said to me, 'Daughter, take heart. You've always found you can trust my word, and I promise you that these winds and high seas will soon die down and the weather will clear, so stop being frightened.' Soon afterwards—God be praised!—the wind blew the ship to the coast of Norway. We landed there on Good Friday and stayed for Easter Saturday, Easter Sunday and Easter Monday.

On the Monday, everyone received communion on board the ship. On Easter Day itself the ship's captain, along with myself and most of the others on board had gone ashore to hear mass at the church. In accordance with local custom, the cross was raised [from the sepulchre] at about midday, and I was filled with devotion and holy thoughts and wept and sobbed as much as if I had been at home. God did not withdraw his grace from me either in church or in the ship or out at sea, nor in any place where I ever went; he was always present in my soul.

After we'd received the sacrament on Easter Monday, as I've already mentioned, our Lord sent us a favourable wind, and we were able to leave Norway and make for Germany, just as we wanted. I got on so well with the captain that he treated me like a mother and gave me food, drink and all my other necessities throughout the voyage. He even lent me his own clothes, otherwise I might have died of cold, because I wasn't as well prepared as the others. I had gone to sea at our Lord's command, and the Master who had told me to go ensured that I managed as well as any of the others. May our Lord be praised and worshipped for it!

Chapter 4

I stayed in Danzig in Germany for about four or five weeks and many people received me well out of love for our Lord. No one was as strongly opposed to me as my daughter-in-law was, despite the fact that as a relative she was bound and obliged to treat me well. I rejoiced in our Lord that people were being so good to me out of love for him, and I was inclined to stay longer. However, our Lord advised me inwardly to leave the district.

I was troubled and bewildered as to how I would carry out God's will, which I didn't in any way want to resist. I had no one of either sex to go with me, and I couldn't go as near to the sea as I would have liked; as I approached it I found that I was too afraid. There was also a problem with the land route because I'd have to pass through districts which were affected by war. What with one thing and another I was thoroughly miserable and I didn't know which way to turn.

I entered a church and prayed that since our Lord had told me to go he would send me help and travelling companions. Suddenly a man came up to me and asked me if I'd make a pilgrimage to a far-off place called Wilsnack, where people venerate the precious blood of our Lord Jesus Christ. It had miraculously oozed out of three hosts which had been consecrated at the altar, and they and the precious blood are worshipped and revered there right to this day by pilgrims who come from far and wide.

I said I'd be more than pleased to go if I'd have good company and I could find some honest man who'd then escort me from Wilsnack to England. He assured me that after making the pilgrimage to Wilsnack with me at his own expense he would see me to the Channel coast, where I'd find companions from my own country, as long as I covered all his costs once we'd left Wilsnack.

He obtained a small ship to take us on our way to the shrine, but as an Englishwoman I couldn't get permission to leave the country. I tried to get permission from one of the Teutonic Knights but I met with a lot of obstruction and hindrance. In the end, our Lord caused a merchant from Lynn to hear of my plight. He came and reassured me, and promised to help me to get away, either secretly or openly. After putting himself to a lot of trouble this good man got permission for me to go where I wanted.

Then I went on board the vessel with the man who'd agreed to look after me. God sent us a light breeze, which pleased me a lot because the sea didn't get choppy. There were others on board who grumbled and groused because they felt we weren't making proper progress. I prayed to our Lord, who sent so much wind that we scudded along and the waves became unpleasantly high. My companions were pleased and delighted but I had a thoroughly miserable time because of the waves. I had only to look at them to be afraid. Our Lord spoke to my spirit and told me to lie down so that I wouldn't see the waves, and that's what I did. Even so, my fears remained and they often made the others impatient with me. So it was that we sailed on our way to a place called Stralsund.

(No one should be surprised if the place-names aren't written correctly. I was more concerned with meditating than studying place-names. As for my scribe, please excuse him, too, as he'd never seen them.)

Chapter 5

When we reached Stralsund we disembarked, and the man and I made our way towards Wilsnack. We were frightened because there were many dangers on the way. There was open war between England and the states we were travelling through, and time and again I begged the man not to abandon me in these foreign lands where the people were hostile. The state of war made me far more afraid than I would have been, but our Lord repeatedly spoke to my mind: 'Why are you afraid?' he asked. 'No one will harm you or anyone you're travelling with. Reassure the man and tell him that no one will hurt him or harm him as long as he's in your company.

'Daughter, you know perfectly well that out of love for a good-looking, handsome husband a woman will go where he wants her to. And, Daughter, there is no one as lovely, as attractive or as good as me, so if you love me you won't shrink from going wherever I want to take you. Daughter, I brought you here and I shall take you safely home to England. Don't worry—just trust me.'

Such holy words and speech in my soul made me weep my eyes out and sob noisily. The more I cried the more the man tired of my company and wanted to abandon me to my own devices. He walked so fast that keeping up was very distressing and tiring for me. He said he was frightened that enemies and thieves might snatch me away and beat him up and steal his things. I did my best to reassure him and I told him I could guarantee that no one would beat him, rob him or even insult him.

Soon after I had said these things there appeared from a wood a tall, well-armed man who looked as if he was ready for a fight.

My man was terrified. 'Look,' he said, 'what's this we can see?'

'Trust in our Lord and don't be afraid of anyone,' I answered, and sure enough the man passed us by and didn't say anything out of the way.

We continued our arduous journey to Wilsnack, but although I didn't have as much stamina as the man, he didn't care what became of me and he wouldn't wait for me. All I could do was struggle on as best I could until such time as illness stopped me from going any further. It was something of a miracle that a lame woman about sixty years old should have kept up for days with a vigorous man who was so impatient to stride on his way.

On the eve of the feast of Corpus Christi we chanced to arrive at a little inn which was quite a way from the nearest town, and the only bedding we could get for ourselves was a little straw. I rested on it throughout the night and all the next day until night fell again. During this time, our Lord sent almost continuous lightning, thunder and rain, which stopped us pursuing our weary way. I was thoroughly glad, because I was really ill and I knew full well that in good weather my companion wouldn't have waited for me—he would have gone. I thanked God for giving him cause to wait though he hadn't meant to.

Because I was ill, arrangements were made for a cart to be ready at Wilsnack, and when the time came I was borne to the Holy Blood of Wilsnack in penitence and great discomfort.

During the journey the local women felt sorry for me, and as we hurried along the roads they frequently told my companion that he was very reprehensible to work me so hard. He only wanted to get rid of me, so he didn't bother about what they said and he didn't spare me in the slightest. Thus through thick and thin our Lord ensured that I reached Wilsnack, where I saw the precious blood which had miraculously oozed from the blessed sacrament of the altar.

Chapter 6

We didn't stay in Wilsnack for long but quickly set off for Aachen by wagon. We soon arrived at a busy ford where people heading for Aachen encountered travellers going in other directions. One of the people there was a monk, a dissolute, irresponsible man who had some young traders or shopkeepers with him.

The monk and the traders were on familiar terms with my guide. They addressed him by name and seemed really friendly towards him. Travelling as a single party, the monk and the traders and me and my companion forded the river together in wagons, and we found ourselves passing a house of Friars Minor. We were very thirsty, and the others told me to go and ask the friars for a jug of wine.

'Sirs,' I replied, 'you'll have to excuse me. If it were a house of nuns I'd be ready to go, but as they're men I'm afraid I won't.'

One of the traders went for the jug of wine. Then one of the friars came out and asked us in to see the blessed sacrament in their church. It was still the eight days of Corpus Christi and it was on display in a glass container for anyone to see if they wanted to. The monk and the other men followed the friars and went inside. I decided I'd like to see the precious sacrament too, so I went as well, though they weren't really keen to have me with them. As soon as I saw it I was filled by the Lord with so much sweetness and devotion that I wept and sobbed uncontrollably with intense feeling. The monk and his companions were angry with me for weeping so much, and as we returned to our wagons they told me off and upbraided me, calling me a hypocrite and making all sorts of nasty remarks. By way of reply, I quoted scripture, citing verses from the psalms: 'They that sow in tears' etc. and 'They that go forth and weep' etc. and others of the sort. At that, they were even angrier; they said I could no longer travel with them and they got my guide to abandon me.

I quietly and gently begged them for the love of God to let me stay with them and not leave me all by myself in a place where there was no one I could turn to and no one who knew me. I pleaded and begged till they let me stay with them as far as a good-sized town, which we reached on the eighth day of Corpus Christi. Once there, they were adamant: come what may, I couldn't stay with them any longer. The man who'd agreed to be my guide and had promised to escort me right to England gave me my gold and other things he was keeping for me, offered to lend me more gold if I wanted him to and said I'd have to fend for myself.

'John,' I replied, 'it wasn't your gold I wanted; in these foreign lands your friendship was worth more to me than anything you possess. What's more, I think you'd please God better if you stayed with me as you promised in Danzig than if you walked all the way to Rome.'

Thus it was that they put me out of their company and left me to make my own way. I said to the man who'd been my guide, 'John, the only reason you're leaving me is that I weep when I see the sacrament or think about our Lord's passion. I'm being forsaken for following God, and I've never known him to let me down so I'm sure he'll meet my needs and keep me safe on the road. May his name be blessed!'

They went off leaving me standing there, and as night fell I felt extremely unhappy at being alone. I didn't know who I could stay with that night or travel with on the following day. I found an inn but a number of local priests came up to me, calling me names like 'English arse' and making other vulgar remarks. I could see the lust in their faces as they asked me whether I fancied having them to escort me. I was terrified for my chastity and thoroughly miserable.

I went to the woman who ran the inn and asked if I could have some of her maids to spend the night with me. She chose two maids, who stayed with me for the whole of the night, but fear of defilement stopped me from sleeping. I lay awake nearly all night long, praying to be saved from any form of sordidness and asking God to find me some wholesome companions who could help me on my way to Aachen. Suddenly, I was inwardly told to go to church early the following day and I'd meet some companions.

I paid for my lodgings first thing in the morning and asked my hosts if they knew of anyone heading for Aachen, but they told me they didn't. I said goodbye and went to the church to meditate and find out whether my inner voice had informed me correctly. As I arrived I saw a group of poor people and I went up to one of them, asking where they were planning to go. When he told me they were going to Aachen I asked him if he'd let me go with them.

'Woman,' he answered, 'haven't you got a man to go with you?'

'No,' I said, 'my man has left me.'

That's how I came to join with some poor folk, and every time we came to a town I bought my food while the others went begging. Out in the country, my companions sometimes removed their clothes and sat there naked, picking fleas off each other. Necessity forced me to bear with them, though it lengthened my journey and put me to much more expense than I would have had otherwise. I felt that it was beneath me to take my clothes off like them, but mixing with them had given me a share of the vermin too, and they bit me and stung me horribly. I suffered morning, noon and night until God sent me some other companions. Despite the discomfort, anguish and delays, I had to stay with the party of poor folk until we reached Aachen.

Chapter 7

On reaching Aachen I met an English monk who was on his way to
Rome. I felt a lot better at having someone I could understand, and we
stayed together for ten or eleven days, during which we viewed our
Lady's smock and other holy relics which were put on display on St
Margaret's Day.

While we were staying there a respectable woman happened to arrive
from London. She was a widow who'd come with a number of servants
to see the holy relics and venerate them. I approached this respectable
woman and told her of my misfortune in having no one to go home to
England with. She promised me everything I could have asked and she
entertained me really well with food and drink.

When St Margaret's Day had come and gone and we'd seen the relics,
this worthy woman and all her servants left Aachen in a hurry. I'd
expected to go with her and I was very unhappy at having my hopes
frustrated like this. I said goodbye to the monk I've mentioned, who was
heading for Rome, and I got on a wagon that was carrying pilgrims. I
did my best to catch the respectable woman up but it wasn't to be.
However, I happened to meet two men, both Londoners, who were on
their way home. I asked them if I could travel with them and they said
I'd be welcome as long as I could manage to go at their speed—they
couldn't tolerate much delay but apart from that they'd be happy to help
me.

It was all I could do to hurry along behind them until we reached a
large town. Here we met some English pilgrims who'd visited the court
of Rome and were returning to England. I begged them to let me join
them, but they told me curtly that they weren't prepared to lengthen
their journey on my account; they'd been robbed and had very little
money to get them home, so they had to take the most demanding
routes and I'd only be welcome if I could manage to keep up with them.
I couldn't see any help for it but to stay with them for as long as I could,
so I left the two men and attached myself to this new party.

We then went to eat and enjoy ourselves. During the meal I glanced
to one side and saw a man who was leaning against the end of a bench.
I asked who it was and they told me it was a friar who belonged to their
party.

'Why isn't he eating with you?' I asked.

'He's been robbed, the same as us, and everyone's got to fend for
themselves as best they can.'

'Well,' I replied, 'I'll give him a share of anything that God sends me.'

(I was certain our Lord would provide us both with whatever we needed.) I gave the monk some food and drink and he cheered up a lot, whereupon we all set out on the road. I followed just behind the rest; I was too old and weak to match their pace. I scampered along and hopped over puddles as fast as I could, but in the end my strength gave out. I had a word with the poor friar I'd helped at the inn and asked him to be my travelling companion as far as Calais, in which case I'd meet his costs and give him something on top to reward his trouble. The friar was more than satisfied and agreed to the deal.

We let the others go ahead and we followed at an easy pace that we could manage. However, the friar got terribly thirsty and he said to me, 'I know this area very well because I've often gone through it on my way to Rome, and I'm certain there's an inn not far from here. Let's go for a drink,' and I happily let him take me there.

When we reached the inn, the hostess felt sorry for me because I was so tired and she said I should travel by cart with other pilgrims, not walk as I was doing with just one male companion. I explained that I had been meaning and fully expecting to travel with a respectable woman from London but had been let down. After resting and having a chat with the hostess we noticed a cart-load of pilgrims going past the inn. The hostess knew the pilgrims who were in the cart, and although they'd gone past she called them back. When she asked them to help me on my way they readily agreed and took me on board.

In due course we reached a good-sized town, and as we passed through I happened to see the woman from London I've already mentioned. I apologized to the other pilgrims and asked them if I could pay a fair price for the time I'd been with them and join my fellow countrywoman, who I'd seen in the town. I explained that we'd agreed, back in Aachen, to travel home to England together.

The pilgrims and I said goodbye and parted on friendly terms. As they went on their way I approached the lady, expecting a warm welcome but getting quite the opposite: she gave me short shrift and spoke to me sharply. 'Why do you think you can travel with me?' the lady demanded. 'I'll have you know that I don't want anything to do with you.'

I was so badly snubbed that I didn't know what to do with myself. I knew no one in the town and no one knew me. I didn't know which way to turn or where the friar was who'd agreed to escort me; whether he'd be coming that way or not I'd no idea. I was very confused and very upset. I felt that this was the lowest I'd been since leaving England. Even so, I put my faith in our Lord's promise and waited in the town for God to send me some sort of help. At last, when it was nearly dusk, I saw the friar approaching the town. I hurried to meet him, complaining of how I had been let down and rebuffed by the woman I'd trusted so much.

The friar did his best to comfort me and he said we'd do no better or worse than God ordained, but he also said that he wouldn't spend the night in the town because he was certain the people presented a threat. We therefore left the town together during the evening, bemoaning our problems as we went and feeling apprehensive and troubled as to where we could shelter during the night.

We happened to be walking beside a wood, darting our eyes all over the place to try and find somewhere where we could rest when by the grace of God we spotted one or two houses. We hurried towards them and found a good man living with his wife and two children. They didn't run an inn or take paying guests but I saw a heap of bracken in the house and I prevailed on them to let me make it my bed for the night. In response to the friar's pleas they let him sleep in the barn, and we thought ourselves lucky to have roofs over our heads.

On the following day we paid for our lodging and struck out for Calais. The going was tiring and difficult: there were two days when we had to cope with hills, valleys and shifting sands. We were thirsty and suffered a lot of discomfort because there weren't many towns on the route we followed and the accommodation was very poor.

I was often most afraid at night. Perhaps I was being afflicted by some unseen enemy, because I was constantly afraid of being raped or defiled. I didn't feel there was a single man who I could trust. With or without good cause I was frightened all the time, and at night I hardly closed my eyes for fear of being molested. Because of this I was always reluctant to go to bed at night unless I had one or two women with me. By the grace of God, there were generally girls who were happy to lie with me in all the places where I stayed, which did a lot to ease my mind.

On the approach to Calais I was so tired and exhausted that I thought I was going to give up the ghost as I tramped along. It was all I could do to reach the town. The friar, who was still at my side, had treated me in a thoroughly pleasant and proper way throughout the journey. Because of this, I rewarded him as best I could and he went on his way seeming very pleased and satisfied.

Chapter 8

In Calais a lot of people—both men and women—treated me kindly, although they'd never seen me before. One good woman invited me into her house and gave me a good wash. She put a new smock on me and looked after me really well. There were other good people who also had me to eat and drink with them.

I had to stay there for three or four days awaiting a ship, and during this time I met a number of old acquaintances. They were waiting for a ship as well, and they gave me the benefit of their kind words and honeyed tongues but they didn't give me anything else.

I wanted to sail to Dover with them but they wouldn't lift a finger to help me and they wouldn't tell me what ship they were using. I enquired and watched to the best of my abilities, and by various means I managed to keep abreast of their plans. In the end I went on board their ship with all my baggage, thinking they would soon be putting to sea, though I didn't know exactly when. However, for a reason I could never discover they suddenly changed to a different ship. By the grace of God I knew they were planning to sail in a hurry, so I left all my things in the boat I was in and with the help of our Lord I was able to get a place on board their new ship. The respectable woman from London who'd previously turned me away was among the other passengers. So it turned out that we all set sail for Dover together.

I could tell from their looks and manner that the others didn't like me very much, so I asked our Lord to help me to keep my dignity and not be sea-sick in front of them, as I didn't want to give them any cause for revulsion. My prayer was answered: while the others were throwing up and spewing, and making plenty of noise and mess, I surprised them all by keeping my composure and doing what I could for them. The woman from London suffered the worst of all when it came to feeling and being sick, so she was the one I did most to help and reassure. I did it for love of our Lord and out of kindness—I didn't have any other motive.

When we reached Dover, those of the passengers who so desired chose companions for the road ahead. I was the only who couldn't—I just wasn't able to get a companion to lighten my journey. I therefore struck out for Canterbury by myself, feeling rather miserable and sad at having no company and also at the fact that I didn't know the way.

One morning I got up early and knocked at the door of a humble cottage. The good fellow who came to see what I wanted had dressed in a hurry—his clothes were untidy and not buttoned up. I told him that if he had a horse I would like him to help me to get to Canterbury, and that I would pay him for his trouble. He wanted to oblige me for the sake of our Lord, so he did as I wanted and led me to Canterbury.

I rejoiced in our Lord, who had helped and relieved me in all my needs, and I thanked him by shedding tears of devotion, sobbing and weeping in almost every place where I called. This was true in places I haven't even mentioned both at home and abroad and by land and by sea. May God be blessed!

Chapter 9

I travelled from Canterbury to London dressed in a sort of apron made of a sheet of canvas. It was rather like wearing a piece of sacking, and was just the same as the thing I'd worn for my journey overseas. When I reached London there were many people who knew who I was. Through lack of money I wasn't dressed as I would have liked and I wanted to avoid being recognized till I'd managed to do some borrowing, so I put a handkerchief over my face. In spite of this, some good-for-nothings recognized me as Margery Kempe of Lynn and by way of insult they said out loud for me to hear: 'Ah, you false flesh—there won't be any good food for you!' I didn't answer and I carried on as if I'd not heard.

I'd never uttered the words above. I'd used them neither of God nor of man, yet people accused me of having done so, and as a result I suffered a lot of condemnation in all sorts of places. They sprang from the Devil, the father of lies, and were cherished, repeated and spread by his minions, false envious people who resented the virtuous way I lived and had no way of doing me harm except with their lying tongues.

No man or woman could ever prove that I'd uttered such words, but they took them on the say-so of other liars, and they made the excuse that they were simply repeating what they'd heard. And that's how these spurious words started going the rounds—thanks to the Devil.

It was shortly after I received God's call that the Devil persuaded one or two people to make the following story up: they said that I was sitting at a good man's table on a day when it was the rule to eat fish. I was served all sorts of fish, including red herring, good quality pike and so on, and they claimed that I'd said to myself, 'Ah, you false flesh, you're going to take the red herring but you won't have your way.' And at that I'd pushed the red herring aside and gone for the pike.

I was supposed to have said other things of the sort, and the words √'False flesh, you'll eat no herring' turned into a catch-phrase that people used at my expense. Other people used the version above, and though there was no truth in any of it the words weren't forgotten and were bandied about in places where I wasn't known and hadn't been heard of.

I went to visit a very respectable widow in London, and for love of our Lord she welcomed me and gave me excellent hospitality. Her house was one of the many places in London where people entertained me well in our Lord's name. May God reward all of them! There was one particular lady who lavished food, drink and other things on me, and on one occasion I dined at her house with various people from all walks of life— people I didn't know and who didn't know me, including some I was later told belonged to the cardinal's household. We had a wonderful feast and we really enjoyed it, but during the merriment some of the guests came out with the words I've quoted above, or others like them— that's to say, 'You false flesh, you won't have any of this fine food.'

I kept quiet and put up with it for a good while. They were busy nattering to one another and making play of the shortcoming of whoever the words related to. When they'd finished bandying the words about I asked them if they knew the person who was supposed to have said them. They answered, 'No, we don't at all, but we've heard that there's a lying hypocrite in Lynn who says that sort of thing. She leaves the plainer kinds of food and waits for all the fancy dishes.'

'Sirs,' I said, 'if you talk about people you should understate any faults you know of, not exaggerate them. In this case—God forgive you— you're saying worse than you know, because I'm the very person you're talking about. I'm used to shame and criticism but as God is my witness I'm not at fault this time.'

When they saw that I wasn't upset, and that rather than wanting to tell them off I simply wanted to put them right in a friendly spirit, they felt the force of my honesty and tried to be conciliatory.

Wherever I went in London I spoke out loud and clear against wrongdoers, including people who swore or cursed or lied. I also spoke out against the showy clothes being worn by men and women alike. I didn't try to spare their feelings or win them round with flattery—not even to make them give me money or food or drinks.

The things I said did a lot of good, and because of this our Lord filled me with devotion when I entered a church to meditate. He thanked me for the fearless way I spoke in his name, denouncing sin and suffering scorn and condemnation for his sake, and he promised me abundant grace in this life and endless joy and bliss in heaven. Our Lord's sweet words gave me so much strength that I couldn't control myself. Instead of obeying my wishes or the guidance of other people, my soul was controlled and guided by our Lord himself, and it expressed itself in noisy sobbing and copious tears, which brought me a great deal of slander and criticism, especially from London's curates and priests.

They refused to let me stay in their churches, and so as not to cause them annoyance I went from one church to another. Many of the ordinary people praised God for being present in me, firmly believing it was God's own goodness that bestowed such mighty grace on my soul.

Chapter 10

Three days before Lammas Day I left London and went to the monastery at Syon in order to obtain my pardon through our Lord's mercy. While I was in the church at Syon I was filled with deep devotion and sublime insight. I shed copious tears of compunction and compassion when I remembered the bitter pains and sufferings which our merciful Lord Jesus Christ endured in the course of his blessed manhood.

Those who saw me weeping and heard my noisy sobs were struck with amazement and wonder as to what it was that was filling my soul. A young man who saw my face and expression was moved by the Holy Spirit to approach me discreetly when he found a suitable moment to do so. He was very keen to understand the cause of my weeping, and he said to me, 'Mother, would you mind telling me why you weep? I've never seen anyone cry as copiously as you, and I've certainly not heard anyone making as much noise sobbing. Mother, though I'm young I want to please our Lord Jesus Christ and follow him as best I can. I'm planning with the help of God to take the habit of the order here, so please try not to be reserved. I'm hoping you'll open your mind and be kind and motherly to me.'

I was gentle and encouraging, and I gladly told him what I thought was appropriate, commending his plans and explaining that part of the reason I wept was that my undaughterly behaviour towards my Maker had often offended against his goodness. It was the great loathing I felt for my sins that made me sob and weep. I was also moved to sob and weep—not surprisingly—by the supreme love of my redeemer, for the passion he'd suffered and the blood he'd shed had saved me from everlasting torment and made me an heir to joy and bliss. I said all sorts of worthwhile things to give him inner strength and power, and for the rest of the time I was there he ate and drank in my company, which he valued highly.

Lammas Day was the main day of pardon, and as I entered the church at Syon I saw the hermit who, as I've already explained, had led me from Lynn with my daughter-in-law on our way to the port. Feeling very glad,

I immediately introduced myself to him, greeting him wholeheartedly and saying to him, 'Ah, Reynald, it's good to see you. I'm sure our Lord must have sent you here, for I'm hoping that having led me from Lynn you'll now escort me back again.'

The hermit seemed unfriendly and wore a scowl on his face—he had no intention of seeing me home to Lynn as I'd hoped. 'I'll have you know your confessor has given you up because you sailed abroad and didn't tell him a word about it,' he told me brusquely. 'You got permission to take your daughter-in-law to the port; you didn't get permission for anything more. None of the friends you had at the time knew what you were planning—so I don't suppose you'll have many friends left when you get back home. Please look somewhere else for an escort; last time I led you on a journey you let me down and I got the blame. I've had enough!'

I urged him and begged him for the love of God not to be annoyed, and I said that those who'd loved me for God's sake before I left would love me for God's sake when I returned. I offered to pay his expenses on the journey home, and in the end he accepted my offer. He escorted me back to London and from there to Lynn, to the glory of God and the benefit of both our souls.

Once I was back in Lynn I submitted myself to my confessor and he spoke to me in no uncertain terms. He was particularly angry because although I was bound to obey him I had undertaken my long journey without his knowledge. However, with the help of our Lord I was soon as highly regarded by him and my other friends as I had been before. May God be praised! Amen.

THE BOOK OF
MARGERY KEMPE

Margery Kempe's Prayers

Margery Kempe's Prayers

For many years I used to begin my prayers like this: when I entered the church I knelt in front of the sacrament to honour the Blessed Trinity (Father, Son and Holy Spirit; one God in three Persons), that glorious virgin the Queen of Mercy our Lady St Mary and the twelve apostles. As I knelt there I recited all the verses of the hymn 'Veni creator spiritus' [Come creator spirit] in the hope that God would illumine my soul as he had illumined the souls of his apostles on the day of Pentecost, endowing me with the gifts of the Holy Spirit so that I would have the grace to understand and do his will, resist the temptations put in my way by my unseen enemies and reject all sin and wickedness.

Once I had said the 'Veni creator spiritus' in full I used to continue as follows: 'I take as my witness the Holy Spirit, our Lady St Mary the Mother of God, the heavenly host and all my confessors here on earth that even if it were possible for me to have complete knowledge and understanding of the mysteries of God, divulged to me by some devil from Hell, I would not want to have it. And as surely as I wouldn't wish to know, hear, see, feel or inwardly apprehend in this life more than God wished, just as surely may God be my help in all my works, in all my thoughts and in all that I say, whether eating, drinking, sleeping or waking.

'Since it's not my will or intention to worship any false devil in place of my God, nor to follow any untrue faith or false beliefs, I renounce the Devil, all his lies and all that I've ever done, said or thought under his influence while believing that I was following God's advice and the inspiration of the Holy Spirit. God, you see and hear the hidden depths of everyone's heart, and inasfar as I've been wrong-minded, forgive me for it and give me in this present life a freely-flowing spring of tears with which to wash away my sins through your mercy and goodness. And, Lord, of your sublime mercy bless me here on earth with all the tears that could make my love for you greater, enlarge my store of merit in heaven and help the souls of my fellow Christians, alive or dead, or bring them advantage. Good Lord, you should no more spare the eyes in my head than you spared the blood in your own body, which you freely shed for the souls of sinners; and give me sufficient pain and sorrow in this world to ensure that I am not prevented from sharing your bliss and seeing your glorious face when I die.

'As for my wailing and sobbing and weeping, Lord God Almighty, you know what scorn, humiliation, contempt and blame they have brought upon me; and you know that it isn't within my own power to weep aloud or silently, no matter what feelings of devotion or sweetness come upon me, since all my tears are a blessing from the Holy Spirit. This being so, Lord, excuse me in the eyes of the world and help people to realize and understand that you do this work and bestow this gift to glorify your name and to make their love for you greater. And, sovereign Lord Christ Jesus, may my crying and weeping save as many people as have scorned me for it, or shall do until the end of the world—many more if that is your will.

'So far as earthly love is concerned, all I want is to love God supremely and to love other creatures for him and in him. This being so, I ask you to quench all carnal desire both in me and in all whose human form has shown me the shape of your own blessed body.

'Lord, suffuse our hearts with a holy fear of you, for the sake of your cruel wounds. Make my confessors fear you in me and love you in me, and by virtue of the grief that you've given me for the sins of others make everyone grieve all the more for their own sins. Good Jesus, make my will yours and your will mine so that I shall have no will but yours alone.

'Good Lord Christ Jesus, I beg you to have mercy on all the lands that belong to Holy Church, on the Pope and all his cardinals, on all archbishops, bishops and all the orders of priests, on all professed religious and especially on all who are working to preserve and defend the teachings of Holy Church. Lord, mercifully bless them, give them victory over their enemies and success in all that they do to bring you glory. Help all who are in a state of grace to remain so right to the end of their lives; make me worthy to have a place in their prayers and they in mine, and each of us in the prayers of the others.

'Have mercy, blessed Lord, on the king of England, all Christian kings and all lords and ladies throughout the world. Lord, help them to use their authority in the way you like best and be lords and ladies in heaven for ever. Lord, I implore you to have mercy on the rich men who are stewards of your goods in this earthly life; give them the grace to use them to your satisfaction.

'Lord, have mercy on Jews, Saracens and all heathen people. Good Lord, bear in mind that there are many saints in heaven who at one time lived as heathens on earth; and just as you have extended your mercy to those in heaven, so extend it to those who are still in this world.

'Lord, you say yourself that no one will come to you without your help and that no one will be called unless you call them. If there's anyone you haven't drawn to you, please may they hear your voice and follow you.

You've called me, Lord, though I never deserved it; you did so because of your great mercy. If everyone knew of all my misdeeds, as you do, Lord, they would wonder and marvel at your goodness towards me. If only they were fit to thank you on my behalf! But you have made worthless creatures good, so make the whole world worthy to give you thanks and praise.

'Lord, have mercy on all misguided heretics and misbelievers, on all tithe-dodgers, thieves, adulterers, prostitutes and criminals. Merciful Lord, forgive them if it's your will to do so, and make them mend their ways all the sooner because of my prayers. Have mercy on all who are tempted and troubled by their unseen enemies, giving them grace to withstand their seductions and ending them when you think it best.

'Have mercy on all my confessors, suffusing their souls with as much grace as I would like you to instil into mine. Have mercy, Lord, on all my children, whether born of my mind or born of my body, and on everyone throughout the world. By my true contrition may you make their sins as if they were mine and forgive their guilt as I would like to have my own guilt pardoned.

'Have mercy, Lord, on all my friends and all my enemies, especially the ones who are ill; and have mercy on all lepers, all bedridden people, all prisoners and all who have spoken about me (or will do so until the end of the world) whether what they say is good or bad. Have mercy on them and treat their souls as graciously as I'd like you to treat mine. Show your sublime mercy to those who have spoken evil of me and forgive them for it. As for those who have spoken in my favour, Lord, reward them because they've done it out of their goodness and not through any merit on my part; you would not be unfair if you let the whole world punish and hate me for having displeased you.

'Have mercy, Lord, on all the suffering souls in purgatory as they await your clemency and the prayers of Holy Church, for surely, Lord, they number among the souls you have chosen. Be as gracious to them as I'd want you to be to my soul if it were going through as much pain as they are.

'Lord Christ Jesus, I thank you for all health and all wealth, for all riches and all poverty, for sickness, scorn, spite, injustice, and all the various troubles which have befallen me or shall do so for as long as I live; and I give you great thanks for any pain you allow me to suffer in this earthly life to atone for my sins and increase my store of merit in heaven. Lord, hear my prayers, for I sincerely have every reason to thank you.

'Even if my soul contained as many hearts and souls as God knew from everlasting would live in heaven eternally, and as many as there are drops of fresh and salt water, pebbles, stones, rocks and blades of grass on the face of the earth, grains of corn, and fish, birds and beasts, leaves on the trees at the height of the season, feathers on birds or hairs on animals, seeds of grass and weeds and flowers both on land and in water when seeds are most plentiful; and even if it contained as many hearts and souls as the number of creatures—past, present and future—which could possibly live, and as many as all the other good things which the earth brings forth, and as many as the stars and angels in the sight of God; and even if each were as holy a soul as our Lady St Mary, who bore Jesus our Saviour, and could think and utter such words of adoration and worship as our Lady St Mary did on this earth, does now in heaven and shall do forever, I could still believe in my heart and say with my mouth to the worship of the Trinity and the heavenly host and to the shame and disgrace of Satan, who fell and could no longer see God's countenance, and of all Satan's demons, that all these hearts and souls could never thank, praise, extol, worship or love God fully, nor could they fully magnify, praise and revere him in accordance with the great mercy he has shown me on earth. As for myself, I cannot do it and I have no way of doing it.

'My Lady, uniquely-chosen Mother of God, fountain of grace, loveliest flower of all women God ever made in the world, the most precious and most highly-prized in his sight, because of your surpassing merits on earth you, more than all souls, supremely deserve to be heard by God. Benign, meek and gracious Lady, adored in heaven with all your holy saints around you, I beg you, out of your love for me, to offer thanks and praise to the blessed Trinity, asking God to show mercy and grace to me and all my confessors, and asking him to help us to persevere until we die in the way of life that pleases him most.

'My soul praises God and all of you who dwell in heaven. May God be blessed in all of you and may you all be blessed in God. Lord, may you be honoured for all your mercies to those in heaven and those on earth. Lord, I especially give you thanks for Mary Magdalene, Mary of Egypt, St Paul and St Augustine. As you showed them your mercy, so show it to me and to all who appeal to your merciful heart.

'May I inherit the peace and repose you left your disciples and those who loved you, and may I enjoy it on earth and in heaven for evermore.

'Lord, remember the woman who was taken in adultery and brought in front of you. You drove all her enemies away and she was left standing all alone with you. I need you to do the same for me: drive away all my enemies, both physical and spiritual, so that I can stand alone in front of you; deaden my soul to all worldly pleasures and make it alive and hungry for the sublime contemplation of all that you are.

'Lord, remember Lazarus who lay in his grave for four days. As well as visiting the holy place where your body was alive and where, for man's sins, it suffered crucifixion and death, I have been where Lazarus was raised from the dead. So, Lord, if any man or woman has died at this hour in mortal sin, and if any prayer can be of avail, then hear my plea on their behalf and bring them to everlasting life.

'Thank you, Lord, for all the sins you have kept me from committing and thank you, Lord, for all the troubles you have made me suffer for those which I have committed. For these and all the other mercies which are necessary for me and for every living creature on earth, I thank you, Lord.

'As for all those who put their faith and trust in my prayers, or shall do so until the end of the world, I ask you, Lord, to grant them, of your abundant mercy, such blessings in spirit or body as they may desire for the good of their souls. Amen.'

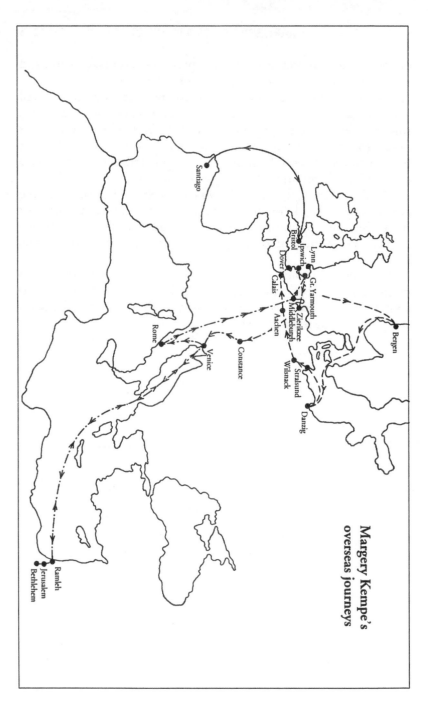

Margery Kempe's overseas journeys

Santiago
Lynn
Bristol
Ipswich
Dover
Calais
Gt. Yarmouth
Zierikzee
Middleburgh
Aachen
Rome
Venice
Constance
Stralsund
Wilsnack
Bergen
Danzig
Ramleh
Jerusalem
Bethlehem

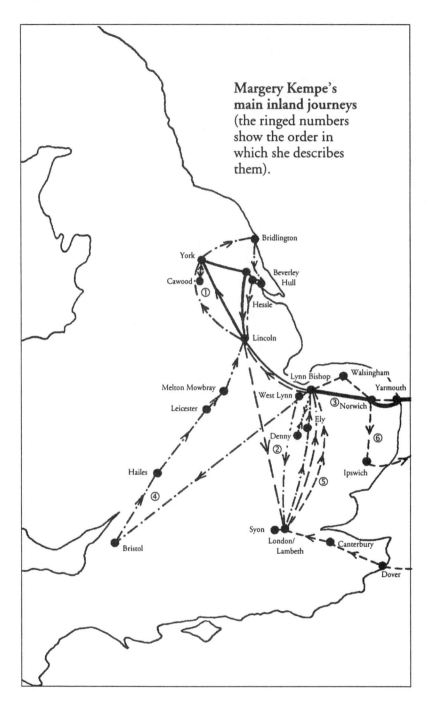

Margery Kempe's
main inland journeys
(the ringed numbers
show the order in
which she describes
them).

Further Reading

Atkinson, C. W., *Mystic and Pilgrim: The Book and World of Margery Kempe* (Cornell, 1983)

Cholmeley, K., *Margery Kempe: Genius and Mystic* (London, 1947)

Collis, L., *The Apprentice Saint* (London, 1964)

Goodman, A., 'The Piety of John Brunham's Daughter, of Lynn', in *Medieval Women*, ed. D. Baker (Oxford, 1978)

Hirsch, J. C., 'Author and Scribe in *The Book of Margery Kempe*', *Medium Aevum*, 44 (1975)

Hirsch, J. C., *The Revelations of Margery Kempe* (Leiden, 1989)

Kempe, M., The Book of Margery Kempe ed. H. E. Allen and S. B. Meech (Oxford, for the Early English Text Society, 1940, 1993)

McEntire, S. J. (ed.), *Margery Kempe: A Book of Essays* (New York and London, 1992)

Osborn, J. M., *The Beginnings of Autobiography in England* (Los Angeles, 1959)

Thornton, M., *Margery Kempe: An Example in the English Pastoral Tradition* (London, 1960)

Watkin, E. I., *On Julian of Norwich, and in Defence of Margery Kempe* (Exeter, 1979)

Weissman, H. P., 'Margery Kempe in Jerusalem: *Hysterica Compassio* in the Late Middle Ages', in *Acts of Interpretation: The Text in its Contexts 700-1600* ed. M. J. Carruthers and E. D. Kirk (Norman, 1982)

What is it that disturbs us so
If wailing, crying, loud moaning?

Do we think it authentic?

Do we want such feeling?
    How can it help - hinder?

Everything attributed to God -

Why would some preach against her?